A
A

Enter Sydney O_____ pre-
dictions for every aspect of your life. With expert readings and forecasts, you can chart a course to romance,
adventure, good health, or career opportunities while
gaining valuable insight into yourself and others. Offering a daily outlook for 18 full months, this fascinating
guide shows you:

- The important dates in your life
- What to expect from an astrological reading
- The initials of people who will be influential in your life
- How the stars can help you stay healthy and fit
- Your lucky lottery numbers
  And more!

Let this expert's sound advice guide you through a year of
heavenly possibilities—for today and for every day of 2000!

SYDNEY OMARR'S DAY-BY-DAY
ASTROLOGICAL GUIDE FOR

ARIES—March 21–April 19
TAURUS—April 20–May 20
GEMINI—May 21–June 20
CANCER—June 21–July 22
LEO—July 23–August 22
VIRGO—August 23–September 22
LIBRA—September 23–October 22
SCORPIO—October 23–November 21
SAGITTARIUS—November 22–December 21
CAPRICORN—December 22–January 19
AQUARIUS—January 20–February 18
PISCES—February 19–March 20

IN 2000

WIN A PERSONALIZED HOROSCOPE FROM SYDNEY OMARR!

Enter the Sydney Omarr Horoscope Sweepstakes!

No Purchase necessary.
Details below.

Name _____

Address _____

City _____ State _____ Zip _____

Mail to:

SYDNEY OMARR HOROSCOPE SWEEPSTAKES
P.O. BOX 9248
Medford, NY 11763

Offer expires August 31, 1999

SYDNEY OMARR'S

DAY-BY-DAY ASTROLOGICAL GUIDE
FOR THE NEW MILLENNIUM

SAGITTARIUS

November 22–December 21

2000

A SIGNET BOOK

SIGNET
Published by New American Library, a division of
Penguin Putnam Inc., 375 Hudson Street,
New York, New York 10014, U.S.A.
Penguin Books Ltd, 27 Wrights Lane,
London W8 5TZ, England
Penguin Books Australia Ltd, Ringwood,
Victoria, Australia
Penguin Books Canada Ltd, 10 Alcorn Avenue,
Toronto, Ontario, Canada M4V 3B2
Penguin Books (N.Z.) Ltd, 182–190 Wairau Road,
Auckland 10, New Zealand

Penguin Books Ltd, Registered Offices:
Harmondsworth, Middlesex, England

First published by Signet, an imprint of New American Library,
a division of Penguin Putnam Inc.

First Printing, July 1999
10 9 8 7 6 5 4 3 2 1

Sydney Omarr is syndicated worldwide by
Los Angeles Times Syndicate.

 REGISTERED TRADEMARK—MARCA REGISTRADA

Printed in the United States of America

CONTENTS

Introduction: The Year
2000—Business as Usual?   1

1. Leaping into the Millennium—Predictions   5

2. The Leap Year Guide to Love   13

3. A User-Friendly Guide to Astrology   26

4. The Planets—Players in Your Personal
   Drama   36

5. How to Decode the Symbols (Glyphs) on
   Your Chart   98

6. Answers to Your Questions   111

7. Your Daily Agenda: Make the Most
   of the Millennium   115

8. What Makes Your Horoscope Special—
   Your Rising Sun   128

9. Stay Healthy and Fit This Millennium Year   136

10. Astrology Adventures on the Internet:
    What's New, What's Exciting, and
    What's *Free*!   146

11. The Sydney Omarr Yellow Pages   154

12. Is Your Life at a Crossroads? Consider a
    Personal Reading   161

13. Your Sagittarius Star Quality   167

14. Show Off the Sagittarius in You   173

15. Unleash Your Sagittarius Potential—Find the
    Work You Love!   176

16. Sagittarius Celebrities—From Hollywood to
    the Halls of Power   179

17. Astrological Outlook for Sagittarius in 2000   183

18. Eighteen Months of Day-by-Day
    Predictions—July 1999 to December 2000   185

INTRODUCTION:

The Year 2000—Business as Usual?

The year 2000 will be ushered in with celebration like never before. However, the very next day could mark one of the biggest snafus in history!

Unless millions of computer users and businesses worldwide have prepared in advance, the change in the initial digits from 19 to 20 of the date 2000 could shut down the technology that regulates every aspect of our lives. Now referred to as the "Y2K bug," this critical flaw that keeps computers locked in the 20th century has nearly every organization that depends on computers racing to beat the clock to avoid a major shutdown. Billions of lines of code must be rewritten before the chimes strike midnight. And suspense will mount during the hours before the century officially closes, as we wait to see what will happen.

The Millennium takes on even more significance when we realize that we're initiating a new era by making critical changes in the technology we've come to depend on. Because of the urgent time factor, everyone from government computer experts to teenage hackers must pull together to guarantee a smooth transition before the midnight deadline. In an extraordinary way, the technology is drawing us together as we make a global effort to resolve this problem.

Astrologers forecasted the union of technology and global cooperation with the entrance of the planet Uranus (technology) into the sign of Aquarius (humanitarian consciousness) in 1996. And it is also the harbinger of the next century, one where remarkable technological advances will be available to more people than ever before; however, the inevitable problems that will occur may also happen on a global scale and require us to work more closely together to discover solutions.

So the stroke of midnight will be a test of whether we are prepared for the challenges of the next century. Will there be shutdowns, accidents, faulty calculations, inaccurate data? Will you just be frustrated temporarily by not being able to use your bank card or by the store losing track of the Christmas gift you returned? Working together for a smooth crossing of the threshold of the Millennium might set the stage for cooperation in other areas, paving the way for better international communications and mutual understanding.

Astrologers have been looking at the horoscope for the Millennium for other clues to what lies ahead. We find that the first day of the Millennium is marked by an alignment of two tiny but powerful forces in astrology, the distant planet Pluto and the tiny planetoid Chiron. In astrology, Pluto is associated with transformation by renewal, Chiron with healing our wounds and helping others to heal. They are aligned in the sign of Sagittarius, which speaks of wide-reaching aspirations and long-term goals, and they are placed in the communications area of the horoscope as the clock chimes 12:01 EST. Let's hope that this Millennium will be a time of global healing and transformation, so that we may greet the new century with hope and enthusiasm.

In this year's guide, we show you some ways that you can harmonize your own life and goals to the rapid changes taking place. For fun, you can compare your planets with our extensive celebrity list, get a new leap-year lease on love, or find out how to use the Internet to connect with the wide world of astrology.

Besides learning the basic information, you can go beyond your sun sign to find out what astrology is all about. Using this book, you can look up your other planets and rising sign and find out what they mean.

2

The sometimes confusing symbols you see on a horoscope are explained in the chapter on the astrological glyphs. And, of course, there is all you need to know about your sun sign.

Let this guide help you use astrology as a valuable tool to create prosperity, happiness, and growth in the Millennium!

CHAPTER 1

Leaping into the Millennium—Predictions

In the U.S. Capitol building, there is a famous frieze of the shooting death of the Indian chief, Tecumseh, who figures prominently in this year's predictions. Every twenty years, there's a fateful lineup of two huge planets, Jupiter and Saturn, which coincides with an old prophecy of gloom and doom known as "Tecumseh's Curse."

Tecumseh, whose name, ironically, means "shooting star," was a brilliant Shawnee chief and orator. Threatened by the rapid territorial expansion of the white man and the concept of land division and property ownership, he attempted to unite the native American tribes to fight off the foreign invaders, but was shot in Canada in 1813 by American forces. Later, William Henry Harrison, who had defeated Indian attacks led by Tecumseh's brother at the famous battle of Tippecanoe, became the first U.S. president to die in office. But some believed that Tecumseh had put a curse on the United States presidency. Seemingly a coincidence, the list of American presidents who did not complete their term in office at twenty-year intervals after Harrison's death gave rise to the legend of "Tecumseh's Curse."

The next conjunction of Jupiter and Saturn after Harrison's term came during Lincoln's term, followed in twenty years by Garfield, then by McKinley, all assassinated by shooting. Both Presidents Harding and Franklin Delano Roosevelt died in office. The seventh president whose term fell under a Jupiter/Saturn conjunction was John F. Kennedy, also assassinated by shooting. And the last was President Reagan, who was shot during his term but survived.

At this writing, the term of current President Bill Clinton lasts until the time of the next conjunction in May 2000. However, he is experiencing a kind of "character assassination" leading to impeachment hearings that threaten his presidency and could result in his leaving office. The president taking office in 2001 will also be under the influence of this conjunction, which happens twice more in that year.

Long before Tecumseh, this conjunction has been regarded as one that brings sweeping and traumatic social and political events, wars, and destruction. The conjunction on May 28, 2000 follows several ominous celestial events and a pileup of seven planets in the sign of Taurus on May 3. So those of you who are born in fixed signs (Taurus, Leo, Scorpio, and Aquarius) can expect to be most influenced.

On a more positive note, it is important to recognize that lineups of planets are not events that happen in isolation. They are part of a natural, cyclical growth process. The stage for the events in the year 2000 has been set in motion by major astrological events in the past. So think of this event in context of what has been building up for some time.

What Types of Experiences Can You Expect?

The Millennium itself produces optimism, forward thinking, and futurism, all encouraged by Jupiter. But then Saturn, the taskmaster of the zodiac, brings reality checks, obstacles, demands for responsibility, duty, organization, structure, and follow-through into the picture. So this year we will all be concerned with the tradeoffs, the prices to be paid for all our growth and expansion. We will be setting limits on negative growth, such as overpopulation, destruction of the environment, and overspending of any kind.

The Saturn/Jupiter conjunction in the fixed earth sign of Taurus suggests that, as in the days of Tecumseh, there will be issues of territory, including land rights and physical boundaries—claiming it, gaining it, expanding it, fighting over it. In 1940–41, when the last Taurus meeting of these two planets happened, World War II was under way. At this moment, in Eastern Europe and in the Middle East, there are rumblings of global involvement in local territorial wars.

In your personal life, big plans run up against obstacles and bureaucratic red tape. You may be at odds with authority figures. In other words, when you try to spread your wings and fly, you may have trouble getting off the ground. Unless you bring practicality and discipline into play, you will run into restrictions that result in frustration.

As you may notice from the glyph chapter in this book, Jupiter's symbol is a variation on Saturn's glyph upside down. This is your clue that the two planets actually complement each other. Saturn, the planet associated with constriction, discipline, rules, obligations, and limitations, is the reverse of Jupiter, which is associated with expansion, optimism, options, opportunities, and luck. Saturn's long-lasting rewards come to you with hard work; Jupiter's rewards come to you with little effort—they're lucky breaks. Without Saturn's limitation, however, Jupiter is like a vehicle with no brakes. Saturn without Jupiter is like a vehicle stalled. In other words, Jupiter's enthusiasm needs Saturn's emphasis on structure and discipline in order to accomplish its goals, and vice versa.

At the same time, these planets can work at cross purposes. Saturn's fears and limitations can dampen Jupiter's hope and enthusiasm. Jupiter's expansion can come to a halt under Saturn's demand for reality checks and authority figures. Saturn can be a real drag on Jupiter.

The key is to find a balance to harmonize both of these complementary principles, bringing dreams down to earth

7

and getting a wider perspective on fears that are the basis of our limitations. When Saturn and Jupiter work together, we can adjust our expectations to reality, give form to our hopes, and overcome our fears. As Franklin D. Roosevelt said, "We have nothing to fear but fear itself." With this conjunction, there should be a dialogue between structure and opportunity, and between ideals and reality, that can be very fruitful in preparing us to meet the challenges of the next century. Together, these planets promise great accomplishments, but there is a tradeoff, a price to be paid by meeting obligations and taking on responsibilities.

Where Might It Affect Your Life?

The people who will be most affected will be those born during the previous conjunction in Taurus (1940–1941), who will have both Saturn and Jupiter returning to their natal positions. This second "Saturn Return" is a time of maturity, of leadership and responsibility, the beginning of assuming the duties of the wise elder of the community.

Here is where the conjunction might most affect your life according to your sun sign and rising sign. First look up your rising sign in the chart on page 134 in this book then read the following descriptions.

If Your Sun or Rising Sign Is Aries—

The principles of expansion vs. contraction will be evident in your second house of possessions, income, and self-esteem. You can make financial progress by combining new ideas with discipline, organization, and structure. Schemes that promise great rewards with no practical basis will not fly. It will also be important to balance your budget, stick to an investment plan, and guard against extravagance.

If Your Sun or Rising Sign Is Taurus—

Since the conjunction, and a major pileup of planets, takes place in your sign in May, you hold the power cards. This means you'll be in an authority position; you may be imposing structures on others or shaking others up. Though you will have many opportunities and a good deal of luck coming your way, you will also be aware that there will be a tradeoff, a price to pay. You'll be highly visible, so be sure that you look and feel your best.

If Your Sun or Rising Sign Is Gemini—

This conjunction falls in your most spiritual and vulnerable place, making this a time to open up and examine past experiences. Many of you may delve deeply into your subconscious. Watch what you put your faith in, for there is a potential for disillusion here. Something you believe in fervently will be tested, but this could take you into a new dimension. More Geminis may be involved with charity, hospitals, prisons, and religious institutions, creating much-needed changes in these places.

If Your Sun or Rising Sign Is Cancer—

The Saturn/Jupiter conjunction will fall in your house of goals, values, and group activities. This is a time when you will test your ideals in relationship to society. You will be forced out of your shell in some way. You will have opportunities to get involved in clubs, unions, or politics, but you may have some conflict between being popular and playing by the rules. You might discover talents you didn't know you had, such as organizing groups or public speaking. It's a year to shine before the public.

If Your Sun or Rising Sign Is Leo—

You will have many new opportunities in your career or public life, but along with the prestige, these bring extra responsibilities and hard work. You may feel that the job of your dreams is at last attainable, only to find that your workload will also be doubled. You'll be especially concerned about your public image, so show yourself at your very best. Keep your energy high by cultivating good habits.

If Your Sun or Rising Sign Is Virgo—

Though you may love your own comfortable home turf, you could find that you are challenged to accept a position in a new and different atmosphere. It is important to open your mind to other cultural or religious points of view. This would be an excellent time to study something new, to apply your mind in a disciplined way. There could be a conflict between new ideas and the traditional ways of thinking, between keeping yourself on the cutting edge versus clinging to the past. Be cautious, but also give way to adventure.

If Your Sun or Rising Sign Is Libra—

The conjunction will fall in the area of life where you share resources with others, and this is where issues of power and control dominate in your financial and most intimate life. This could complicate investments, savings, and the cost of living. It is a very important time to deal with funds from outside sources, inheritance, or with tax matters. You could be pushing to increase your income as this year begins, but not getting the backing or funding you need, or the funds may come with restrictions. Wheeling and dealing will face many challenges, but the results could bring you long-term security.

If Your Sun or Rising Sign Is Scorpio—

You'll get more accomplished if you do it with someone else. The pileup of planets in Taurus in May falls in your partnership sector, where you'll be making some lasting and permanent changes. Go for long-term benefits, perhaps turning over the reins to another for a while. The emphasis is on changing or improving relationships, making and meeting commitments, and on legal issues.

If Your Sun or Rising Sign Is Sagittarius—

Pay special attention to the care and maintenance department of your life. This is not the time to take your health for granted or burn the candle at both ends, so listen to your body and make sure everything is in working order. Consider alternate methods of healing that are pleasurable and uplifting as well as effective. Take courses to improve yourself. The events of May 2000 mean that you will be rethinking your job situation. Routine may weigh you down, but you can enhance your reputation by getting the job done and upgrading your skills if necessary. Don't promise more than you can deliver.

If Your Sun or Rising Sign Is Capricorn—

Since Capricorn is a Saturn-ruled sign, you may be especially favored by this conjunction, benefiting from the up-side of both planets. Your self-expression and creativity can take leaps forward now. It's an excellent time to expose your talents to a larger audience. Though you may have extra opportunities for romance, there may also be restrictions involved. The object of your affections may have other obligations or you may attract lovers who are not free to follow their hearts. Matters involving children—both the joys and responsibilities of their upbringing—will be more important than ever to you.

If Your Sun or Rising Sign Is Aquarius—

Your home and personal life will be emphasized by this conjunction, which could give you conflicting emotions

11

about your domestic scene. Perhaps you'll want to move or sell, yet there will be an equally strong pull that might hold you back from taking the decisive step. The grass may look greener elsewhere, but not prove to be so. You may have some wonderful ideas about practical home products or interior design, and you could be highly successful here. You could also resolve some long-standing family issues if you keep an open mind.

If Your Sun or Rising Sign Is Pisces—

How you communicate with others will be emphasized by this conjunction. The buildup of planets in Taurus, a fixed earth sign, indicates a tendency toward stubbornness, so make an extra effort to be flexible and to listen to other points of view. Friends and relatives could be more demanding, perhaps imposing extra duties and responsibilities for their care. There may be elderly friends or family that require your attention. There may be some changes in your neighborhood that require you to get involved. Take extra care of your car and matters concerning local transportation. Taking up new studies or hobbies now could be especially beneficial. Consider learning a new language or computer skills, or taking a writing course to broaden your horizons. The discipline of Saturn and the good luck of Jupiter might help you write that novel or play you've had on the back burner.

CHAPTER 2

The Leap Year Guide to Love

Though the year 2000 is a leap year, when ladies traditionally make the first romantic moves, today it's no longer unusual for women to chase the object of their desire aggressively, no matter what the year. One of the main reasons women turn to astrology is to help them attract a lover or to figure out what's going wrong in a relationship.

Probably the question astrologers hear most is: What sign is best for me in love? Or: I'm a Taurus and my lover is a Gemini. What are our prospects? You might be wondering if you can trust that first spark of chemistry—should you lower your expectations if you're a Leo with a fatal attraction to a sexy Scorpio? Old-fashioned astrologers would warn ominously, "This relationship is doomed from the start!" It used to be that some sun-sign combinations were treated like champagne and tomato juice—never the twain should meet. Others were considered blessed by the stars with perfect compatibility. Today's astrologers are more realistic, acknowledging that, though some combinations will be more challenging, there are too many long-lasting relationships between so-called incompatible sun signs to brand any combination as totally unworkable. We've gone far beyond stereotyping to respecting and enjoying the differences between people and using astrology to help us get along with them.

Each sun sign does have certain predictable characteristics in love, however, which can help you better understand the dynamics of the relationship. But we must be careful not to oversimplify. Just because someone is a so-called "incompatible" sign is no reason the relationship can't work out. For a true in-depth comparison, an astrologer considers the interrelationships of all the planets and houses (where they fall in your respective horoscopes).

Since romantic bonds between other planets can offset difficulties between sun signs, it's worthwhile to analyze several of the most important ones. You can do this by making a very simple chart that compares the moon, Mars, and Venus, as well as the sun signs of the partners in a relationship. You can find the signs for Mars and Venus in the tables in this book. Unfortunately complete moon tables are too long for a book of this size, so it might be worth your while to consult an astrological ephemeris (a book of planetary tables) in your local library or to have a computer chart cast to find out each other's moon placement.

Simply look up the signs of Mars and Venus in this book (and the moon, if possible) for each person and list them, with the sun sign, next to each other. Then add the element (earth, air, fire, or water) of each sign. The earth signs are Taurus, Virgo, and Capricorn. The air signs are Gemini, Libra, and Aquarius. The fire signs are Aries, Leo, and Sagittarius. And the water signs are Cancer, Scorpio, and Pisces.

Here's an example:

	SUN	MOON	MARS	VENUS
ROMEO	Aries/Fire	Leo/Fire	Scorpio/Water	Taurus/Earth
JULIET	Pisces/Water	Leo/Fire	Aries/Fire	Aquarius/ Air

As a rule of thumb, signs of the *same* element or *complementary* elements (fire with air and earth with water) get along best. So you can see that this particular Romeo and Juliet could have some challenges ahead, with an emotional bond (the moon) creating a strong tie.

14

The Lunar Link—
The Person You Need

The planet in your chart that governs your emotions is
the moon. (Note: The moon is not technically a planet,
but is usually referred to as one by astrologers.) So you
would naturally take this into consideration when evaluating a potential romantic partnership. If a person's moon
is in a good relationship to your sun, moon, Venus, or
Mars, preferably in the same sign or element, you should
relate well on some emotional level. Your needs will
be compatible; you'll understand each other's feelings
without much effort. If the moon is in a compatible element, such as earth with water or fire with air, you may
have a few adjustments, but you will be able to make
them easily. With a water–fire or earth–air combination,
you'll have to make a considerable effort to understand
where the other is coming from emotionally.

The Venus Attraction—
The One You Want

Venus is what you respond to, so if you and your partner
have a good Venus aspect, you should have much in
common. You'll enjoy doing things together. The same
type of lovemaking will turn you both on, so you'll have
no trouble pleasing each other.

Look up both partners' Venus placements in the
charts on page 78. Your lover's Venus in the same sign
or a sign of the same element as your own Venus, Mars,
moon, or sun is best. Second-best is a sign of a compatible element (earth with water, air with fire). Venus in
water with air, or earth with fire means that you may
have to make a special effort to understand what appeals
to each other. And you'll have to give each other plenty
of space to enjoy activities that don't particularly appeal
to you. By the way, this chart can work not only for

lovers, but for any relationship where compatibility of tastes is important to you.

The Mars Connection— This One Lights Your Fire!

Mars positions reveal your sexual energy—how often you like to make love, for instance. It also shows your temper—do you explode or do a slow burn? Here you'll find out if your partner is direct, aggressive, and hot-blooded or more likely to take the cool, mental approach. Mutually supportive partners have their Mars working together in the same or complementary elements. But *any* contacts between Mars and Venus in two charts can strike sexy sparks. Even the difficult aspects—your partner's Mars three or six signs away from your sun, Mars, or Venus—can offer sexual stimulation. Who doesn't get turned on by a challenge from time to time? Sometimes the easy Mars relationships can drift into dullness.

The Solar Bond

The sun is the focus of our personality and therefore the most powerful component involved in astrology. Once again, earth and water or fire and air combinations will have an easier time together. Mixtures earth and water with fire and air can be much more challenging. However, each pair of sun signs has special lessons to teach and learn from each other. There is a negative side to the most ideal couple and a positive side to the most unlikely match—Each has an up and a down side. So if the outlook for you and your beloved (or business associate) seems like an uphill struggle, take heart! Such legendary lovers as Juan and Eva Peron, Ronald and Nancy Reagan, Harry and Bess Truman, Julius Caesar and Cleopatra, Billy and Ruth Graham, and George and

Martha Washington are among the many who have made successful partnerships between supposedly incompatible sun signs.

How to Seduce Every Sign . . .

The Aries Lover

It's not easy to make the first move on an Aries, since this sign always likes to be first. Try challenging your Aries in some way—this sign loves the chase almost as much as the conquest. So don't be too easy or accommodating—let them feel a sense of accomplishment when they've won your heart.

Be sure your interests and appearance are up to the minute. You can wear the latest style off the fashion show runway with an Aries, especially if it's bright red. Aries is a pioneer, an adventurer, always ahead of the pack. Play up your frontier spirit. Present the image of the two of you as an unbeatable team, one that can conquer the world, and you'll keep this courageous sign at your side.

Since they tend to idealize their lovers, Aries is especially disillusioned when their mates flirt. Be sure they always feel like number one in your life.

The Taurus Lover

Taurus is often seduced by surface physical beauty alone. Their five senses are highly susceptible, so find ways to appeal to all of them! Your home should be a restful haven from the outside world. Get a great sound system, some comfortable furniture to sink into, and keep the refrigerator stocked with treats. Most Taureans would rather entertain on their own turf than gad about town, so it helps if you're a good host or hostess.

Taurus like a calm, contented, committed relationship. This is not a sign to trifle with. Don't flirt or tease if you want to please. Don't rock the boat or try to make

17

this sign jealous. Instead, create a steady, secure environment with lots of shared pleasures.

Taurus is an extremely sensual, affectionate, nurturing lover, but can be quite possessive. Taurus likes to "own" you, so don't hold back with them or play power games. If you need more space in the relationship, be sure to set clear boundaries, letting them know exactly where they stand. When ambiguity in a relationship makes Taurus uneasy, they may go searching for someone more solid and substantial. A Taurus romance works best where the limits are clearly spelled out. Taurus needs physical demonstrations of affection—so don't hold back on hugs.

The Gemini Lover

Variety is the spice of life to this flirtatious sign. Guard against jealousy—it is rarely justified. Provide a stimulating sex life—this is a very experimental sign—to keep them interested. Be a bit unpredictable. Don't let lovemaking become a routine. Most of all, sharing lots of laughs together can make Gemini take your relationship very seriously.

Keeping Gemini interested is like walking a tightrope. Though this sign needs stability and a strong home base to accomplish their goals, they also require a great deal of personal freedom. A great role model is Barbara Bush, a Gemini successfully married to another Gemini.

This is a sign that loves to communicate, so sit down and talk things over. Be interested in your partner's doings, but have a life of your own and ideas to contribute. Since this is a gadabout social sign, don't insist on quiet nights at home when your Gemini is in a party mood.

Gemini needs a steady hand, but at the same time plenty of rope. Focus on common goals and abstract ideals. Gemini likes to share, so be a twin soul and do things together. Keep up on their latest interests. Stay in touch mentally and physically, using both your mind and your hands to communicate.

18

The Cancer Lover

The song "Try a Little Tenderness" must have been written by a Cancer. This is probably the water sign that requires the most TLC. Cancers tend to be very private people who may take some time to open up. They are extremely self-protective and will rarely tell you what is truly bothering them. They operate indirectly, like the movements of the crab. You may have to divine their problem by following subtle clues, then draw them out gently and try to voice any criticism in the most tactful, supportive way possible.

Family ties are especially strong for Cancer. They will rarely break a strong family bond. Create an intimate family atmosphere, with the emphasis on food and family get-togethers. You can get valuable clues to Cancer appeal from their mothers and their early family situation. If their early life was unhappy, it's even more important that they feel they have found a close family with you.

Encouraging their creativity can counter Cancer's moodiness, which is also a sure sign of emotional insecurity. Find ways to distract them from negative moods. Calm them with a good meal for instance, or a trip to the seashore. Cancers are usually quite nostalgic and attached to the past. So be careful not to throw out their old treasures or photos.

The Leo Lover

Appeal to Leo pride by treating this sign royally. Be well groomed and dressed, someone they're proud to show off.

Leo thinks big, and likes to live like a king, so don't you be petty or miserly. Remember special occasions with a beautifully wrapped gift or flowers. Make an extra effort to treat them royally. Keep a sense of fun and playfulness, and loudly applaud Leo's creative efforts. React, respond, be a good audience! If Leo's ignored, this sign will seek a more appreciative audience—fast!

(Cheating Leos are almost always looking for an ego boost.)

Be generous with compliments. You can't possibly overdo here. Always accentuate the positive. Make them feel important by asking for advice and consulting them often. Leo enjoys a charming sociable companion, but be sure to make them the center of attention in your life.

The Virgo Lover

Virgos love to feel needed, so give them a job to do in your life. They are great fixer-uppers. Take their criticism as a form of love and caring, of noticing what you do. Bring them out socially—they're often very shy. Calm their nerves with good food, a healthy environment, trips to the country.

Virgos may seem cool and conservative on the surface, but underneath you'll find a sensual romantic. Think of Raquel Welch, Sophia Loren, Jacqueline Bisset, Garbo—it's amazing how seductive this practical sign can be! They are idealists, however, looking for someone who meets their high standards. If you've measured up, they'll do anything to serve and please you.

Mental stimulation is a turn-on to this Mercury-ruled sign. An intellectual discussion could lead to romantic action, so stay on your toes and keep well informed. This sign often mixes business with pleasure, so it helps if you share the same professional interests—you'll get to see more of your busy mate. With Virgo, the couple who works and plays together, stays together.

The Libra Lover

Do not underestimate Libra's need for beauty and harmony. To keep them happy, avoid scenes. Opt for calm, impersonal discussion of problems (or a well-reasoned debate) over an elegant dinner. Pay attention to the niceties of life. Send little gifts on Valentines Day and don't forget birthdays and anniversaries. Play up the romance to the hilt—with all the lovely gestures and trimmings—but tone down intensity and emotional drama (Aries, Scorpio take note). Surround your Libra with a physically tasteful atmosphere—elegant, well-designed furnishings and calm colors. Be well groomed and tastefully dressed and be sure to emphasize good conversation and good manners.

Bear in mind that Libra truly enjoys life with a mate and needs the harmony of a steady relationship. Outside affairs can throw them off balance. However, members of this sign are natural charmers who love to surround themselves with admirers, and this can cause a very possessive partner to feel insecure. Most of the time, Librans are only testing their charms with harmless flirtations and will rarely follow through, unless they are not getting enough attention or there is an unattractive atmosphere at home.

Mental compatibility is what keeps Libra in tune. Unfortunately this sign, like Taurus, often falls for physical beauty or someone who provides an elegant lifestyle, rather than someone who shares their ideals and activities, the kind of compatibility that will keep you together in the long run.

The Scorpio Lover

Pluto-ruled Scorpio is fascinated by power and control in all its forms. They don't like to compromise—it's "all or nothing." They don't trust or respect anything that comes too easily, so be a bit of a challenge and keep them guessing. Maintain your own personal identity in spite of Scorpio's desire to probe your innermost secrets.

Sex is especially important to this sign, which will demand fidelity from you (though they may not deliver it themselves). Communication on this level is critical. Explore Scorpio's fantasies together. Scorpio is a detective, so watch your own flirtations—don't play with fire. This is a jealous and vengeful sign, so you'll live to regret it. Scorpios rarely flirt for the fun of it themselves. There is usually a strong motive behind their actions.

Scorpios are often deceptively cool and remote on the

outside, but don't be fooled: This sign always has a hidden agenda and feels very intensely about most things. The disguise is necessary because Scorpio does not trust easily; but when they do, they are devoted and loyal and will stick with you through the toughest times. You can lean on this very intense and focused sign. The secret is in first establishing that basic trust through mutual honesty and respect.

Scorpio has a fascination with the dark, mysterious side of life. If unhappy, they are capable of carrying on a secret affair. So try to emphasize positive, constructive solutions with them. Don't fret if they need time alone to sort out problems. They may also prefer time alone with you to socializing with others, so plan romantic getaways together to a private beach or a secluded wilderness spot.

The Sagittarius Lover

Be a mental and spiritual traveling companion. Sagittarius is a footloose adventurer whose ideas know no boundaries, so don't try to fence them in. Sagittarians resent restrictions of any kind. For a long-lasting relationship, be sure you are in harmony with Sagittarius's ideals and spiritual beliefs. They like to feel that their life is constantly being elevated and taken to a higher level. Since down-to-earth matters often get put aside in the Sagittarian's scheme of things, get finances under control (money matters upset more relationships with Sagittarians than any other problem), but try to avoid being the stern disciplinarian in this relationship (find a good accountant).

Sagittarius is not generally a homebody—unless there are several homes. Be ready and willing to take off on the spur of the moment, or they'll go without you! Sports, outdoor activities, and physical fitness are important—stay in shape with some of Sagittarius Jane Fonda's tapes. Dress with flair and style—it helps if you look especially good in sportswear. Sagittarius men like beautiful legs, so play up yours. And this is one of the

22

great animal lovers, so try to get along with the dog, cat, or horse.

The Capricorn Lover

Capricorns are ambitious, even if they are the stay-at-home partner in your relationship. They will be extremely active, have a strong sense of responsibility to their partner, and take commitments seriously. However, they might look elsewhere if the relationship becomes too dutiful. They also need romance, fun, lightness, humor, and adventure!

Generation gaps are not unusual in Capricorn romances, when the older Capricorn partner works hard all through life and seeks pleasurable rewards with a young partner, or the young Capricorn gets a taste of luxury and instant status from an older lover. This is one sign that grows more interested in romance as they age! Younger Capricorns often tend to put business way ahead of pleasure.

Capricorn is impressed by those who entertain well, have "class," and can advance their status in life. Keep improving yourself and cultivate important people. Stay on the conservative side. Extravagant or frivolous loves don't last—Capricorn keeps a weather eye on the bottom line. Even the wildest Capricorns, such as Elvis Presley, Rod Stewart, or David Bowie, show a conservative streak in their personal lives. It's also important to demonstrate a strong sense of loyalty to your family, especially older members. This reassures Capricorn, who'll be happy to grow old along with you!

The Aquarius Lover

Aquarius is one of the most independent, least domestic signs. Finding time alone with this sign may be one of your greatest challenges. They are everybody's buddy, usually surrounded by people they collect—some of whom may be old lovers who are now "just friends." However, it is unlikely that old passions will be rekindled if you manage to become Aquarius's number-one best friend as well as lover, and if you get actively involved in other important aspects of Aquarius's life, such as the political or charitable causes they believe in.

Aquarius needs a supportive backup person who encourages them but is not overly possessive when their natural charisma attracts admirers by the dozen. Take a leaf from Joanne Woodward, whose marriage to perennial Aquarius heartthrob Paul Newman has lasted more than 30 years. Encourage them to develop their original ideas. Don't rain on their parade if they decide suddenly to market their spaghetti sauce and donate the proceeds to their favorite charity, or drive racing cars. Share their goals and be their fan, or you'll never see them.

You may be called on to give them grounding where needed. Aquarius needs someone who can keep track of their projects. But always remember, it's basic friendship—with the tolerance and common ideals that implies—that will hold you together.

The Pisces Lover

They are great fantasists and extremely creative lovers, so use your imagination to add drama and spice to your times together. You can let your fantasies run wild with this sign—and they'll go you one better! They enjoy variety in lovemaking, so try never to let it become routine.

To keep a Pisces hooked, don't hold the string too tight! This is a sensitive, creative sign that may appear to need someone to manage their lives or point the direction out of their Neptunian fog, but if you fall into that role, expect your Pisces to rebel against any strong-arm tactics. Pisces is more susceptible to a play for sympathy than a play for power. They are suckers for a sob story, the most empathetic sign of the zodiac. More than one Pisces has been seduced and held by someone who plays the underdog role.

Long-term relationships work best if you can bring Pisces down to earth and, at the same time, encourage their creative fantasies. Deter them from escapism into alcohol or substance abuse by helping them to get counseling, if needed. Pisces will seek a soulmate who provides positive energy, self-confidence, and a safe harbor from the storms of life.

CHAPTER 3

A User-Friendly Guide to Astrology

Astrology is like a fascinating foreign country with a language all its own and territory that's easy to get lost in. This chapter is a brief introduction to the basics of astrology, to help you find your way around in later travels. Bear in mind, as you discover the difference between signs, houses, and constellations, that the information we share so readily was in ancient times a carefully guarded secret of scholar–priests entrusted with timing sacred ceremonies. While it takes years of study and practice to become an expert, you can derive pleasure and self-knowledge by learning how astrology works. Whether you're planning a brief visit or a long study, this user-friendly guide can give you the basic lay of the land, an overview that will help you get off on the road to understanding your own horoscope.

What Do We Mean by a "Sign"?

Signs are the "real estate" of astrology. They are segments of territory located on the *zodiac,* an imaginary 360-degree belt circling the earth. This belt is divided into twelve equal 30-degree portions, which are the *signs*.

There's a lot of confusion about the difference between the *signs* and the *constellations* of the zodiac. *Constellations* are patterns of stars that originally marked the twelve divisions of the zodiac, like sign posts. Though each *sign* is named after the constellation which once marked the same area, over hundreds of years, the earth's orbit has shifted, so that from our point of view here on earth, the constellations have "moved" and are no longer valid sign posts. However the 30-degree territory that belonged to each sign remains the same. (Most Western astrologers use the 12-equal-part division of the zodiac. But some methods of astrology do still use the constellations instead of the signs.)

Most people think of themselves in terms of their sun sign. A *sun sign* refers to the sign the sun is orbiting through at a given moment (from our point of view here on earth). For instance, "I'm an Aries" means that the sun was passing through Aries when that person was born. However, there are nine other planets (plus asteroids, fixed stars, and sensitive points) which also form our total astrological personality, and some or many of these will be located in other signs. No one is completely "Aries," with all their astrological components in one sign! (Please note that in astrology, the sun and moon are usually referred to as "planets," though of course they're not.)

What Makes a Sign Special?

What makes the sign of Aries associated with go-getters and Taureans savvy with money? And Geminis talk a blue streak and Sagittarians footloose? It is important to note that characteristics associated with the signs are not accidental. They are derived from combinations of four basic components: a sign's element, quality, polarity, and place on the zodiac.

For example, take the element of fire: It's hot, passionate. Then add an active cardinal mode. Give it a jolt of positive energy and place it first in line. And doesn't that sound like the active, me-first, driving, hotheaded, energetic Aries?

Then take the element of earth, practical, sensual, the

place where things grow. Add the fixed, stable mode. Give it energy that reacts to its surroundings, that settles in. Put it after Aries. Now you've got a good idea of how sensual, earthy Taurus operates.

Another way to grasp the idea is to pretend you're doing a magical puzzle based on the numbers that can divide into twelve (the number of signs): 4, 3, and 2. There are four "building blocks" or elements, three ways a sign operates (qualities) and two polarities. These alternate in turn around the zodiac, with a different combination coming up for each sign. Here's how they add up.

THE FOUR ELEMENTS

These describe the physical concept of the sign. Is it fiery (dynamic), earthy (practical), airy (mental), water (emotional)? There are three zodiac signs of each of the four elements: fire (Aries, Leo, Sagittarius), earth (Taurus, Virgo, Capricorn), air (Gemini, Libra, Aquarius), water (Cancer, Scorpio, Pisces). These are the same elements that make up our planet: earth, air, fire and water. But astrology uses the elements as *symbols* that link our body and psyche to the rhythms of the planets. Fire signs spread warmth and enthusiasm. They are able to fire up or motivate others. They have hot tempers. These are people who make ideas catch fire and spring into existence. Earth signs are the builders of the zodiac who follow through after the initiative of fire signs to make things happen. These people are solid, practical realists who enjoy material things and sensual pleasures. They are interested in ideas that can be used to achieve concrete results. Air signs are mental people, great communicators. Following the consolidating earth signs, they'll reach out to inspire others through the use of words, social contacts, discussion, and debate. Water signs complete each four-sign series, adding the ingredients of emotion, compassion, and imagination. Water-sign people are nonverbal communicators who attune themselves to their surroundings and react through the medium of feelings.

A SIGN'S QUALITY

The second consideration when defining a sign is how it will operate. Will it take the initiative, or move slowly and deliberately, or adapt easily? Its *quality* (or modality) will tell. There are three qualities and four signs of each quality: cardinal, fixed, and mutable.

Cardinal signs are the start-up signs that begin each season (Aries, Cancer, Libra, Capricorn). These people love to be active, involved in projects. They are usually on the fast track to success, impatient to get things under way. *Fixed signs* (Taurus, Leo, Scorpio, Aquarius) move steadily, always in control. They happen in the middle of a season, after the initial character of the season is established. Fixed signs are naturally more centered. They tend to move more deliberately, doing things slowly but thoroughly. They govern parts of your horoscope where you take root and integrate your experiences. *Mutable signs* (Gemini, Virgo, Sagittarius, Pisces) embody the principle of distribution. These are the signs that break up the cycle, prepare the way for a change by distributing the energy to the next group. Mutables are flexible, adaptable, communicative. They can move in many directions easily, darting around obstacles.

A SIGN'S POLARITY

In addition to an element and a quality, each sign has a polarity, either a positive or negative electrical charge that generates energy around the zodiac like a giant battery. Polarity refers to opposites, which you could also define as masculine/feminine, yin/yang, active/reactive. Alternating around the zodiac, the six fire and air signs are positive, active, masculine, and yang in polarity. These signs are open, expanding outward. The six earth and water signs are reactive, negative, and yin—in other words, nurturing and receptive in polarity, which allows the energy to develop and take shape. All positive energy would be like a car without brakes. All negative energy would be like a stalled vehicle, going nowhere. Both polarities are needed in balanced proportion.

Finally we must consider the order of the signs. This

is vital to the balance of the zodiac and the transmission of energy throughout the zodiac. Each sign is quite different from its neighbors on either side. Yet each seems to grow out of its predecessor like links in a chain, transmitting a synthesis of energy gathered along the chain to the following sign, beginning with the fire-powered active positive cardinal sign of Aries and ending with watery mutable, reactive Pisces.

The Layout of a Horoscope Chart

A horoscope chart is a graphic map of the heavens at a given moment in time. It looks somewhat like a wheel divided with twelve spokes. The territory marked off by each "spoke" is a section called a *house*. The houses are extremely important in astrological interpretation because each house is associated with a different area of life and is influenced (or *ruled*) by a sign and a planet assigned to that house.

In addition, the house is colored by the sign passing over the spoke (or cusp) at the moment of the horoscope. The sequence of the houses begins at the left center spoke (or the 9 position if you were reading a clock) and follows reading counter-clockwise around the chart.

The First House—Home of Aries and Mars

This is the house of "firsts"—the first impression you make, how you initiate matters, the image you choose to project. This is your advertisement to the world. Planets that fall here will intensify the way you come across to others. Often a person's first house will project an entirely different type of personality than the sun sign. For instance, a Capricorn with Leo in the first house will come across as much more flamboyant than the average Capricorn. The sign passing over the cusp of this house at the time of your birth is known as your ascendant or rising sign.

The Second House—Home of Taurus and Venus

This is how you experience the material world—what you value. Here is your contact with the material world—your attitudes about money, possessions, finances, whatever belongs to you, and what you own, as well as your earning and spending capacity. As a Venus-ruled house, it describes your sensuality, your delight in physical pleasures. On a deeper level, this house reveals your sense of self-esteem—how you value yourself.

The Third House—Home of Gemini and Mars

This is how well you communicate with others—are you understood? This house shows how you reach out to others nearby and interact with the immediate environment. Here is how your thinking process works, how you communicate. This house shows your first relationships, your experiences with brothers and sisters, as well as how well you deal with people close to you now, such as your neighbors or pals. It's where you take short trips, write letters, or use the telephone. It shows how your mind works in terms of left-brain logical and analytical functions.

The Fourth House—Home of Cancer and the Moon

This is how you are nurtured and made to feel secure— your roots! At the bottom of the chart, the fourth house, like the home, shows the foundation of life and its psychological underpinnings. Here is where you have the deepest confrontations with who you are and how you make yourself feel secure. It shows your early home environment and the circumstances at the end of your life—your final "home"—as well as the place you call home now. Astrologers look here for information about the parental nurturers in your life.

The Fifth House—Home of Leo and the Sun

This is how you express yourself creatively—your idea of play. The Leo house is where the creative potential develops. Here you express yourself and procreate, in the sense that children are outgrowths of your creative ability. But this house most represents your inner childlike self, who delights in play. If inner security has been established by the time you reach this house, you are now free to have fun, romance, and love affairs, and to give of yourself. This is also the place astrologers look for playful love affairs, flirtations, and brief romantic encounters (rather than long-term commitments).

The Sixth House—Home of Virgo and Mercury

This is how you function in daily life. The sixth house has been called the "repair and maintenance" department. Here is where you get things done, how you look after others and fulfill responsibilities, such as taking care of pets. Here is your daily survival, your "job" routine and organization (as opposed to your career, which is the domain of the tenth house), your diet, and your health and fitness regimens. This house shows how you take care of your body and organize yourself so you can perform efficiently in the world.

The Seventh House—Home of Libra and Venus

This is how you form a partnership. Here is the way you commit to others, as well as your close, intimate, one-on-one relationships (including open enemies—those you "face off" with). This house shows your attitude toward partners and those with whom you enter commitments, contracts, or agreements. Open hostilities, lawsuits, divorces, and marriages happen here. If the first house represents the "I" in your horoscope, the seventh or opposite house is the "not-I"—the complementary partner you attract by the way you come across. If you are having trouble with partnerships, consider what you are attracting by the energies of your first and seventh houses.

The Eighth House—Home of Scorpio and Pluto (also Mars)

This is how you merge with something greater than yourself. Here is where you deal with issues of power and control, where you share with others and merge your energy with another to become something greater. Here are your attitudes toward sex, shared resources, and taxes (what you share with the government). Because this house involves what belongs to others, there can be power struggles or there can be a deep psychological transformation as you bond with another. Here you transcend yourself with the occult, dreams, drugs, or psychic experiences that reflect the collective unconscious.

The Ninth House—Home of Sagittarius and Jupiter

This is how you search for wisdom and higher knowledge. As the third house represents the "lower mind," its opposite on the wheel, the ninth house, is the "higher mind"—the abstract, intuitive, spiritual mind that asks big questions like why are we here, how everything fits together, what it all means. The ninth house shows what you believe in. After the third house explored what was close at hand, the ninth stretches out to explore more exotic territory, either by traveling, broadening mentally

33

with higher education, or stretching spiritually with religious activity. Here is where you write a book or an extensive thesis, where you pontificate, philosophize, or preach.

The Tenth House—Home of Capricorn and Saturn

This is your public image and how you handle authority. This house is located directly overhead at the "high noon" position. This is the most "visible" house in the chart, the one where the world sees you. It deals with your public image, your career (but not your routine "job"), and your reputation. Here is where you go public and take on responsibilities (as opposed to the fourth house, where you stay home). This will affect the career you choose and your "public relations." This house is also associated with your father figure or whoever else was the authority figure in your life.

The Eleventh House—Home of Aquarius and Uranus

This is your support system, how you relate to society and your goals. This house is where you define what you really want, the kinds of friends you have, your teammates, your political affiliations, and the kind of groups you identify with as an equal. Here is where you could become a socially conscious humanitarian—or a party-going social butterfly. It's where you look to others to stimulate you and discover your kinship to the rest of humanity. The sign on this house can help you understand what you gain and lose from friendships, how concerned you are with social approval, and with what others think.

The Twelfth House—Home of Pisces and Neptune

Here is where the boundaries between yourself and others become blurred, where you become selfless. In your trip around the zodiac, you've gone from the "I" of self-assertion in the first house to the final house symbolizing the dissolution that happens before rebirth, a place where the accumulated experiences are processed in the unconscious. Spiritually oriented astrologers look to this house for your past lives and karma. Places where we go to be alone and do spiritual or reparatory work belong here, such as retreats, religious institutions, hospitals. Here is also where we withdraw from society—or are forced to withdraw because of antisocial activity. Selfless giving through charitable acts is part of this house. In your daily life, the twelfth house reveals your deepest intimacies and your best-kept secrets, especially those you hide from yourself and keep repressed deep in the unconscious. It is where we surrender a sense of a separate self to a deep feeling of wholeness, such as selfless service in religion or any activity that involves merging with the greater whole. Many sports stars have important planets in the twelfth house that enable them to find an inner, almost mystical, strength that transcends their limits.

Who's Home in Your Houses?

Houses are stronger or weaker depending on how many planets are inhabiting them and the condition of those planets. If there are many planets in a given house, it follows that the activities of that house will be especially important in your life. If the planet that rules the house is also located there, this too adds power to the house.

CHAPTER 4

The Planets—Players in Your Personal Drama

Once you understand the basic territory of astrology—what defines a sign and the layout of a horoscope chart—you're ready to meet the cast of characters who make the chart come alive. Nothing happens without the planets, which relate to each other to create the action in a chart.

The ten planets in your chart will play starring or supporting roles, depending on their position in your horoscope. A planet in the first house, particularly one that's close to your rising sign, is sure to be a featured player. Planets that are grouped together usually operate together like a team, playing off each other, rather than expressing their energy singularly. A planet that stands alone, away from the others, is usually outstanding and sometimes steals the show.

Each planet has two signs where it is especially at home. These are called its *dignities*. The most favorable place for a planet is in the sign or signs it rules; the next best place is in a sign where it is *exalted,* or especially harmonious. On the other hand, there are places in the horoscope where a planet has to work harder to play its role. These places are called the planet's *detriment* and *fall*. The sign opposite a planet's rulership, which embodies the opposite area of life, is its detriment. The sign opposite its exaltation is called its fall. Though the terms may suggest unfortunate circumstances for the planet, that is not always the case. In fact, a planet that is debilitated can actually be more complete, because it must stretch itself to meet the challenges of living in a more difficult sign. Like world leaders who've had to struggle for greatness, this planet may actually develop great strength and character.

Here's a list of the best places for each planet to be, in the signs they rule. Note that, as new planets were discovered in this century, they replaced the traditional rulers of signs that best complimented their energies.

ARIES—Mars
TAURUS—Venus, in its most sensual form
GEMINI—Mercury, in its communicative role
CANCER—the moon
LEO—the sun
VIRGO—Mercury, in its critical capacity
LIBRA—Venus, in its aesthetic, judgmental form
SCORPIO—Pluto, replacing the sign's original ruler, Mars
SAGITTARIUS—Jupiter
CAPRICORN—Saturn
AQUARIUS—Uranus, replacing Saturn, its original ruler
PISCES—Neptune, replacing Jupiter, its original ruler

A person who has many planets in exalted signs is lucky indeed, for here is where the planet can accomplish the most, and be its most influential and creative.

SUN—Exalted in Aries, where its energy creates action
MOON—Exalted in Taurus, where instincts and reactions operate on a highly creative level
MERCURY—Exalted in Virgo, which it also rules, and where it can reach analytical heights
VENUS—Exalted in Pisces, a sign whose sensitivity encourages love and creativity
MARS—Exalted in Capricorn, a sign that puts energy to work
JUPITER—Exalted in Cancer, where it encourages nurturing and growth
SATURN—At home in Libra, where it steadies the scales of justice and promotes balanced, responsible judgment

37

URANUS—Powerful in Scorpio, where it promotes transformation

NEPTUNE—Especially favored in Cancer, where it gains the security to transcend to a higher state

PLUTO—Exalted in Pisces, where it dissolves the old cycle to make way for transition to the new

The Sun is Always Center Stage

Your sun sign is where you directly express yourself, displaying the part of you that shines brightest, even when you're accompanied by strong costars, or you're dressed modestly, or sharing a house with several other planets. When you know a person's sun sign, you already know some very useful generic qualities. Then, after you add the other planets, you'll have an accurate profile of that person and will be more able to predict how that individual will act in a given situation. The sun's just one actor on the stage, but a very powerful one—a good reason why sun-sign astrology works for so many people.

The sun rules the sign of Leo, gaining strength through the pride, dignity, and confidence of the fixed-fire personality. It is exalted in "me-first" Aries. In its detriment, Aquarius, the sun-ego is strengthened through group participation and social consciousness, rather than through self-centeredness. Note how many Aquarius people are involved in politics, social work, public life, following the demands of their sun sign to be spokesperson for a group. In its fall, Libra, the sun needs the strength of a partner—an "other"—to enhance balance and self-expression.

Like your sun sign, each of the other nine planet's personalities is colored by the sign it is passing through at the time. For example, Mercury, the planet that rules the way you communicate, will express itself in a dynamic, headstrong Aries way if it was passing through the sign of Aries when you were born. You would communicate in a much different way if it were passing through the slower, more patient sign of Taurus. Here's a rundown of the planets and how they behave in every sign.

The Moon—The Oscar Nominee

The Moon's role is to dig beneath the surface to reflect your needs, your longings, and the kind of childhood conditioning you had. In a man's chart, the moon position also describes his female, receptive, emotional side, and the woman in his life who will have the deepest effect. (Venus reveals the kind of woman who attracts him physically).

The sign the moon was passing through at your birth reflects your instinctive emotional nature and the things that appeal to you subconsciously. Since accurate moon tables are too extensive for this book, check through these descriptions to find the moon sign that feels most familiar—or better yet, have your chart calculated by a computer service to get your accurate moon placement.

The moon rules maternal Cancer and is exalted in Taurus—both comforting, home-loving signs where the natural emotional energies of the moon are easily and productively expressed. But when the moon is in the opposite signs—in its Capricorn detriment and its Scorpio fall—it leaves the comfortable nest and deals with emotional issues of power and achievement in the outside world. Those of you with the moon in these signs will find your emotional role more challenging in life.

Moon in Aries

Emotionally, you are independent and ardent. You are an idealistic, impetuous person who falls in and out of love easily. You respond to a challenge, but could cool down once your quarry is captured. To avoid continuous "treat 'em rough" situations, you should work on cultivating patience and tolerance. Be wary of responding to excitement for its own sake.

39

Moon in Taurus

This is a strong position for the moon, so emotional satisfaction will be an important factor in your life. You are a huggy, sentimental soul who is very fond of the good life and gravitates toward solid, secure relationships. You like frequent displays of affection and creature comforts—all the tangible trappings of a cozy atmosphere. You are sensual and steady emotionally, but very stubborn and determined. You can't be pushed and tend to protect your turf.

Moon in Gemini

You crave mental stimulation and variety in life, which you usually get through either a varied social life, the excitement of flirtation, and/or multiple professional involvements. You may marry more than once and have a rather chaotic emotional life due to your difficulty with commitment and settling down. Be sure to find a partner who is as outgoing as you are. You will have to learn at some point to focus your energies because you tend to be somewhat fragmented—you may do two things at once, or have two careers, homes, or even two lovers. If you can find a creative way to express your many-faceted nature, you'll be ahead of the game.

Moon in Cancer

This is the most powerful lunar position, which is sure to have a deep imprint on your character. Your needs are very much associated with your reaction to the needs of others. You are very sensitive and self-protective, though some of you may mask this with a hard shell. This placement also gives an excellent memory and an uncanny ability to psyche out the needs of others. All of the lunar phases will affect you, especially full moons and eclipses, so be sure to mark them on your calendar. You are happiest at home and may work at home or turn your office into a second home, where you can nurture and comfort people (you may tend to "mother the world"). This psychic, intuitive moon might draw you to occult work in some way. Or you may professionally provide food and shelter to others.

Moon in Leo

This is a warm, passionate moon that takes everything to heart. You are attracted to all that is noble, generous, and aristocratic in life and may be a bit of a snob. You have an innate ability to take command emotionally, but you need strong support, loyalty, and loud applause from those you love. You are possessive of your loved ones and your turf, and you will roar if anyone threatens to take over your territory.

Moon in Virgo

You are rather cool until you decide if others measure up. But once someone or something meets your ideal standards, you hold up your end of the arrangement perfectly. You may, in fact, drive yourself too hard to attain some notion of perfection. Try to be a bit easier on yourself and others. Don't always act the critic! You love to be the teacher and are drawn to situations where you can change others for the better. But sometimes you must learn to accept others for what they are and enjoy what you have.

Moon in Libra

This is a partnership-oriented placement—you may find it difficult to be alone or to do things alone. But you must learn to lean on yourself first. When you have learned emotional balance, you can have excellent relationships. Avoid extremes in your love life—you thrive in a rather conservative, traditional, romantic relationship, where your partner provides attention and flattery—but not possessiveness. You'll be your most charming in an elegant, harmonious atmosphere.

Moon in Scorpio

This is a moon that enjoys and responds to intense, passionate feelings. You may go to extremes and have a very dramatic emotional life, full of ardor, suspicion, jealousy, and obsession. It would be much healthier to channel your need for power and control into meaningful work. This is a good position for anyone in the fields of medicine, police work, research, the occult, psychoanalysis, or intuitive work, because life-and-death situations are not as likely to faze you. However, you do take personal disappointments very hard.

Moon in Sagittarius

You take life's ups and downs with good humor and the proverbial grain of salt. You'll love 'em and leave 'em, and take off on a great adventure at a moment's notice. "Born free" could be your slogan, for you can't stand to be possessed emotionally by anyone. Attracted by the exotic, you have wanderlust mentally and physically. You may be too much in search of new mental and spiritual stimulation to ever settle down.

Moon in Capricorn

Are you ever accused of being too cool and calculating? You have an earthy side, but you take prestige and position very seriously. Your strong drive to succeed extends to your romantic life, where you will be devoted to improving your lifestyle and rising to the top. A structured situation where you can advance methodically makes you feel wonderfully secure. You may be attracted to someone older or very much younger or from a different social world. It may be difficult to look at the lighter side of emotional relationships, but the "up" side of this moon in its detriment is that you tend to be very dutiful and responsible to those you care for.

Moon in Aquarius

You are a people collector with many friends of all backgrounds. You are happiest surrounded by people and may feel slightly uneasy when left alone. Though intense emotions could be unsettling, you usually stay friends with those with whom you get involved. You're tolerant and understanding, but sometimes you can be emotionally unpredictable. You don't like anything to be too rigid and you may resist working on schedule. You may even have a very unconventional love life. With plenty of space, you will be able to sustain relationships, but you'll blow away from possessive demanding types.

Moon in Pisces

You are very responsive and empathetic to others, especially if they have problems, but be on guard against attracting too many people with sob stories. You'll be happiest if you can find a way to express your creative imagination in the arts or in the spiritual or healing professions. You may tend to escape to a fantasy world or be attracted to exotic places or people. You need an emotional anchor, as you are very sensitive to the moods of others. You are happiest near water, working in a field that gives you emotional variety. But steer clear of too much escapism (especially in alcohol) or reclusiveness. Keep a firm foothold in reality.

Mercury—The Scriptwriter

Mercury shows how you think and speak, and how logically your mind works. It stays close to the sun—never more than a sign away—and very often it shares the same sign as the sun, reinforcing the sun's communicative talents. Mercury functions easily in the naturally analytical signs Gemini and Virgo, which it rules. Yet Mercury in Sagittarius and Pisces, where logic often takes second place to visionary ideas, and where Mercury is debilitated, can provide visionary thinking and poetic expression. But this planet must be properly harnessed. Check your sun sign and the signs preceding and following it to see which Mercury position most applies to you.

Mercury in Aries

Your mind is very active and assertive. You never hesitate to say what you think; you never shy away from a battle. In fact, you may relish a verbal confrontation. Tact is not your strong point, so you may have to learn not to trip over your tongue.

Mercury in Taurus

You may be a slow learner, but you have good concentration and mental stamina. You want to make your ideas really happen. You'll attack a problem methodically and consider every angle thoroughly, never jumping to conclusions. You'll stick with a subject until you master it.

Mercury in Gemini

You are a wonderful communicator with great facility for expressing yourself both verbally and in writing. You talk and talk, and you love gathering all kinds of information. You probably finish other people's sentences and talk with hand gestures. You can talk to anybody anytime—and you probably have the phone bills to prove it. You read anything from sci-fi to Shakespeare, and you might need an extra room just for your book collection. Though you learn fast, you may lack focus and discipline. Watch a tendency to jump from subject to subject.

Mercury in Cancer

You rely on intuition more than logic. Your mental processes are usually colored by your emotions, so you may seem shy or hesitant to voice your opinions. But this placement gives you the advantage of great imagination and empathy in the way you communicate with others.

Mercury in Leo

You are enthusiastic and very dramatic in the way you express yourself. You like to hold the attention of groups and could be a great public speaker. You think big, preferring to deal with the overall picture rather than the details.

Mercury in Virgo

This is one of the best places for Mercury. It should give you the ability to think critically, pay attention to details, and analyze thoroughly. Your mind focuses on the practical side of things, making you well suited to teaching or editing.

Mercury in Libra

You are a born diplomat who smoothes over ruffled feathers. You may be a talented debater or lawyer, but constantly weighing the pros and cons of situations makes you vacillate when making decisions.

Mercury in Scorpio

Yours is an investigative mind that stops at nothing to get the answers. You may have a sarcastic, stinging wit, and a gift for the cutting remark. But there's always a grain of truth to your verbal sallies, thanks to your penetrating insight.

Mercury in Sagittarius

You are a super salesman with a tendency to expound. Though you are very broad minded, you can be dogmatic when it comes to telling others what's good for them. You won't hesitate to tell the truth as you see it, so watch a tendency toward tactlessness. On the plus side, you have a great sense of humor. This position of Mercury is often considered by astrologers to be at a disadvantage because Sagittarius opposes Gemini, the sign Mercury rules, and squares off with Virgo, another Mercury-ruled sign. What often happens is that Mercury in Sagittarius oversteps its bounds and loses sight of the facts in a situation. Do a reality check before making promises that you may not be able to deliver.

Mercury in Capricorn

This placement endows good mental discipline. You have a love of learning and a very orderly approach to your subjects. You will patiently plod through the facts and figures until you have mastered the tasks. You grasp structured situations easily, but may be short on creativity.

Mercury in Aquarius

With Uranus and Neptune in Aquarius now energizing your Mercury, you're sure to be on the cutting edge of new ideas. An independent, original thinker, you'll have more far-out ideas than the average person and be quick to check out any unusual opportunities. Your opinions are so well researched and grounded in fact that once your mind is made up, it is difficult to change.

Mercury in Pisces

You have the psychic intuitive mind of a natural poet. You should learn to make use of your creative imagination. You think in terms of helping others, but check a tendency to be vague and forgetful of details.

Venus—The Romantic Heroine

Venus is the planet of romantic love, pleasure, and artistry. It shows what you react to, your tastes, and what (or who) turns you on. It is naturally at home in Libra, the sign of partnerships, or Taurus, the sign of physical pleasures, both of which it rules. Yet in Aries, its detriment, Venus, daring and full of energy, is negatively self-serving. In Pisces, where Venus is exalted, this planet can go overboard, loving to the point of self-sacrifice. While Venus in Virgo, its fall, can be the perfectionist in love, it can also offer affectionate service and true support.

You can find your Venus placement on the charts in this book. Look for the year of your birth in the left-hand column, then follow the line across the page until you read the time period of your birthday. The sign heading that column will be your Venus. If you were born on a day when Venus was changing signs, check the signs preceding or following that day. Here are the roles your Venus plays—and the songs it sings.

Venus in Aries

Scarlett O'Hara could embody this placement. You can't stand to be bored, confined, or ordered around. But a good challenge—maybe even a rousing row—turns you on. Confess—don't you pick a fight now and then just to get someone stirred up? You're attracted by the chase, not the catch, which could cause some problems in your love life if the object of your affection becomes too attainable. You like to wear red and be first with the latest fashion. You'll spot a trend before anyone else.

Venus in Taurus

All your senses work in high gear, making this the perfect placement for a "Material Girl." You love to be surrounded by glorious tastes, smells, textures, sounds, and sights—austerity is not for you. Neither is being rushed, for you like time to enjoy your pleasures. Soothing surroundings with plenty of creature comforts are your cup of tea. You like to feel secure in your nest, with no sudden jolts or surprises. You like familiar objects—in fact, you may hate to let anything or anyone go.

Venus in Gemini

You are a lively, sparkling personality who "Loves the Night Life," thriving in constant variety and a frequent change of scenery. A varied social life is important to you, with plenty of stimulation and a chance to engage in some light flirtation. Commitment may be difficult because playing the field is so much fun.

Venus in Cancer

An atmosphere where you feel protected, coddled, and mothered is best for you. You'd love to be surrounded by children in a cozy, homelike situation. You are attracted to those who are tender and nurturing, who make you feel secure and well provided for—your "Heart Belongs to Daddy" (or Mommy). You may be secretive about your emotional life or attracted to clandestine relationships.

Venus in Leo

You're an "Uptown Girl" or boy who loves "Puttin' on the Ritz" to consort with elegant people, dress up, and be the center of attraction. First-class attention in large doses turns you on, and so does the glitter of real gold and the flash of mirrors. You like to feel like a star at all times, surrounded by your admiring audience. But you may be attracted to flatterers and tinsel, while the real gold requires some digging.

Venus in Virgo

Everything neatly in its place? On the surface, you are attracted to an atmosphere where everything is in perfect order, but underneath are some basic, earthy urges. You are attracted to those who appeal to your need to teach, serve, or play out a Pygmalion fantasy. You are at your best when you are busy doing something useful.

Venus in Libra

"I Feel Pretty" could be your theme song. Elegance and harmony are your key words—you can't abide an atmosphere of contention. Your taste tends toward the classic, with light harmonies of color—nothing clashing, trendy, or outrageous. You love doing things with a partner and should be careful to pick one who is decisive, but patient enough to let you weigh the pros and cons. Steer clear of argumentative types.

Venus in Scorpio

Hidden mysteries intrigue you—in fact, anything that is too open and above board is a bit of a bore. You surely have a stack of whodunits by the bed, along with an erotic magazine or two. You like to solve puzzles, and you may also be fascinated with the occult, crime, or scientific research. Intense, "All or Nothing at All" situations add spice to your life, and you love to ferret out the secrets of others. But you could get burned by your flair for living on the edge. The color black, spicy food, dark wood furniture, and heady perfume all get you in the right mood.

Venus in Sagittarius

"Like a Rolling Stone" sums up your Venus personality. If you are not actually a world traveler, your surroundings are sure to reflect your love of faraway places. You like a casual outdoor atmosphere and a dog or two to pet. There should be plenty of room for athletic equipment and suitcases. You're attracted to kindred souls who love to travel and who share your freedom-loving philosophy of life. Athletics, as well as spiritual or New Age pursuits, could be your other interests.

Venus in Capricorn

"Diamonds Are a Girl's Best Friend" could be the theme song of this ambitious Venus. You want substance in life and you are attracted to whatever will help you get where you are going. Status objects turn you on, and so do those who have a serious, responsible, businesslike approach, or who remind you of a beloved parent. It is characteristic of this placement to be attracted to someone of a different generation. Antiques, traditional clothing, and dignified behavior favor you.

Venus in Aquarius

"Just Friends, Lovers No More" is often what happens to this Venus. You like to be in a group, particularly one pushing a worthy cause. You feel quite at home surrounded by people, remaining detached from any intense commitment. Original ideas and unpredictable people fascinate you. You don't like everything to be planned out in advance, preferring spontaneity and delightful surprises.

Venus in Pisces

"Why Not Take all of Me?" pleads this Venus, who loves to give of yourself—and you find plenty of takers. Stray animals and people appeal to your heart and your pocketbook, but be careful to look at their motives realistically once in a while. You are extremely vulnerable to sob stories of all kinds. Fantasy, theater, and psychic or spiritual activities also speak to you.

Mars—The Conquering Hero

Mars is the mover and shaker in your life. It shows how you pursue your goals and whether you have energy to burn or proceed in a slow, steady pace. Or perhaps you are nervous, restless, and unable to sit still. Your Mars placement will also show how you get angry: Do you explode, do a slow burn, or hold everything inside, then get revenge later?

In Aries, which it rules, and Scorpio, which it corules, Mars is at its most powerful. Yet this drive can be self-serving and impetuous. In Libra, the sign of its detriment, Mars demands cooperation in a relationship. In Capricorn, where it is exalted, Mars becomes an ambitious achiever headed for the top. But in Cancer, the sign of its fall, Mars's aggression becomes tempered by feelings, especially those involving self-protection and security, which are always considered first. The end can never justify the means for Mars in Cancer.

To find your Mars, turn to the chart on page 86. Find your birth year in the left-hand column and trace the line across horizontally until you come to the column headed by the month of your birth. There you will find an abbreviation of your Mars sign. If the description of your Mars sign doesn't ring true, read the description of the sign preceding and following it. You may have been born on a day when Mars was changing signs, and your Mars would then be in the adjacent sign.

Mars in Aries

In the sign it rules, Mars shows its brilliant, fiery nature. You have an explosive temper and can be quite impatient, but on the other hand you have tremendous cour-

51

age, energy, and drive. You'll let nothing stand in your way as you race to be first! Obstacles are met head on and broken through by force. However, those that require patience and persistence can have you exploding in rage. You're a great starter, but not necessarily around for the finish.

Mars in Taurus

Slow, steady, concentrated energy gives you the power. You've great stamina and you never give up, as you wear away obstacles with your persistence. Often you come out a winner because you've had the patience to hang in there. When angered, you do a slow burn.

Mars in Gemini

You can't sit still for long; this Mars craves variety. You often have two or more things going on at once—it's all an amusing game to you. Your life can get very complicated, but that only adds spice and stimulation. What drives you into a nervous, hyper state? Boredom, sameness, routine, and confinement. You can do wonderful things with your hands and you have a way with words.

Mars in Cancer

You rarely attack head on—instead, you'll keep things to yourself, make plans in secret, and always cover your actions. This might be interpreted by some as manipulative, but you are only being self-protective. You get furious when anyone knows too much about you, but you do like to know all about others. Your mothering and feeding instincts can be put to good use if you work in the food, hotel, or child-care industry. You may have to overcome your fragile sense of security, which prompts you not to take risks and to get physically upset when criticized. Don't take things so personally!

Mars in Leo

You have a very dominant personality that takes center stage—modesty is not one of your traits, nor is taking a back seat. You prefer giving the orders and have been known to make a dramatic scene if they are not obeyed. Properly used, this Mars confers leadership ability, endurance, and courage.

Mars in Virgo

You are the fault finder of the zodiac, who notices every little detail. Mistakes of any kind make you very nervous. You may worry even if everything is going smoothly. You may not express your anger directly, but you sure can nag. You have definite likes and dislikes and you are sure you can do the job better than anyone else. You are certainly more industrious and detail oriented than other signs. Your Mars energy is often most positively expressed in some kind of teaching role.

Mars in Libra

This Mars will have a passion for beauty, justice, and art. Generally, you will avoid confrontations at all costs, preferring to spend your energy finding a diplomatic solution or weighing the pros and cons. Your other techniques are using passive aggression or charm to get people to do what you want.

Mars in Scorpio

This is a powerful placement, so intense that it demands careful channeling into worthwhile activities. Otherwise, you could become obsessed with your sexuality or might use your need for power and control to manipulate others. You are strong willed, shrewd, and very private about your affairs, and you'll usually have a secret agenda behind your actions. Your great stamina, focus, and discipline would be excellent assets for careers in the military or medical fields, especially research or surgery. When angry, you don't get mad—you get even!

Mars in Sagittarius

This expansive Mars often propels people into sales, travel, athletics, or philosophy. Your energies function well when you are on the move. You have a hot temper and are inclined to say what you think before you consider the consequences. You shoot for high goals—and talk endlessly about them—but you may be weak on groundwork. This Mars needs a solid foundation. Watch a tendency to take unnecessary risks.

Mars in Capricorn

This is an ambitious Mars with an excellent sense of timing. You have the drive for success and the discipline to achieve it. You have an eye for those who can be of use to you, and you may dismiss people ruthlessly when you're angry. But you drive yourself hard and deliver full value. This is a good placement for an executive. You'll aim for status and a high material position in life, and keep climbing despite the odds. A great Mars to have!

Mars in Aquarius

This is the most rebellious Mars. You seem to have a drive to assert yourself against the status quo. You may enjoy provoking people, shocking them out of traditional views. Or this placement could express itself in an off-beat sex life—somehow you often find yourself in unconventional situations. You enjoy being a leader of an active group that pursues forward-looking studies, politics, or goals.

Mars in Pisces

This Mars is a good actor who knows just how to appeal to the sympathies of others. You create and project wonderful fantasies or use your sensitive antennae to crusade for those less fortunate. You get what you want through creating a veil of illusion and glamour. This is a good Mars for someone in the creative fields—a dancer, performer, or photographer—or for someone in the motion-picture industry. Many famous film stars have this placement. Watch a tendency to manipulate by making others feel sorry for you.

Jupiter—The Jolly Giant

Jupiter is often viewed as the "Santa Claus" of the horoscope, a jolly happy planet that brings good luck, gifts, success, and opportunities. Jupiter also embodies the functions of the higher mind, where you do complex, expansive thinking and deal with the big overall picture rather than the specifics (the role of Mercury). This big, bright, swirling mass of gases is associated with the kind of windfall you get without too much hard work. You're optimistic under Jupiter's influence—anything seems possible. You'll travel, expand your mind with higher education, and publish to share your knowledge widely. But a strong Jupiter has its down side, too. Jupiter's influence is neither discriminating nor disciplined. It represents the principle of growth without judgment, and could result in extravagance, weight gain, laziness, and carelessness if not kept in check.

Be sure to look up your Jupiter in the tables in this book. When the current position of Jupiter is favorable, you may get that lucky break. At any rate, it's a great time to try new things, take risks, travel, or get more education. Opportunities seem to open up at this time, so take advantage of them. Once a year, Jupiter changes signs. That means you are due for an expansive time every twelve years, when Jupiter travels through your sun sign. You'll also have "up" periods every four years, when Jupiter is in the same element as your sun sign.

Jupiter in Aries

You are the soul of enthusiasm and optimism. Your luckiest times are when you are getting started on an exciting project or selling an ideal that you really believe in, but don't be arrogant with those who do not share your enthusiasm. You follow your impulses, often ignoring budget or other common sense limitations. To produce real, solid benefits, you'll need patience and follow-through wherever this Jupiter falls in your horoscope.

Jupiter in Taurus

You'll spend on beautiful material things, especially items made of natural materials, such as rare woods, pure fabrics, or precious gems. You can't have too much comfort or too many sensual pleasures. Watch a tendency to overindulge in good food, or to overpamper yourself with nothing but the best. Spartan living is not for you! You may be especially lucky in matters of real estate.

Jupiter in Gemini

You are the great talker of the zodiac, and you may be a great writer, too. But restlessness could be your weak point. You jump around, talk too much, and could be a jack of all trades. Keeping a secret is especially difficult, so you'll also have to watch a tendency to spill the beans. Since you love to be at the center of a beehive of activity, you'll have a vibrant social life. Your best opportunities will come through your talent for language—speaking, writing, communicating, and selling.

Jupiter in Cancer

You are luckiest in situations where you can find emotional closeness or deal with basic security needs, such as food, nurturing, or shelter. You may be a great collector and you may simply love to accumulate things—you are the one who stashed things away for a rainy day. You probably have a very good memory and love children—in fact, you may have many children to care for. The food, hotel, child-care, or shipping business hold good opportunities for you.

Jupiter in Leo

You are a natural showman who loves to live in a larger-than-life way. Yours is a personality full of color that always find its way into the limelight. You can't have too much attention or applause. Show biz is a natural place for you, and so is any area where you can play to a crowd. Exercising your flair for drama, your natural playfulness, and your romantic nature brings you good fortune. But watch a tendency to be overly extravagant or to monopolize center stage.

Jupiter in Virgo

You actually love those minute details others find boring. To you, they make all the difference between the perfect and the ordinary. You are the fine craftsman who spots every flaw. You expand your awareness by finding the most efficient methods and by being of service to others. Many will be drawn to medical or teaching fields. You'll also have luck in publishing, crafts, nutrition, and service professions. Watch out for a tendency to overwork.

Jupiter in Libra

This is an other-directed Jupiter that develops best with a partner, for the stimulation of others helps you grow.

You are also most comfortable in harmonious, beautiful situations, and you work well with artistic people. You have a great sense of fair play and an ability to evaluate the pros and cons of a situation. You usually prefer to play the role of diplomat rather than adversary.

Jupiter in Scorpio

You love the feeling of power and control, of taking things to their limit. You can't resist a mystery, and your shrewd, penetrating mind sees right through to the heart of most situations and people. You have luck in work that provides for solutions to matters of life and death. You may be drawn to undercover work, behind-the-scenes intrigue, psychotherapy, the occult, and sex-related ventures. Your challenge will be to develop a sense of moderation and tolerance for other beliefs—this Jupiter can be fanatical. You may have luck in handling other people's money—insurance, taxes, and inheritance can bring you a windfall.

Jupiter in Sagittarius

Independent, outgoing, and idealistic, you'll shoot for the stars. This Jupiter compels you to travel far and wide, both physically and mentally, via higher education. You may have luck while traveling in an exotic place. You also have luck with outdoor ventures, exercise, and animals, particularly horses. Since you tend to be very open about your opinions, watch a tendency to be tactless and to exaggerate. Instead, use your wonderful sense of humor to make your point.

Jupiter in Capricorn

Jupiter is much more restrained in Capricorn, the sign of rules and authority. Here, Jupiter can make you overwork and heighten your ambition or sense of duty. You'll expand in areas that advance your position, putting you farther up the social or corporate ladder. You are lucky working within the establishment in a very structured situation, where you can show off your ability to organize and reap rewards for your hard work.

Jupiter in Aquarius

This is another freedom-loving Jupiter, with great tolerance and originality. You are at your best when you are working for a humanitarian cause and in the company of many supporters. This is a good Jupiter for a political career, for you'll relate to all kinds of people on all social levels. You have an abundance of original ideas, but you are best off away from routine and any situation that imposes rigid rules. You need mental stimulation!

Jupiter in Pisces

You are a giver whose feelings and pocketbook are easily touched by others, so choose your companions with care. You could be the original sucker for a hard-luck story—better find a worthy hospital or charity to appreciate your selfless support. You have a great creative imagination and may attract good fortune in fields related to oil, perfume, pharmaceuticals, petroleum, dance, footwear, and alcohol. But beware of overindulgence in alcohol—focus on a creative outlet instead.

Saturn—The "Heavy"

Jupiter speeds you up with lucky breaks, then along comes Saturn to slow you down with the disciplinary brakes. Saturn has unfairly been called a malefic planet, one of the bad guys of the zodiac. On the contrary, Saturn is one of our best friends, the kind who tells you what's wrong with you for your own good. Under a Saturn transit, we grow up, take responsibility for our lives, and emerge from whatever test this planet has in store, far wiser, more capable, and mature.

When Saturn hits a critical point in your horoscope, you can count on an experience that will make you slow down, pull back, and reexamine your life. It is a call to eliminate what is not working and to shape up. By the end of its 28-year trip around the zodiac, Saturn will have tested you in all areas of your life. The major tests usually happen in seven-year cycles, when Saturn passes over the angles of your chart—your rising sun, midheaven, descendant, and nadir. This is when the real life-changing experiences happen. But you are also in for a testing period whenever Saturn passes a planet in your chart or stresses that planet from a distance. Therefore it is useful to check your planetary positions with the travel schedule of Saturn in order to prepare in advance, or at least to brace yourself.

When Saturn returns to its location at the time of your birth, at approximately age 28, you'll have your first Saturn return. At this time, a person usually takes stock or settles down to find his mission in life and assume full adult duties and responsibilities.

Another way Saturn helps us is to reveal the karmic lessons from previous lives and give us the chance to overcome them. So look at Saturn's challenges as much-needed opportunities for self-improvement. Under a Jupiter influence, you'll have more fun, but Saturn gives you solid, long-lasting results.

Look up your natal Saturn in the tables in this book for clues on where you need work.

Saturn in Aries

Saturn here puts the brakes on Aries' natural drive and enthusiasm. You don't let anyone push you around and you know what's best for yourself. Following orders is not your strong point, and neither is diplomacy. You tend to be quick to go on the offensive in relationships, attacking first, before anyone attacks you. Because no one quite lives up to your standards, you often wind up doing everything yourself. You'll have to learn to cooperate and tone down self-centeredness.

Saturn in Taurus

A big issue is getting control of the cash flow. There will be lean periods that can be frightening, but you have the patience and endurance to stick them out and the methodical drive to prosper in the end. Learn to take a philosophical attitude like Ben Franklin, who also had this placement and who said, "A penny saved is a penny earned."

Saturn in Gemini

You are a serious student of life who may have difficulty communicating or sharing your knowledge. You may be shy, speak slowly, or have fears about communicating, like Eleanor Roosevelt. You dwell in the realms of science, theory, or abstract analysis, even when you are dealing with the emotions, like Sigmund Freud, who also had this placement.

Saturn in Cancer

Your tests come with establishing a secure emotional base. In doing so, you may have to deal with some very basic fears centering on your early home environment. Most of your Saturn tests will have emotional roots in those early childhood experiences. You may have difficulty remaining objective in terms of what you try to achieve, so it will be especially important for you to deal with negative feelings such as guilt, paranoia, jealousy, resentment, and suspicion. Galileo and Michelangelo also navigated these murky waters.

Saturn in Leo

This is an authoritarian Saturn, a strict, demanding parent who may deny the pleasure principle in your zeal to see that rules are followed. Though you may feel guilty about taking the spotlight, you are very ambitious and loyal. You have to watch a tendency toward rigidity, as well as a leaning toward overwork and holding back affection. Joseph Kennedy and Billy Graham share this placement.

Saturn in Virgo

This is a cautious, exacting Saturn, intensely hard on yourself. Most of all, you give yourself the roughest time with your constant worries about every little detail, often making yourself sick. You may have difficulties setting priorities and getting the job done. Your tests will come in learning tolerance and understanding of others. Charles de Gaulle and Nathaniel Hawthorne had this meticulous Saturn.

Saturn in Libra

Saturn is exalted here, which makes this planet an ally. You may choose very serious, older partners in life, perhaps stemming from a fear of dependency. You need to learn to stand solidly on your own before you commit to another. You are extremely cautious as you deliberate every involvement—with good reason. It is best that you find an occupation that makes good use of your sense of duty and honor. Steer clear of fly-by-night situations. Khrushchev and Mao Tse-tung had this placement, too.

Saturn in Scorpio

You have great staying power. This Saturn tests you in situations involving the control of others. You may feel drawn to some kind of intrigue or undercover work, like J. Edgar Hoover. Or there may be an air of mystery surrounding your life and death, like Marilyn Monroe and Robert Kennedy, who had this placement. There are lessons to be learned from your sexual involvements—often sex is used for manipulation or is somehow out of the ordinary. The Roman emperor Caligula and the transvestite Christine Jorgensen are extreme cases.

Saturn in Sagittarius

Your challenges and lessons will come from tests of your spiritual and philosophical values, as happened to Martin Luther King and Gandhi. You are high minded and sincere with the reflective, moral placement. Uncompromising in your ethical standards, you could become a benevolent despot.

Saturn in Capricorn

With the help of Saturn at maximum strength, your judgment will improve with age. And, like Spencer Tracy's screen image, you'll be the gray-haired hero with a strong sense of responsibility. You advance in life slowly but steadily, always with a strong hand at the helm and an eye for the advantageous situation. Negatively, you may be a loner, prone to periods of melancholy.

Saturn in Aquarius

Do you care too much about what others think? Do you feel like an outsider, as Greta Garbo did? You may fear being different from others and therefore slight your own unique, forward-looking gifts, or, like Lord Byron and Howard Hughes, you may take the opposite tack and rebel in the extreme. You can apply discipline to accomplish great humanitarian goals, as Albert Schweitzer did.

Saturn in Pisces

Your fear of the unknown and the irrational may lead you to the safety and protection of an established institution. Some of you may avoid looking too deeply inside at all costs. Jesse James, who had this placement, spent his life on the run. Or you might go in the opposite, more positive direction by developing a discipline that puts you more in control of your feelings. Some of you will take refuge in work with hospitals, charities, or religious institutions.

Queen Victoria, who had this placement, symbolized an era when charitable institutions of all kinds were founded. Discipline applied to artistic work, especially poetry and dance, or spiritual work, such as yoga or meditation, might be helpful.

Uranus, Neptune, and Pluto— The Character Roles

These three outer planets are slow moving but powerful forces in your life. Since they stay in a sign at least seven years, you'll share the sign placement with everyone you went to school with and perhaps your brothers and sisters. However, the area of life (house) where the planet operates in your chart is what makes its influence unique to you. When one of these distant planets changes signs, there is a definite shift in the atmosphere, bringing the feeling of the end of an era.

Since these planets are so far away from the sun—too distant to be seen by the naked eye—they pick up signals from the universe at large. These planetary receivers literally link the sun with distant energies, and then perform a similar function in your horoscope by linking your central character with intuitive, spiritual, transformative forces from the cosmos. Each planet has a special domain and will reflect this in the area of your life where it falls.

Uranus—The Revolutionary, the Techie

Uranus is the brilliant, highly unpredictable genius who shakes us out of our rut and propels us forward. There is nothing ordinary about this quirky green planet that seems to be traveling on its side, surrounded by a swarm of at least fifteen moons. Is it any wonder that astrologers assigned it to Aquarius, the most eccentric and gregarious sign? Uranus seems to wend its way around the sun, marching to its own tune.

Uranus energy is electrical, happening in sudden flashes. It is not influenced by karma or past events, nor does it regard tradition, sex, or sentiment. The Uranian key words are "surprise" and "awakening." Suddenly, there's that flash of inspiration, that bright idea, that totally new approach that turns around whatever scheme you were undertaking. The Uranus place in your life is where you awaken and become your own person, and it is probably the most unconventional place in your chart.

Look up the sign of Uranus at the time of your birth and see where you follow your own tune.

Uranus in Aries

BIRTH DATES:
March 30, 1927–November 4, 1927
January 13, 1928—June 6, 1934
October 10, 1934—March 28, 1935

Your generation is original, creative, and pioneering. It developed the computer, the airplane, and the cyclotron. You let nothing hold you back from exploring the unknown and you have a powerful mixture of fire and electricity behind you. Women of your generation were among the first to be liberated. You are the unforgettable style setters, with a surprise in store for everyone. Like Yoko Ono, Grace Kelly, and Jacqueline Onassis, your life may be jolted by sudden and violent changes.

Uranus in Taurus

BIRTH DATES:
June 6, 1934–October 10, 1934
March 28, 1935–August 7, 1941
October 5, 1941–May 15, 1942

You are probably self-employed or would like to be. You have original ideas about making money, and you brace yourself for sudden changes of fortune. This Uranus can cause shakeups, particularly in finances, but it can also make you a born entrepreneur.

Uranus in Gemini

BIRTH DATES:
August 7, 1941–October 5, 1941
May 15, 1942–August 30, 1948
November 12, 1948–June 10, 1949
You were the first children to be influenced by television and in your adult years, your generation stocks up on answering machines, cordless phones, car phones, computers, and fax machines—any new way you can communicate. You have an inquiring mind, but your interests are rather short lived. This Uranus can be easily fragmented if there is no structure and focus.

Uranus in Cancer

BIRTH DATES:
August 30, 1948–November 12, 1948
June 10, 1949–August 24, 1955
January 28, 1956–June 10, 1956
This generation came at a time when divorce was becoming commonplace, so your home image is unconventional. You may have an unusual relationship with your parents; you may have come from a broken home or an unconventional one. You'll have unorthodox ideas about parenting, intimacy, food, and shelter. You may also be interested in dreams, psychic phenomena, and memory work.

Uranus in Leo

BIRTH DATES:
August 24, 1955–January 28, 1956
June 10, 1956–November 1, 1961
January 10, 1962–August 10, 1962
This generation understood how to use electronic media. Many of your group are now leaders in the high-tech

industries, and you also understand how to use the new media to promote yourself. Like Isadora Duncan, you may have a very eccentric kind of charisma and a life that is sparked by unusual love affairs. Your children, too, may have traits that are out of the ordinary. Where this planet falls in your chart, you'll have a love of freedom, be a bit of an egomaniac, and show the full force of your personality in a unique way, like tennis great Martina Navratilova.

Uranus in Virgo

BIRTH DATES:
November 1, 1961–January 10, 1962
August 10, 1962–September 28, 1968
May 20, 1969–June 24, 1969

You'll have highly individual work methods, and many of you will be finding newer, more practical ways to use computers. Like Einstein, who had this placement, you'll break the rules brilliantly. Your generation came at a time of student rebellions, the civil rights movement, and the general acceptance of health foods. Chances are, you're concerned about pollution and cleaning up the environment. You may also be involved with nontraditional healing methods. Heavyweight champ Mike Tyson has this placement.

Uranus in Libra

BIRTH DATES:
September 28, 1968–May 20, 1969
June 24, 1969–November 21, 1974
May 1, 1975–September 8, 1975.

Your generation is likely to have unconventional relationships. Born during the time when women's liberation was a major issue, many of your generation came from broken homes and have no clear image of what a committed relationship entails. There may be sudden splits and experiments before you settle down. Your generation will be much involved in legal and political reforms and in changing artistic and fashion looks.

Uranus in Scorpio

BIRTH DATES:
November 21, 1974–May 1, 1975
September 8, 1975–February 17, 1981
March 20, 1981–November 16, 1981

Interest in transformation, meditation, and life after death signaled the beginning of New Age consciousness. Your generation recognizes no boundaries, no limits, and no external controls. You'll have new attitudes toward death and dying, psychic phenomena, and the occult. Like Mae West and Casanova, you'll shock 'em sexually, too.

Uranus in Sagittarius

BIRTH DATES:
February 17, 1981–March 20, 1981
November 16, 1981–February 15, 1988
Mary 27, 1988–December 2, 1988

Could this generation be the first to travel in outer space? The last generation with this placement included Charles Lindbergh—at that time, the first Zeppelins and the Wright Brothers were conquering the skies. Uranus here forecasts great discoveries, mind expansion, and long-distance travel. Like Galileo and Martin Luther, this generation will generate new theories about the cosmos and man's relation to it.

Uranus in Capricorn

BIRTH DATES:
December 20, 1903–January 30, 1912
September 4, 1912–November 12, 1912

February 15, 1988–May 27, 1988
December 2, 1988–April 1, 1995
June 9, 1995–January 12, 1996

This generation will challenge traditions with the help of electronic gadgets. In these years, we got organized with the help of technology put to practical use. Great leaders, movers and shakers of history like Julius Caesar and Henry VIII, were born under this placement.

Uranus in Aquarius

BIRTH DATES:
January 30, 1912–September 4, 1912
November 12, 1912–April 1, 1919
August 16, 1919–January 22, 1920
April 1, 1995–June 9, 1995
January 12, 1996–March 10, 2003

The last generation with this placement produced great innovative minds such as Leonard Bernstein and Orson Welles. The next will become another radical breakthrough generation, much concerned with global issues that involve all humanity. Intuition, innovation, and sudden changes will surprise everyone when Uranus is in its home sign. This will be a time of experimentation on every level.

Uranus in Pisces

BIRTH DATES:
April 1, 1919–August 16, 1919
January 22, 1920–March 31, 1927
November 4, 1927–January 12, 1928

In this century, Uranus in Pisces focused attention on the rise of electronic entertainment—radio and the cinema, and the secretiveness of Prohibition. This produced a generation of idealists exemplified by Judy Garland's theme, "Somewhere Over the Rainbow."

Neptune—The Glamour Girl

Under Neptune's influence, you see what you want to see. Neptune is the planet of illusion, dissolution (it dissolves hard reality), and makeup. Neptune is not interested in the world at face value—it dons tinted glasses or blurs the facts with the haze of an intoxicating substance.

But Neptune also encourages you to create, to let your fantasies and daydreams run free, to break through your ordinary perceptions and go to another level of reality, where you can experience either confusion or ecstasy. Neptune's force can pull you off course, like this planet affects its neighbor, Uranus, but only if you allow this to happen. Those who use Neptune wisely can translate their daydreams into poetry, theater, design, or inspired moves in the business world, avoiding the tricky "con artist" side of this planet.

Find your Neptune listed here:

Neptune in Cancer

BIRTH DATES:
July 19, 1901–December 25, 1901
May 21, 1902–September 23, 1914
December 14, 1914–July 19, 1915
March 19, 1916–May 2, 1916

Dreams of the homeland, idealistic patriotism, and glamorization of the nurturing assets of women characterized this time. You who were born here have unusual psychic ability and deep insights into the basic needs of others.

Neptune in Leo

BIRTH DATES:
September 23, 1914–December 14, 1914
July 19, 1915–March 19, 1916

May 2, 1916–September 21, 1928
February 19, 1929–July 24, 1929

Neptune here brought us the glamour and high living of the 1920s and the big spenders of that time, when Neptunian temptations of gambling, seduction, theater, and lavish entertaining distracted from the realities of the age. Those born in that generation also made great advances in the arts.

Neptune in Virgo

BIRTH DATES:

September 21, 1928–February 19, 1929
July 24, 1929–October 3, 1942
April 17, 1943–August 2, 1943

Neptune in Virgo encompassed the Great Depression and World War II, while those born at this time later spread the gospel of health and fitness. This generation's devotion to spending hours at the office inspired the term "workaholic." Health-care concerns of the elderly will come to the forefront of national consciousness as this generation ages, changing the way we think about growing old.

Neptune in Libra

BIRTH DATES:

October 3, 1942–April 17, 1943
August 2, 1943–December 24, 1955
March 12, 1956–October 19, 1956
June 15, 1957–August 6, 1957

Neptune in Libra was the romantic generation who would later be concerned with relating. As this generation matured, there was a new trend toward marriage and commitment. Racial and sexual equality became important issues, as they redesigned traditional male and female roles to suit modern times.

Neptune in Scorpio

BIRTH DATES:

December 24, 1955–March 12, 1956

October 19, 1956–June 15, 1957

August 6, 1957–January 4, 1970

May 3, 1970–November 6, 1970

Neptune in Scorpio brought in a generation that would become interested in transformative power. Born in an era that glamorized sex, drugs, rock and roll, and Eastern religion, they matured in a more sobering time of AIDS, cocaine abuse, and New Age spirituality. As they evolve, they will become active in healing the planet from the results of the abuse of power.

Neptune in Sagittarius

BIRTH DATES:

January 4, 1970–May 3, 1970

November 6, 1970–January 19, 1984

June 23, 1984–November 21, 1984

Neptune in Sagittarius was the time when space travel became a reality. The Neptune influence glamorized new approaches to mysticism, religion, and mind expansion. This generation will take a new approach to spiritual life, with emphasis on visions, mysticism, and clairvoyance.

Neptune in Capricorn

BIRTH DATES:

January 19, 1984–June 23, 1984

November 21, 1984–January 29, 1998

Neptune in Capricorn, which began in 1984 and would stay until 1998, brought a time when delusions about material power were first glamorized, then dashed on the rocks of reality. It was also a time when the psychic and occult worlds spawned a new category of business enterprise and sold services on television.

Neptune in Aquarius

BIRTH DATES:
Starting January 29, 1998 through the end of the century

This should be a time of breakthroughs, when the creative influence of Neptune reaches a universal audience. This is a time of dissolving barriers, when we truly become one world.

Pluto—The Private Eye

Pluto deals with the underworld of our personality, digging out our secrets to effect a total transformation as it brings deep subconscious feelings to the surface. Nothing escapes—or is sacred—with Pluto. When this tiny planet zaps a strategic point in your horoscope, your life changes so dramatically that there's no going back.

While Mars governs the visible power, Pluto is the power behind the scenes, where you can transform, heal, and affect the unconscious needs of the masses. Pluto governs your need to control, as well as your attitudes toward death and immortality. Much of the strength of your Pluto will depend on its position in your chart and the aspects it makes to other planets.

Because Pluto was discovered only recently, the signs of its exaltation and fall are debated. However, it was given the rulership of Scorpio. As it passed through Scorpio from 1984 to 1995 under the rule of Pluto, we were able to witness this planet's fullest effect. Because of its eccentric path, the length of time Pluto stays in any given sign can vary from 13 to 32 years.

Pluto in Gemini

BIRTH DATES:
Late 1800s–May 28, 1914

This was a time of mass suggestion and breakthroughs in communications, when many brilliant writers, such as Ernest Hemingway and F. Scott Fitzgerald, were born. Henry Miller, D. H. Lawrence, and James Joyce scandalized society by using explicit sexual images and language in their literature. "Muckraking" journalists exposed corruption. Pluto-ruled Scorpio President Theodore Roosevelt said, "Speak softly, but carry a big stick." This generation had an intense need to communicate and made major breakthroughs in knowledge. A compulsive restlessness and a thirst for a variety of experiences characterizes many of this generation.

Pluto in Cancer

BIRTH DATES:
May 28, 1914–June 14, 1939

Pluto in Cancer suggests great emotional (Cancer) power. During this time period dictators and mass media arose to manipulate the emotions of the masses. Women's rights were obtained as Pluto transited this lunar-ruled sign, transforming the position of women in society. Deep sentimental feelings, acquisitiveness, and possessiveness characterize these times and the people who were born then.

Pluto in Leo

BIRTH DATES:
June 14, 1939–August 19, 1957

The performing arts, under Leo's rule, never wielded more power over the masses than during this era. Pluto in Leo transforms via creative self-expression, exemplified by the almost shamanistic rock and roll stars such as Mick Jagger and John Lennon, who were born at this time. (So were Bill and Hillary Clinton.) People born with Pluto in Leo often tend to be self-centered and love to "do their own thing"—for better or for worse.

Pluto in Virgo

BIRTH DATES:
August 19, 1957–October 5, 1971
April 17, 1972–July 30, 1972

This became the "yuppie" generation that sparked a mass clean-up shape-up movement toward fitness, health, and obsessive careerism. It's a much more sober, serious, driven generation than the fun-loving Pluto in Leos. During this time, inventions took on a practical turn, as answering machines, fax machines, car phones, and home office equipment have all transformed the workplace.

Pluto in Libra

BIRTH DATES:
October 5, 1971–April 17, 1972
July 30, 1972–August 28, 1984

A mellower generation, people born at this time are concerned with partnerships, working together, and finding diplomatic solutions to problems. Marriage is important to this generation, who redefine it along more traditional, but equal-partnership lines. This was a time of women's liberation, gay rights, ERA, and legal battles over abortion, all of which transformed our ideas about relationships.

Pluto in Scorpio

BIRTH DATES:
August 28, 1984–January 17, 1995

Pluto was in its ruling sign for a comparatively short period of time. In 1989, it was at its perihelion, or the closest point to the sun and Earth. We have all felt this transforming power somewhere in our lives. This was a time of record achievements, destructive sexually transmitted diseases, nuclear power controversies, and explosive political issues. Pluto destroys in order to create new understanding—think of it as a phoenix rising from the ashes, which should be some consolation for those of you who have felt Pluto's force before 1995. Sexual shockers were par for the course during these intense years, when black clothing, transvestites, body piercing, tattoos, and sexually explicit advertising pushed the boundaries of good taste.

Pluto in Sagittarius

BIRTH DATES:
January 17, 1995–January 27, 2008

During our current Pluto transit through Sagittarius, we are being pushed to expand our horizons and find deeper meaning in life. For many of us, this will mean traveling the globe via our modems as we explore the vastness of the Internet. It signals a time of spiritual transformation and religion will exert much power in politics as well. Since Sagittarius is the sign that rules travel, there's a good possibility that Pluto, the planet of extremes, will make space travel a reality for some of us. Discovery of life on Mars, traveling here as minute life forms on meteors, could transform our ideas about where we came from. At this writing, a giant telescope in Puerto Rico has been reactivated to search the faraway galaxies for pulsing hints of life.

New dimensions in electronic publishing, concern with animal rights and the environment, and an increasing emphasis on extreme forms of religion are signs of Pluto in Sagittarius. Look for charismatic religious leaders to arise now. We'll also be developing far-reaching philosophies designed to elevate our lives with a new sense of purpose.

Look Up Your Planets

The following tables are provided so that you can look up the signs of seven major planets—Venus, Mars, Saturn, Jupiter, Uranus, Neptune, and Pluto. We do not have room for tables for the moon and Mercury, which change signs often.

How to Use the Venus Table

Find the year of your birth in the vertical column on the left, then follow across the page until you find the correct date. Your Venus sign is at the top of that column.

VENUS SIGNS 1901–2000

	Aries	Taurus	Gemini	Cancer	Leo	Virgo
1901	3/29–4/22	4/22–5/17	5/17–6/10	6/10–7/5	7/5–7/29	7/29–8/23
1902	5/7–6/3	6/3–6/30	6/30–7/25	7/25–8/19	8/19–9/13	9/13–10/7
1903	2/28–3/24	3/24–4/18	4/18–5/13	5/13–6/9	6/9–7/7	7/7–8/17
						9/6–11/8
1904	3/13–5/7	5/7–6/1	6/1–6/25	6/25–7/19	7/19–8/13	8/13–9/6
1905	2/3–3/6	3/6–4/9	7/8–8/6	8/6–9/1	9/1–9/27	9/27–10/21
	4/9–5/28	5/28–7/8				
1906	3/1–4/7	4/7–5/2	5/2–5/26	5/26–6/20	6/20–7/16	7/16–8/11
1907	4/27–5/22	5/22–6/16	6/16–7/11	7/11–8/4	8/4–8/29	8/29–9/22
1908	2/14–3/10	3/10–4/5	4/5–5/5	5/5–9/8	9/8–10/8	10/8–11/3
1909	3/29–4/22	4/22–5/16	5/16–6/10	6/10–7/4	7/4–7/29	7/29–8/23
1910	5/7–6/3	6/4–6/29	6/30–7/24	7/25–8/18	8/19–9/12	9/13–10/6
1911	2/28–3/23	3/24–4/17	4/18–5/12	5/13–6/8	6/9–7/7	7/8–11/8
1912	4/13–5/6	5/7–5/31	6/1–6/24	6/24–7/18	7/19–8/12	8/13–9/5
1913	2/3–3/6	3/7–5/1	7/8–8/5	8/6–8/31	9/1–9/26	9/27–10/20
	5/2–5/30	5/31–7/7				
1914	3/14–4/6	4/7–5/1	5/2–5/25	5/26–6/19	6/20–7/15	7/16–8/10
1915	4/27–5/21	5/22–6/15	6/16–7/10	7/11–8/3	8/4–8/28	8/29–9/21
1916	2/14–3/9	3/10–4/5	4/6–5/5	5/6–9/8	9/9–10/7	10/8–11/2
1917	3/29–4/21	4/22–5/15	5/16–6/9	6/10–7/3	7/4–7/28	7/29–8/21
1918	5/7–6/2	6/3–6/28	6/29–7/24	7/25–8/18	8/19–9/11	9/12–10/5
1919	2/27–3/22	3/23–4/16	4/17–5/12	5/13–6/7	6/8–7/7	7/8–11/8
1920	4/12–5/6	5/7–5/30	5/31–6/23	6/24–7/18	7/19–8/11	8/12–9/4
1921	2/3–3/6	3/7–4/25	7/8–8/5	8/6–8/31	9/1–9/25	9/26–10/20
	4/26–6/1	6/2–7/7				
1922	3/13–4/6	4/7–4/30	5/1–5/25	5/26–6/19	6/20–7/14	7/15–8/9
1923	4/27–5/21	5/22–6/14	6/15–7/9	7/10–8/3	8/4–8/27	8/28–9/20
1924	2/13–3/8	3/9–4/4	4/5–5/5	5/6–9/8	9/9–10/7	10/8–11/12
1925	3/28–4/20	4/21–5/15	5/16–6/8	6/9–7/3	7/4–7/27	7/28–8/21

Libra	Scorpio	Sagittarius	Capricorn	Aquarius	Pisces
8/23–9/17	9/17–10/12	10/12–1/16	1/16–2/9	2/9–3/5	3/5–3/29
			11/7–12/5	12/5–1/11	
10/7–10/31	10/31–11/24	11/24–12/18	12/18–1/11	2/6–4/4	1/11–2/6
					4/4–5/7
8/17–9/6	12/9–1/5			1/11–2/4	2/4–2/28
11/8–12/9					
9/6–9/30	9/30–10/25	1/5–1/30	1/30–2/24	2/24–3/19	3/19–4/13
		10/25–11/18	11/18–12/13	12/13–1/7	
10/21–11/14	11/14–12/8	12/8–1/1/06			1/7–2/3
8/11–9/7	9/7–10/9	10/9–12/15	1/1–1/25	1/25–2/18	2/18–3/14
	12/15–12/25	12/25–2/6			
9/22–10/16	10/16–11/9	11/9–12/3	2/6–3/6	3/6–4/2	4/2–4/27
			12/3–12/27	12/27–1/20	
11/3–11/28	11/28–12/22	12/22–1/15			1/20–2/4
8/23–9/17	9/17–10/12	10/12–11/17	1/15–2/9	2/9–3/5	3/5–3/29
			11/17–12/5	12/5–1/15	
10/7–10/30	10/31–11/23	11/24–12/17	12/18–12/31	1/1–1/15	1/16–1/28
				1/29–4/4	4/5–5/6
11/19–12/8	12/9–12/31		1/1–1/10	1/11–2/2	2/3–2/27
9/6–9/30	1/1–1/4	1/5–1/29	1/30–2/23	2/24–3/18	3/19–4/12
	10/1–10/24	10/25–11/17	11/18–12/12	12/13–12/31	
10/21–11/13	11/14–12/7	12/8–12/31		1/1–1/6	1/7–2/2
8/11–9/6	9/7–10/9	10/10–12/5	1/1–1/24	1/25–2/17	2/18–3/13
	12/6–12/30	12/31			
9/22–10/15	10/16–11/8	1/1–2/6	2/7–3/6	3/7–4/1	4/2–4/26
		11/9–12/2	12/3–12/26	12/27–12/31	
11/3–11/27	11/28–12/21	12/22–12/31		1/1–1/19	1/20–2/13
8/22–9/16	9/17–10/11	1/1–1/14	1/15–2/7	2/8–3/4	3/5–3/28
		10/12–11/6	11/7–12/5	12/6–12/31	
10/6–10/29	10/30–11/22	11/23–12/16	12/17–12/31	1/1–4/5	4/6–5/6
11/9–12/8	12/9–12/31		1/1–1/9	1/10–2/2	2/3–2/26
9/5–9/30	1/1–1/3	1/4–1/28	1/29–2/22	2/23–3/18	3/19–4/11
	9/31–10/23	10/24–11/17	11/18–12/11	12/12–12/31	
10/21–11/13	11/14–12/7	12/8–12/31		1/1–1/6	1/7–2/2
8/10–9/6	9/7–10/10	10/11–11/28	1/1–1/24	1/25–2/16	2/17–3/12
	11/29–12/31				
9/21–10/14	1/1	1/2–2/6	2/7–3/5	3/6–3/31	4/1–4/26
	10/15–11/7	11/8–12/1	12/2–12/25	12/26–12/31	
11/13–11/26	11/27–12/21	12/22–12/31		1/1–1/19	1/20–2/12
8/22–9/15	9/16–10/11	1/1–1/14	1/15–2/7	2/8–3/3	3/4–3/27
		10/12–11/6	11/7–12/5	12/6–12/31	

VENUS SIGNS 1901–2000

	Aries	Taurus	Gemini	Cancer	Leo	Virgo
1926	5/7–6/2	6/3–6/28	6/29–7/23	7/24–8/17	8/18–9/11	9/12–10/5
1927	2/27–3/22	3/23–4/16	4/17–5/11	5/12–6/7	6/8–7/7	7/8–11/9
1928	4/12–5/5	5/6–5/29	5/30–6/23	6/24–7/17	7/18–8/11	8/12–9/4
1929	2/3–3/7 4/20–6/2	3/8–4/19 6/3–7/7	7/8–8/4	8/5–8/30	8/31–9/25	9/26–10/19
1930	3/13–4/5	4/6–4/30	5/1–5/24	5/25–6/18	6/19–7/14	7/15–8/9
1931	4/26–5/20	5/21–6/13	6/14–7/8	7/9–8/2	8/3–8/26	8/27–9/19
1932	2/12–3/8	3/9–4/3	4/4–5/5 7/13–7/27	5/6–7/12 7/28–9/8	9/9–10/6	10/7–11/1
1933	3/27–4/19	4/20–5/28	5/29–6/8	6/9–7/2	7/3–7/26	7/27–8/20
1934	5/6–6/1	6/2–6/27	6/28–7/22	7/23–8/16	8/17–9/10	9/11–10/4
1935	2/26–3/21	3/22–4/15	4/16–5/10	5/11–6/6	6/7–7/6	7/7–11/8
1936	4/11–5/4	5/5–5/28	5/29–6/22	6/23–7/16	7/17–8/10	8/11–9/4
1937	2/2–3/8 4/14–6/3	3/9–4/13 6/4–7/6	7/7–8/3	8/4–8/29	8/30–9/24	9/25–10/18
1938	3/12–4/4	4/5–4/28	4/29–5/23	5/24–6/18	6/19–7/13	7/14–8/8
1939	4/25–5/19	5/20–6/13	6/14–7/8	7/9–8/1	8/2–8/25	8/26–9/19
1940	2/12–3/7	3/8–4/3	4/4–5/5 7/5–7/31	5/6–7/4 8/1–9/8	9/9–10/5	10/6–10/31
1941	3/27–4/19	4/20–5/13	5/14–6/6	6/7–7/1	7/2–7/26	7/27–8/20
1942	5/6–6/1	6/2–6/26	6/27–7/22	7/23–8/16	8/17–9/9	9/10–10/3
1943	2/25–3/20	3/21–4/14	4/15–5/10	5/11–6/6	6/7–7/6	7/7–11/8
1944	4/10–5/3	5/4–5/28	5/29–6/21	6/22–7/16	7/17–8/9	8/10–9/2
1945	2/2–3/10 4/7–6/3	3/11–4/6 6/4–7/6	7/7–8/3	8/4–8/29	8/30–9/23	9/24–10/18
1946	3/11–4/4	4/5–4/28	4/29–5/23	5/24–6/17	6/18–7/12	7/13–8/8
1947	4/25–5/19	5/20–6/12	6/13–7/7	7/8–8/1	8/2–8/25	8/26–9/18
1948	2/11–3/7	3/8–4/3	4/4–5/6 6/29–8/2	5/7–6/28 8/3–9/7	9/8–10/5	10/6–10/31
1949	3/26–4/19	4/20–5/13	5/14–6/6	6/7–6/30	7/1–7/25	7/26–8/19
1950	5/5–5/31	6/1–6/26	6/27–7/21	7/22–8/15	8/16–9/9	9/10–10/3
1951	2/25–3/21	3/22–4/15	4/16–5/10	5/11–6/6	6/7–7/7	7/8–11/9

Libra	Scorpio	Sagittarius	Capricorn	Aquarius	Pisces
10/6–10/29	10/30–11/22	11/23–12/16	12/17–12/31	1/1–4/5	4/6–5/6
11/10–12/8	12/9–12/31	1/1–1/7	1/8	1/9–2/1	2/2–2/26
9/5–9/28	1/1–1/3	1/4–1/28	1/29–2/22	2/23–3/17	3/18–4/11
	9/29–10/23	10/24–11/16	11/17–12/11	12/12–12/31	
10/20–11/12	11/13–12/6	12/7–12/30	12/31	1/1–1/5	1/6–2/2
8/10–9/6	9/7–10/11	10/12–11/21	1/1–1/23	1/24–2/16	2/17–3/12
	11/22–12/31				
9/20–10/13	1/1–1/3	1/4–2/6	2/7–3/4	3/5–3/31	4/1–4/25
	10/14–11/6	11/7–11/30	12/1–12/24	12/25–12/31	
11/2–11/25	11/26–12/20	12/21–12/31		1/1–1/18	1/19–2/11
8/21–9/14	9/15–10/10	1/1–1/13	1/14–2/6	2/7–3/2	3/3–3/26
		10/11–11/5	11/6–12/4	12/5–12/31	
10/5–10/28	10/29–11/21	11/22–12/15	12/16–12/31	1/1–4/5	4/6–5/5
11/9–12/7	12/8–12/31		1/1–1/7	1/8–1/31	2/1–2/25
9/5–9/27	1/1–1/2	1/3–1/27	1/28–2/21	2/22–3/16	3/17–4/10
	9/28–10/22	10/23–11/15	11/16–12/10	12/11–12/31	
10/19–11/11	11/12–12/5	12/6–12/29	12/30–12/31	1/1–1/5	1/6–2/1
8/9–9/6	9/7–10/13	10/14–11/14	1/1–1/22	1/23–2/15	2/16–3/11
	11/15–12/31				
9/20–10/13	1/1–1/3	1/4–2/5	2/6–3/4	3/5–3/30	3/31–4/24
	10/14–11/6	11/7–11/30	12/1–12/24	12/25–12/31	
11/1–11/25	11/26–12/19	12/20–12/31		1/1–1/18	1/19–2/11
8/21–9/14	9/15–10/9	1/1–1/12	1/13–2/5	2/6–3/1	3/2–3/26
		10/10–11/5	11/6–12/4	12/5–12/31	
10/4–10/27	10/28–11/20	11/21–12/14	12/15–12/31	1/1–4/4	4/6–5/5
11/9–12/7	12/8–12/31		1/1–1/7	1/8–1/31	2/1–2/24
9/3–9/27	1/1–1/2	1/3–1/27	1/28–2/20	2/21–3/16	3/17–4/9
	9/28–10/21	10/22–11/15	11/16–12/10	12/11–12/31	
10/19–11/11	11/12–12/5	12/6–12/29	12/30–12/31	1/1–1/4	1/5–2/1
8/9–9/6	9/7–10/15	10/16–11/7	1/1–1/21	1/22–2/14	2/15–3/10
	11/8–12/31				
9/19–10/12	1/1–1/4	1/5–2/5	2/6–3/4	3/5–3/29	3/30–4/24
	10/13–11/5	11/6–11/29	11/30–12/23	12/24–12/31	
11/1–11/25	11/26–12/19	12/20–12/31		1/1–1/17	1/18–2/10
8/20–9/14	9/15–10/9	1/1–1/12	1/13–2/5	2/6–3/1	3/2–3/25
		10/10–11/5	11/6–12/5	12/6–12/31	
10/4–10/27	10/28–11/20	11/21–12/13	12/14–12/31	1/1–4/5	4/6–5/4
11/10–12/7	12/8–12/31		1/1–1/7	1/8–1/31	2/1–2/24

	Aries	Taurus	Gemini	Cancer	Leo	Virgo
1952	4/10–5/4	5/5–5/28	5/29–6/21	6/22–7/16	7/17–8/9	8/10–9/3
1953	2/2–3/3 4/1–6/5	3/4–3/31 6/6–7/7	7/8–8/3	8/4–8/29	8/30–9/24	9/25–10/18
1954	3/12–4/4	4/5–4/28	4/29–5/23	5/24–6/17	6/18–7/13	7/14–8/8
1955	4/25–5/19	5/20–6/13	6/14–7/7	7/8–8/1	8/2–8/25	8/26–9/18
1956	2/12–3/7	3/8–4/4	4/5–5/7 6/24–8/4	5/8–6/23 8/5–9/8	9/9–10/5	10/6–10/31
1957	3/26–4/19	4/20–5/13	5/14–6/6	6/7–7/1	7/2–7/26	7/27–8/19
1958	5/6–5/31	6/1–6/26	6/27–7/22	7/23–8/15	8/16–9/9	9/10–10/3
1959	2/25–3/20	3/21–4/14	4/15–5/10	5/11–6/6	6/7–7/8 9/21–9/24	7/9–9/20 9/25–11/9
1960	4/10–5/3	5/4–5/28	5/29–6/21	6/22–7/15	7/16–8/9	8/10–9/2
1961	2/3–6/5	6/6–7/7	7/8–8/3	8/4–8/29	8/30–9/23	9/24–10/17
1962	3/11–4/3	4/4–4/28	4/29–5/22	5/23–6/17	6/18–7/12	7/13–8/8
1963	4/24–5/18	5/19–6/12	6/13–7/7	7/8–7/31	8/1–8/25	8/26–9/18
1964	2/11–3/7	3/8–4/4	4/5–5/9 6/18–8/5	5/10–6/17 8/6–9/8	9/9–10/5	10/6–10/31
1965	3/26–4/18	4/19–5/12	5/13–6/6	6/7–6/30	7/1–7/25	7/26–8/19
1966	5/6–6/31	6/1–6/26	6/27–7/21	7/22–8/15	8/16–9/8	9/9–10/2
1967	2/24–3/20	3/21–4/14	4/15–5/10	5/11–6/6	6/7–7/8 9/10–10/1	7/9–9/9 10/2–11/9
1968	4/9–5/3	5/4–5/27	5/28–6/20	6/21–7/15	7/16–8/8	8/9–9/2
1969	2/3–6/6	6/7–7/6	7/7–8/3	8/4–8/28	8/29–9/22	9/23–10/17
1970	3/11–4/3	4/4–4/27	4/28–5/22	5/23–6/16	6/17–7/12	7/13–8/8
1971	4/24–5/18	5/19–6/12	6/13–7/6	7/7–7/31	8/1–8/24	8/25–9/17
1972	2/11–3/7	3/8–4/3	4/4–5/10 6/12–8/6	5/11–6/11 8/7–9/8	9/9–10/5	10/6–10/30
1973	3/25–4/18	4/18–5/12	5/13–6/5	6/6–6/29	7/1–7/25	7/26–8/19
1974	5/5–5/31	6/1–6/25	6/26–7/21	7/22–8/14	8/15–9/8	9/9–10/2
1975	2/24–3/20	3/21–4/13	4/14–5/9	5/10–6/6	6/7–7/9 9/3–10/4	7/10–9/2 10/5–11/9

Libra	Scorpio	Sagittarius	Capricorn	Aquarius	Pisces
9/4–9/27	1/1–1/2	1/3–1/27	1/28–2/20	2/21–3/16	3/17–4/9
	9/28–10/21	10/22–11/15	11/16–12/10	12/11–12/31	
10/19–11/11	11/12–12/5	12/6–12/29	12/30–12/31	1/1–1/5	1/6–2/1
8/9–9/6	9/7–10/22	10/23–10/27	1/1–1/22	1/23–2/15	2/16–3/11
	10/28–12/31				
9/19–10/13	1/1–1/6	1/7–2/5	2/6–3/4	3/5–3/30	3/31–4/24
	10/14–11/5	11/6–11/30	12/1–12/24	12/25–12/31	
11/1–11/25	11/26–12/19	12/20–12/31		1/1–1/17	1/18–2/11
8/20–9/14	9/15–10/9	1/1–1/12	1/13–2/5	2/6–3/1	3/2–3/25
		10/10–11/5	11/6–12/6	12/7–12/31	
10/4–10/27	10/28–11/20	11/21–12/14	12/15–12/31	1/1–4/6	4/7–5/5
11/10–12/7	12/8–12/31		1/1–1/7	1/8–1/31	2/1–2/24
9/3–9/26	1/1–1/2	1/3–1/27	1/28–2/20	2/21–3/15	3/16–4/9
	9/27–10/21	10/22–11/15	11/16–12/10	12/11–12/31	
10/18–11/11	11/12–12/4	12/5–12/28	12/29–12/31	1/1–1/5	1/6–2/2
8/9–9/6	9/7–12/31		1/1–1/21	1/22–2/14	2/15–3/10
9/19–10/12	1/1–1/6	1/7–2/5	2/6–3/4	3/5–3/29	3/30–4/23
	10/13–11/5	11/6–11/29	11/30–12/23	12/24–12/31	
11/1–11/24	11/25–12/19	12/20–12/31		1/1–1/16	1/17–2/10
8/20–9/13	9/14–10/9	1/1–1/12	1/13–2/5	2/6–3/1	3/2–3/25
		10/10–11/5	11/6–12/7	12/8–12/31	
10/3–10/26	10/27–11/19	11/20–12/13	2/7–2/25	1/1–2/6	4/7–5/5
			12/14–12/31	2/26–4/6	
11/10–12/7	12/8–12/31		1/1–1/6	1/7–1/30	1/31–2/23
9/3–9/26	1/1	1/2–1/26	1/27–2/20	2/21–3/15	3/16–4/8
	9/27–10/21	10/22–11/14	11/15–12/9	12/10–12/31	
10/18–11/10	11/11–12/4	12/5–12/28	12/29–12/31	1/1–1/4	1/5–2/2
8/9–9/7	9/8–12/31		1/1–1/21	1/22–2/14	2/15–3/10
9/18–10/11	1/1–1/7	1/8–2/5	2/6–3/4	3/5–3/29	3/30–4/23
	10/12–11/5	11/6–11/29	11/30–12/23	12/24–12/31	
	11/25–12/18	12/19–12/31		1/1–1/16	1/17–2/10
10/31–11/24					
8/20–9/13	9/14–10/8	1/1–1/12	1/13–2/4	2/5–2/28	3/1–3/24
		10/9–11/5	11/6–12/7	12/8–12/31	
			1/30–2/28	1/1–1/29	
10/3–10/26	10/27–11/19	11/20–12/13	12/14–12/31	3/1–4/6	4/7–5/4
			1/1–1/6	1/7–1/30	1/31–2/23
11/10–12/7	12/8–12/31				

VENUS SIGNS 1901–2000

	Aries	Taurus	Gemini	Cancer	Leo	Virgo
1976	4/8–5/2	5/2–5/27	5/27—6/20	6/20–7/14	7/14–8/8	8/8–9/1
1977	2/2–6/6	6/6–7/6	7/6–8/2	8/2–8/28	8/28–9/22	9/22–10/17
1978	3/9–4/2	4/2–4/27	4/27–5/22	5/22–6/16	6/16–7/12	7/12–8/6
1979	4/23–5/18	5/18–6/11	6/11–7/6	7/6–7/30	7/30–8/24	8/24–9/17
1980	2/9–3/6	3/6–4/3	4/3–5/12 6/5–8/6	5/12–6/5 8/6–9/7	9/7–10/4	10/4–10/30
1981	3/24–4/17	4/17–5/11	5/11–6/5	6/5–6/29	6/29–7/24	7/24–8/18
1982	5/4–5/30	5/30–6/25	6/25–7/20	7/20–8/14	8/14–9/7	9/7–10/2
1983	2/22–3/19	3/19–4/13	4/13–5/9	5/9–6/6	6/6–7/10 8/27–10/5	7/10–8/27 10/5–11/9
1984	4/7–5/2	5/2–5/26	5/26–6/20	6/20–7/14	7/14–8/7	8/7–9/1
1985	2/2–6/6	6/7–7/6	7/6–8/2	8/2–8/28	8/28–9/22	9/22–10/16
1986	3/9–4/2	4/2–4/26	4/26–5/21	5/21–6/15	6/15–7/11	7/11–8/7
1987	4/22–5/17	5/17–6/11	6/11–7/5	7/5–7/30	7/30–8/23	8/23–9/16
1988	2/9–3/6	3/6–4/3	4/3–5/17 5/27–8/6	5/17–5/27 8/28–9/22	9/7–10/4 9/22–10/16	10/4–10/29
1989	3/23–4/16	4/16–5/11	5/11–6/4	6/4–6/29	6/29–7/24	7/24–8/18
1990	5/4–5/30	5/30–6/25	6/25–7/20	7/20–8/13	8/13–9/7	9/7–10/1
1991	2/22–3/18	3/18–4/13	4/13–5/9	5/9–6/6	6/6–7/11 8/21–10/6	7/11–8/21 10/6–11/9
1992	4/7–5/1	5/1–5/26	5/26–6/19	6/19–7/13	7/13–8/7	8/7–8/31
1993	2/2–6/6	6/6–7/6	7/6–8/1	8/1–8/27	8/27–9/21	9/21–10/16
1994	3/8–4/1	4/1–4/26	4/26–5/21	5/21–6/15	6/15–7/11	7/11–8/7
1995	4/22–5/16	5/16–6/10	6/10–7/5	7/5–7/29	7/29–8/23	8/23–9/16
1996	2/9–3/6	3/6–4/3	4/3–8/7	8/7–9/7	9/7–10/4	10/4–10/29
1997	3/23–4/16	4/16–5/10	5/10–6/4	6/4–6/28	6/28–7/23	7/23–8/17
1998	5/3–5/29	5/29–6/24	6/24–7/19	7/19–8/13	8/13–9/6	9/6–9/30
1999	2/21–3/18	3/18–4/12	4/12–5/8	5/8–6/5	6/5–7/12 8/15–10/7	7/12–8/15 10/7–11/9
2000	4/6–5/1	5/1–5/25	5/25–6/13	6/13–7/13	7/13–8/6	8/6–8/31

Libra	Scorpio	Sagittarius	Capricorn	Aquarius	Pisces
9/1–9/26	9/26–10/20	1/1–1/26	1/26–2/19	2/19–3/15	3/15–4/8
		10/20–11/14	11/14–12/8	12/9–1/4	
10/17–11/10	11/10–12/4	12/4–12/27	12/27–1/20/78		1/4–2/2
8/6–9/7	9/7–1/7			1/20–2/13	2/13–3/9
9/17–10/11	10/11–11/4	1/7–2/5	2/5–3/3	3/3–3/29	3/29–4/23
		11/4–11/28	11/28–12/22	12/22–1/16/80	
10/30–11/24	11/24–12/18	12/18–1/11/81			1/16–2/9
8/18–9/12	9/12–10/9	10/9–11/5	1/11–2/4	2/4–2/28	2/28–3/24
			11/5–12/8	12/8–1/23/82	
10/2–10/26	10/26–11/18	11/18–12/12	1/23–3/2	3/2–4/6	4/6–5/4
			12/12–1/5/83		
11/9–12/6	12/6–1/1/84			1/5–1/29	1/29–2/22
9/1–9/25	9/25–10/20	1/1–1/25	1/25–2/19	2/19–3/14	3/14–4/7
		10/20–11/13	11/13–12/9	12/10–1/4	
10/16–11/9	11/9–12/3	12/3–12/27	12/28–1/19		1/4–2/2
8/7–9/7	9/7–1/7			1/20–2/13	2/13–3/9
9/16–10/10	10/10–11/3	1/7–2/5	2/5–3/3	3/3–3/28	3/28–4/22
		11/3–11/28	11/28–12/22	12/22–1/15	
10/29–11/23	11/23–12/17	12/17–1/10			1/15–2/9
8/18–9/12	9/12–10/8	10/8–11/5	1/10–2/3	2/3–2/27	2/27–3/23
			11/5–12/10	12/10–1/16/90	
10/1–10/25	10/25–11/18	11/18–12/12	1/16–3/3	3/3–4/6	4/6–5/4
			12/12–1/5		
11/9–12/6	12/6–12/31	12/31–1/25/92		1/5–1/29	1/29–2/22
8/31–9/25	9/25–10/19	10/19–11/13	1/25–2/18	2/18–3/13	3/13–4/7
			11/13–12/8	12/8–1/3/93	
10/16–11/9	11/9–12/2	12/2–12/26	12/26–1/19		1/3–2/2
8/7–9/7	9/7–1/7			1/19–2/12	2/12–3/8
9/16–10/10	10/10–11/13	1/7–2/4	2/4–3/2	3/2–3/28	3/28–4/22
		11/3–11/27	11/27–12/21	12/21–1/15	
10/29–11/23	11/23–12/17	12/17–1/10/97			1/15–2/9
8/17–9/12	9/12–10/8	10/8–11/5	1/10–2/3	2/3–2/27	2/27–3/23
			11/5–12/12	12/12–1/9	
9/30–10/24	10/24–11/17	11/17–12/11	1/9–3/4	3/4–4/6	4/6–5/3
11/9–12/5	12/5–12/31	12/31–1/24		1/4–1/28	1/28–2/21
8/31–9/24	9/24–10/19	10/19–11/13	1/24–2/18	2/18–3/12	3/13–4/6
			11/13–12/8	12/8	

How to Use the Mars, Jupiter, and Saturn Tables

Find the year of your birth on the left side of each column. The dates when the planet entered each sign are listed on the right side of each column. (Signs are abbreviated to the first three letters.) Your birthday should fall on or between each date listed, and your planetary placement should correspond to the earlier sign of that period.

MARS SIGN 1901–2000

Year	Mon	Day	Sign		Year	Mon	Day	Sign
1901	MAR	1	Leo		1905	JAN	13	Scp
	MAY	11	Vir			AUG	21	Sag
	JUL	13	Lib			OCT	8	Cap
	AUG	31	Scp			NOV	18	Aqu
	OCT	14	Sag			DEC	27	Pic
	NOV	24	Cap		1906	FEB	4	Ari
1902	JAN	1	Aqu			MAR	17	Tau
	FEB	8	Pic			APR	28	Gem
	MAR	19	Ari			JUN	11	Can
	APR	27	Tau			JUL	27	Leo
	JUN	7	Gem			SEP	12	Vir
	JUL	20	Can			OCT	30	Lib
	SEP	4	Leo			DEC	17	Scp
	OCT	23	Vir		1907	FEB	5	Sag
	DEC	20	Lib			APR	1	Cap
1903	APR	19	Vir			OCT	13	Aqu
	MAY	30	Lib			NOV	29	Pic
	AUG	6	Scp		1908	JAN	11	Ari
	SEP	22	Sag			FEB	23	Tau
	NOV	3	Cap			APR	7	Gem
	DEC	12	Aqu			MAY	22	Can
1904	JAN	19	Pic			JUL	8	Leo
	FEB	27	Ari			AUG	24	Vir
	APR	6	Tau			OCT	10	Lib
	MAY	18	Gem			NOV	25	Scp
	JUN	30	Can		1909	JAN	10	Sag
	AUG	15	Leo			FEB	24	Cap
	OCT	1	Vir			APR	9	Aqu
	NOV	20	Lib			MAY	25	Pic

	JUL	21	Ari	AUG	19	Can
	SEP	26	Pic	OCT	7	Leo
	NOV	20	Ari	1916 MAY	28	Vir
1910	JAN	23	Tau	JUL	23	Lib
	MAR	14	Gem	SEP	8	Scp
	MAY	1	Can	OCT	22	Sag
	JUN	19	Leo	DEC	1	Cap
	AUG	6	Vir	1917 JAN	9	Aqu
	SEP	22	Lib	FEB	16	Pic
	NOV	6	Scp	MAR	26	Ari
	DEC	20	Sag	MAY	4	Tau
1911	JAN	31	Cap	JUN	14	Gem
	MAR	14	Aqu	JUL	28	Can
	APR	23	Pic	SEP	12	Leo
	JUN	2	Ari	NOV	2	Vir
	JUL	15	Tau	1918 JAN	11	Lib
	SEP	5	Gem	FEB	25	Vir
	NOV	30	Tau	JUN	23	Lib
1912	JAN	30	Gem	AUG	17	Scp
	APR	5	Can	OCT	1	Sag
	MAY	28	Leo	NOV	11	Cap
	JUL	17	Vir	DEC	20	Aqu
	SEP	2	Lib	1919 JAN	27	Pic
	OCT	18	Scp	MAR	6	Ari
	NOV	30	Sag	APR	15	Tau
1913	JAN	10	Cap	MAY	26	Gem
	FEB	19	Aqu	JUL	8	Can
	MAR	30	Pic	AUG	23	Leo
	MAY	8	Ari	OCT	10	Vir
	JUN	17	Tau	NOV	30	Lib
	JUL	29	Gem	1920 JAN	31	Scp
	SEP	15	Can	APR	23	Lib
1914	MAY	1	Leo	JUL	10	Scp
	JUN	26	Vir	SEP	4	Sag
	AUG	14	Lib	OCT	18	Cap
	SEP	29	Scp	NOV	27	Aqu
	NOV	11	Sag	1921 JAN	5	Pic
	DEC	22	Cap	FEB	13	Ari
1915	JAN	30	Aqu	MAR	25	Tau
	MAR	9	Pic	MAY	6	Gem
	APR	16	Ari	JUN	18	Can
	MAY	26	Tau	AUG	3	Leo
	JUL	6	Gem	SEP	19	Vir

	NOV	6	Lib		APR	7	Pic
	DEC	26	Scp		MAY	16	Ari
1922	FEB	18	Sag		JUN	26	Tau
	SEP	13	Cap		AUG	9	Gem
	OCT	30	Aqu		OCT	3	Can
	DEC	11	Pic		DEC	20	Gem
1923	JAN	21	Ari	1929	MAR	10	Can
	MAR	4	Tau		MAY	13	Leo
	APR	16	Gem		JUL	4	Vir
	MAY	30	Can		AUG	21	Lib
	JUL	16	Leo		OCT	6	Scp
	SEP	1	Vir		NOV	18	Sag
	OCT	18	Lib		DEC	29	Cap
	DEC	4	Scp	1930	FEB	6	Aqu
1924	JAN	19	Sag		MAR	17	Pic
	MAR	6	Cap		APR	24	Ari
	APR	24	Aqu		JUN	3	Tau
	JUN	24	Pic		JUL	14	Gem
	AUG	24	Aqu		AUG	28	Can
	OCT	19	Pic		OCT	20	Leo
	DEC	19	Ari	1931	FEB	16	Can
1925	FEB	5	Tau		MAR	30	Leo
	MAR	24	Gem		JUN	10	Vir
	MAY	9	Can		AUG	1	Lib
	JUN	26	Leo		SEP	17	Scp
	AUG	12	Vir		OCT	30	Sag
	SEP	28	Lib		DEC	10	Cap
	NOV	13	Scp	1932	JAN	18	Aqu
	DEC	28	Sag		FEB	25	Pic
1926	FEB	9	Cap		APR	3	Ari
	MAR	23	Aqu		MAY	12	Tau
	MAY	3	Pic		JUN	22	Gem
	JUN	15	Ari		AUG	4	Can
	AUG	1	Tau		SEP	20	Leo
1927	FEB	22	Gem		NOV	13	Vir
	APR	17	Can	1933	JUL	6	Lib
	JUN	6	Leo		AUG	26	Scp
	JUL	25	Vir		OCT	9	Sag
	SEP	10	Lib		NOV	19	Cap
	OCT	26	Scp		DEC	28	Aqu
	DEC	8	Sag	1934	FEB	4	Pic
1928	JAN	19	Cap		MAR	14	Ari
	FEB	28	Aqu		APR	22	Tau

88

	JUN	2	Gem	AUG	19	Vir
	JUL	15	Can	OCT	5	Lib
	AUG	30	Leo	NOV	20	Scp
	OCT	18	Vir	1941 JAN	4	Sag
	DEC	11	Lib	FEB	17	Cap
1935	JUL	29	Scp	APR	2	Aqu
	SEP	16	Sag	MAY	16	Pic
	OCT	28	Cap	JUL	2	Ari
	DEC	7	Aqu	1942 JAN	11	Tau
1936	JAN	14	Pic	MAR	7	Gem
	FEB	22	Ari	APR	26	Can
	APR	1	Tau	JUN	14	Leo
	MAY	13	Gem	AUG	1	Vir
	JUN	25	Can	SEP	17	Lib
	AUG	10	Leo	NOV	1	Scp
	SEP	26	Vir	DEC	15	Sag
	NOV	14	Lib	1943 JAN	26	Cap
1937	JAN	5	Scp	MAR	8	Aqu
	MAR	13	Sag	APR	17	Pic
	MAY	14	Scp	MAY	27	Ari
	AUG	8	Sag	JUL	7	Tau
	SEP	30	Cap	AUG	23	Gem
	NOV	11	Aqu	1944 MAR	28	Can
	DEC	21	Pic	MAY	22	Leo
1938	JAN	30	Ari	JUL	12	Vir
	MAR	12	Tau	AUG	29	Lib
	APR	23	Gem	OCT	13	Scp
	JUN	7	Can	NOV	25	Sag
	JUL	22	Leo	1945 JAN	5	Cap
	SEP	7	Vir	FEB	14	Aqu
	OCT	25	Lib	MAR	25	Pic
	DEC	11	Scp	MAY	2	Ari
1939	JAN	29	Sag	JUN	11	Tau
	MAR	21	Cap	JUL	23	Gem
	MAY	25	Aqu	SEP	7	Can
	JUL	21	Cap	NOV	11	Leo
	SEP	24	Aqu	DEC	26	Can
	NOV	19	Pic	1946 APR	22	Leo
1940	JAN	4	Ari	JUN	20	Vir
	FEB	17	Tau	AUG	9	Lib
	APR	1	Gem	SEP	24	Scp
	MAY	17	Can	NOV	6	Sag
	JUL	3	Leo	DEC	17	Cap

1947	JAN	25	Aqu		MAR	20	Tau
	MAR	4	Pic		MAY	1	Gem
	APR	11	Ari		JUN	14	Can
	MAY	21	Tau		JUL	29	Leo
	JUL	1	Gem		SEP	14	Vir
	AUG	13	Can		NOV	1	Lib
	OCT	1	Leo		DEC	20	Scp
	DEC	1	Vir	1954	FEB	9	Sag
1948	FEB	12	Leo		APR	12	Cap
	MAY	18	Vir		JUL	3	Sag
	JUL	17	Lib		AUG	24	Cap
	SEP	3	Scp		OCT	21	Aqu
	OCT	17	Sag		DEC	4	Pic
	NOV	26	Cap	1955	JAN	15	Ari
1949	JAN	4	Aqu		FEB	26	Tau
	FEB	11	Pic		APR	10	Gem
	MAR	21	Ari		MAY	26	Can
	APR	30	Tau		JUL	11	Leo
	JUN	10	Gem		AUG	27	Vir
	JUL	23	Can		OCT	13	Lib
	SEP	7	Leo		NOV	29	Scp
	OCT	27	Vir	1956	JAN	14	Sag
	DEC	26	Lib		FEB	28	Cap
1950	MAR	28	Vir		APR	14	Aqu
	JUN	11	Lib		JUN	3	Pic
	AUG	10	Scp		DEC	6	Ari
	SEP	25	Sag	1957	JAN	28	Tau
	NOV	6	Cap		MAR	17	Gem
	DEC	15	Aqu		MAY	4	Can
1951	JAN	22	Pic		JUN	21	Leo
	MAR	1	Ari		AUG	8	Vir
	APR	10	Tau		SEP	24	Lib
	MAY	21	Gem		NOV	8	Scp
	JUL	3	Can		DEC	23	Sag
	AUG	18	Leo	1958	FEB	3	Cap
	OCT	5	Vir		MAR	17	Aqu
	NOV	24	Lib		APR	27	Pic
1952	JAN	20	Scp		JUN	7	Ari
	AUG	27	Sag		JUL	21	Tau
	OCT	12	Cap		SEP	21	Gem
	NOV	21	Aqu		OCT	29	Tau
	DEC	30	Pic	1959	FEB	10	Gem
1953	FEB	8	Ari		APR	10	Can

	JUN	1	Leo		NOV	14	Cap
	JUL	20	Vir		DEC	23	Aqu
	SEP	5	Lib	1966	JAN	30	Pic
	OCT	21	Scp		MAR	9	Ari
	DEC	3	Sag		APR	17	Tau
1960	JAN	14	Cap		MAY	28	Gem
	FEB	23	Aqu		JUL	11	Can
	APR	2	Pic		AUG	25	Leo
	MAY	11	Ari		OCT	12	Vir
	JUN	20	Tau		DEC	4	Lib
	AUG	2	Gem	1967	FEB	12	Scp
	SEP	21	Can		MAR	31	Lib
1961	FEB	5	Gem		JUL	19	Scp
	FEB	7	Can		SEP	10	Sag
	MAY	6	Leo		OCT	23	Cap
	JUN	28	Vir		DEC	1	Aqu
	AUG	17	Lib	1968	JAN	9	Pic
	OCT	1	Scp		FEB	17	Ari
	NOV	13	Sag		MAR	27	Tau
	DEC	24	Cap		MAY	8	Gem
1962	FEB	1	Aqu		JUN	21	Can
	MAR	12	Pic		AUG	5	Leo
	APR	19	Ari		SEP	21	Vir
	MAY	28	Tau		NOV	9	Lib
	JUL	9	Gem		DEC	29	Scp
	AUG	22	Can	1969	FEB	25	Sag
	OCT	11	Leo		SEP	21	Cap
1963	JUN	3	Vir		NOV	4	Aqu
	JUL	27	Lib		DEC	15	Pic
	SEP	12	Scp	1970	JAN	24	Ari
	OCT	25	Sag		MAR	7	Tau
	DEC	5	Cap		APR	18	Gem
1964	JAN	13	Aqu		JUN	2	Can
	FEB	20	Pic		JUL	18	Leo
	MAR	29	Ari		SEP	3	Vir
	MAY	7	Tau		OCT	20	Lib
	JUN	17	Gem		DEC	6	Scp
	JUL	30	Can	1971	JAN	23	Sag
	SEP	15	Leo		MAR	12	Cap
	NOV	6	Vir		MAY	3	Aqu
1965	JUN	29	Lib		NOV	6	Pic
	AUG	20	Scp		DEC	26	Ari
	OCT	4	Sag	1972	FEB	10	Tau

Year	Mo	Day	Sign	Year	Mo	Day	Sign
	MAR	27	Gem	1978	JAN	26	Can
	MAY	12	Can		APR	10	Leo
	JUN	28	Leo		JUN	14	Vir
	AUG	15	Vir		AUG	4	Lib
	SEP	30	Lib		SEP	19	Scp
	NOV	15	Scp		NOV	2	Sag
	DEC	30	Sag		DEC	12	Cap
1973	FEB	12	Cap	1979	JAN	20	Aqu
	MAR	26	Aqu		FEB	27	Pic
	MAY	8	Pic		APR	7	Ari
	JUN	20	Ari		MAY	16	Tau
	AUG	12	Tau		JUN	26	Gem
	OCT	29	Ari		AUG	8	Can
	DEC	24	Tau		SEP	24	Leo
1974	FEB	27	Gem		NOV	19	Vir
	APR	20	Can	1980	MAR	11	Leo
	JUN	9	Leo		MAY	4	Vir
	JUL	27	Vir		JUL	10	Lib
	SEP	12	Lib		AUG	29	Scp
	OCT	28	Scp		OCT	12	Sag
	DEC	10	Sag		NOV	22	Cap
1975	JAN	21	Cap		DEC	30	Aqu
	MAR	3	Aqu	1981	FEB	6	Pic
	APR	11	Pic		MAR	17	Ari
	MAY	21	Ari		APR	25	Tau
	JUL	1	Tau		JUN	5	Gem
	AUG	14	Gem		JUL	18	Can
	OCT	17	Can		SEP	2	Leo
	NOV	25	Gem		OCT	21	Vir
1976	MAR	18	Can		DEC	16	Lib
	MAY	16	Leo	1982	AUG	3	Scp
	JUL	6	Vir		SEP	20	Sag
	AUG	24	Lib		OCT	31	Cap
	OCT	8	Scp		DEC	10	Aqu
	NOV	20	Sag	1983	JAN	17	Pic
1977	JAN	1	Cap		FEB	25	Ari
	FEB	9	Aqu		APR	5	Tau
	MAR	20	Pic		MAY	16	Gem
	APR	27	Ari		JUN	29	Can
	JUN	6	Tau		AUG	13	Leo
	JUL	17	Gem		SEP	30	Vir
	SEP	1	Can		NOV	18	Lib
	OCT	26	Leo	1984	JAN	11	Scp

Year	Month	Day	Sign		Year	Month	Day	Sign
	AUG	17	Sag			JUL	12	Tau
	OCT	5	Cap			AUG	31	Gem
	NOV	15	Aqu			DEC	14	Tau
	DEC	25	Pic		1991	JAN	21	Gem
1985	FEB	2	Ari			APR	3	Can
	MAR	15	Tau			MAY	26	Leo
	APR	26	Gem			JUL	15	Vir
	JUN	9	Can			SEP	1	Lib
	JUL	25	Leo			OCT	16	Scp
	SEP	10	Vir			NOV	29	Sag
	OCT	27	Lib		1992	JAN	9	Cap
	DEC	14	Scp			FEB	18	Aqu
1986	FEB	2	Sag			MAR	28	Pic
	MAR	28	Cap			MAY	5	Ari
	OCT	9	Aqu			JUN	14	Tau
	NOV	26	Pic			JUL	26	Gem
1987	JAN	8	Ari			SEP	12	Can
	FEB	20	Tau		1993	APR	27	Leo
	APR	5	Gem			JUN	23	Vir
	MAY	21	Can			AUG	12	Lib
	JUL	6	Leo			SEP	27	Scp
	AUG	22	Vir			NOV	9	Sag
	OCT	8	Lib			DEC	20	Cap
	NOV	24	Scp		1994	JAN	28	Aqu
1988	JAN	8	Sag			MAR	7	Pic
	FEB	22	Cap			APR	14	Ari
	APR	6	Aqu			MAY	23	Tau
	MAY	22	Pic			JUL	3	Gem
	JUL	13	Ari			AUG	16	Can
	OCT	23	Pic			OCT	4	Leo
	NOV	1	Ari			DEC	12	Vir
1989	JAN	19	Tau		1995	JAN	22	Leo
	MAR	11	Gem			MAY	25	Vir
	APR	29	Can			JUL	21	Lib
	JUN	16	Leo			SEP	7	Scp
	AUG	3	Vir			OCT	20	Sag
	SEP	19	Lib			NOV	30	Cap
	NOV	4	Scp		1996	JAN	8	Aqu
	DEC	18	Sag			FEB	15	Pic
1990	JAN	29	Cap			MAR	24	Ari
	MAR	11	Aqu			MAY	2	Tau
	APR	20	Pic			JUN	12	Gem
	MAY	31	Ari			JUL	25	Can

Year	Mon	Day	Sign		Year	Mon	Day	Sign
	SEP	9	Leo			NOV	27	Lib
	OCT	30	Vir		1999	JAN	26	Scp
1997	JAN	3	Lib			MAY	5	Lib
	MAR	8	Vir			JUL	5	Scp
	JUN	19	Lib			SEP	2	Sag
	AUG	14	Scp			OCT	17	Cap
	SEP	28	Sag			NOV	26	Aqu
	NOV	9	Cap		2000	JAN	4	Pic
	DEC	18	Aqu			FEB	12	Ari
1998	JAN	25	Pic			MAR	23	Tau
	MAR	4	Ari			MAY	3	Gem
	APR	13	Tau			JUN	16	Can
	MAY	24	Gem			AUG	1	Leo
	JUL	6	Can			SEP	17	Vir
	AUG	20	Leo			NOV	4	Lib
	OCT	7	Vir			DEC	23	Scp

JUPITER SIGN 1901–2000

Year	Mon	Day	Sign		Year	Mon	Day	Sign
1901	JAN	19	Cap			OCT	26	Ari
1902	FEB	6	Aqu		1917	FEB	12	Tau
1903	FEB	20	Pic			JUN	29	Gem
1904	MAR	1	Ari		1918	JUL	13	Can
	AUG	8	Tau		1919	AUG	2	Leo
	AUG	31	Ari		1920	AUG	27	Vir
1905	MAR	7	Tau		1921	SEP	25	Lib
	JUL	21	Gem		1922	OCT	26	Scp
	DEC	4	Tau		1923	NOV	24	Sag
1906	MAR	9	Gem		1924	DEC	18	Cap
	JUL	30	Can		1926	JAN	6	Aqu
1907	AUG	18	Leo		1927	JAN	18	Pic
1908	SEP	12	Vir			JUN	6	Ari
1909	OCT	11	Lib			SEP	11	Pic
1910	NOV	11	Scp		1928	JAN	23	Ari
1911	DEC	10	Sag			JUN	4	Tau
1913	JAN	2	Cap		1929	JUN	12	Gem
1914	JAN	21	Aqu		1930	JUN	26	Can
1915	FEB	4	Pic		1931	JUL	17	Leo
1916	FEB	12	Ari		1932	AUG	11	Vir
	JUN	26	Tau		1933	SEP	10	Lib

Year	Month	Day	Sign		Year	Month	Day	Sign
1934	OCT	11	Scp			OCT	5	Sag
1935	NOV	9	Sag		1960	MAR	1	Cap
1936	DEC	2	Cap			JUN	10	Sag
1937	DEC	20	Aqu			OCT	26	Cap
1938	MAY	14	Pic		1961	MAR	15	Aqu
	JUL	30	Aqu			AUG	12	Cap
	DEC	29	Pic			NOV	4	Aqu
1939	MAY	11	Ari		1962	MAR	25	Pic
	OCT	30	Pic		1963	APR	4	Ari
	DEC	20	Ari		1964	APR	12	Tau
1940	MAY	16	Tau		1965	APR	22	Gem
1941	MAY	26	Gem			SEP	21	Can
1942	JUN	10	Can			NOV	17	Gem
1943	JUN	30	Leo		1966	MAY	5	Can
1944	JUL	26	Vir			SEP	27	Leo
1945	AUG	25	Lib		1967	JAN	16	Can
1946	SEP	25	Scp			MAY	23	Leo
1947	OCT	24	Sag			OCT	19	Vir
1948	NOV	15	Cap		1968	FEB	27	Leo
1949	APR	12	Aqu			JUN	15	Vir
	JUN	27	Cap			NOV	15	Lib
	NOV	30	Aqu		1969	MAR	30	Vir
1950	APR	15	Pic			JUL	15	Lib
	SEP	15	Aqu			DEC	16	Scp
	DEC	1	Pic		1970	APR	30	Lib
1951	APR	21	Ari			AUG	15	Scp
1952	APR	28	Tau		1971	JAN	14	Sag
1953	MAY	9	Gem			JUN	5	Sc
1954	MAY	24	Can			SEP	11	Sag
1955	JUN	13	Leo		1972	FEB	6	Cap
	NOV	17	Vir			JUL	24	Sag
1956	JAN	18	Leo			SEP	25	Cap
	JUL	7	Vir		1973	FEB	23	Aqu
	DEC	13	Lib		1974	MAR	8	Pic
1957	FEB	19	Vir		1975	MAR	18	Ari
	AUG	7	Lib		1976	MAR	26	Tau
1958	JAN	13	Scp			AUG	23	Gem
	MAR	20	Lib			OCT	16	Tau
	SEP	7	Scp		1977	APR	3	Gem
1959	FEB	10	Sag			AUG	20	Can
	APR	24	Scp			DEC	30	Gem

Year	Mon	Day	Sign	Year	Mon	Day	Sign
1978	APR	12	Can	1989	MAR	11	Gem
	SEP	5	Leo		JUL	30	Can
1979	FEB	28	Can	1990	AUG	18	Leo
	APR	20	Leo	1991	SEP	12	Vir
	SEP	29	Vir	1992	OCT	10	Lib
1980	OCT	27	Lib	1993	NOV	10	Scp
1981	NOV	27	Scp	1994	DEC	9	Sag
1982	DEC	26	Sag	1996	JAN	3	Cap
1984	JAN	19	Cap	1997	JAN	21	Aqu
1985	FEB	6	Aqu	1998	FEB	4	Pic
1986	FEB	20	Pic	1999	FEB	13	Ari
1987	MAR	2	Ari		JUN	28	Tau
1988	MAR	8	Tau		OCT	23	Ari
	JUL	22	Gem	2000	FEB	14	Tau
	NOV	30	Tau		JUN	30	Gem

SATURN SIGN 1903–2000

Year	Mon	Day	Sign	Year	Mon	Day	Sign
1903	JAN	19	Aqu		SEP	13	Scp
1905	APR	13	Pic	1926	DEC	2	Sag
	AUG	17	Aqu	1929	MAR	15	Cap
1906	JAN	8	Pic		MAY	5	Sag
1908	MAR	19	Ari		NOV	30	Cap
1910	MAY	17	Tau	1932	FEB	24	Aqu
	DEC	14	Ari		AUG	13	Cap
1911	JAN	20	Tau		NOV	20	Aqu
1912	JUL	7	Gem	1935	FEB	14	Pic
	NOV	30	Tau	1937	APR	25	Ari
1913	MAR	26	Gem		OCT	18	Pic
1914	AUG	24	Can	1938	JAN	14	Ari
	DEC	7	Gem	1939	JUL	6	Tau
1915	MAY	11	Can		SEP	22	Ari
1916	OCT	17	Leo	1940	MAR	20	Tau
	DEC	7	Can	1942	MAY	8	Gem
1917	JUN	24	Leo	1944	JUN	20	Can
1919	AUG	12	Vir	1946	AUG	2	Leo
1921	OCT	7	Lib	1948	SEP	19	Vir
1923	DEC	20	Scp	1949	APR	3	Leo
1924	APR	6	Lib		MAY	29	Vir

					JUN	5	Leo
1950	NOV	20	Lib	1977	NOV	17	Vir
1951	MAR	7	Vir	1978	JAN	5	Leo
	AUG	13	Lib		JUL	26	Vir
1953	OCT	22	Scp	1980	SEP	21	Lib
1956	JAN	12	Sag	1982	NOV	29	Scp
	MAY	14	Scp	1983	MAY	6	Lib
	OCT	10	Sag		AUG	24	Scp
1959	JAN	5	Cap	1985	NOV	17	Sag
1962	JAN	3	Aqu	1988	FEB	13	Cap
1964	MAR	24	Pic		JUN	10	Sag
	SEP	16	Aqu		NOV	12	Cap
	DEC	16	Pic	1991	FEB	6	Aqu
1967	MAR	3	Ari	1993	MAY	21	Pic
1969	APR	29	Tau		JUN	30	Aqu
1971	JUN	18	Gem	1994	JAN	28	Pic
1972	JAN	10	Tau	1996	APR	7	Ari
	FEB	21	Gem	1998	JUN	9	Tau
1973	AUG	1	Can		OCT	25	Ari
1974	JAN	7	Gem	1999	MAR	1	Tau
	APR	18	Can	2000	AUG	10	Gem
1975	SEP	17	Leo		OCT	16	Tau
1976	JAN	14	Can				

CHAPTER 5

How to Decode the Symbols (Glyphs) on Your Chart

Astrology has its own special symbolic language, which has evolved over thousands of years. For beginners, it looks like a mysterious code . . . and it is! When you first try to decipher your chart, you may recognize the tiny moon and the symbol for your sign. Perhaps you'll also recognize Mars and Venus, since they are often used as male and female gender symbols outside of astrology. But the other marks could look as strange as Japanese to the uninitiated. Those little characters, called glyphs (or sigils) were created centuries ago, and any astrologer from Russia to Argentina could read your chart and know what it means. So a chart set up in Moscow can be interpreted by an astrologer in New York. And, since there are only 12 signs and 10 planets (not counting a few asteroids and other space creatures some astrologers use), it's a lot easier than learning to read Japanese!

You may well ask why you should bother to put in the effort at all. There are several good reasons. First, it's interesting. The glyphs are much more than little drawings—they are magical codes that contain within them keys to the meanings of the planets. Cracking the code can teach you immediately, in a visual way, much about the deeper meaning of a planet or sign.

If you ever get your horoscope chart done by computer, the printout will be written in glyphs. Though many charts have a list of the planets in plain English, many do not, leaving you mystified if you can't read the glyphs. You might pick out the symbol for the sun and the trident of Neptune . . . but then there's Jupiter (is that a number 4?) and Mercury, who looks like Venus wearing a hat.

Here's a code-cracker for the glyphs, beginning with the glyphs for the planets. To those who already know their glyphs . . . don't just skim over the chapter! There are hidden meanings to discover, so test your glyph-ese.

The Glyphs for the Planets

Almost all the glyphs of the planets are combinations of the most basic forms: the circle, the half-circle or arc, and the cross. Artists and glyph designers have stylized these forms over the years, but the basic concept is always visible. Each component of the glyph has a special meaning in relation to the others, which combines to create the meaning of the completed symbol.

For instance, the circle, which has no beginning or end, is one of the oldest symbols of spirit or spiritual forces. All of the early diagrams of the heavens—the spiritual territory—are shown in circular form. The semicircle or arc symbolizes the receptive, finite soul, which contains spiritual potential in the curving line. The vertical line symbolizes movement from heaven to earth. The horizontal line describes temporal movement, here and now, in time and space. Superimposed together, the vertical and horizontal planes symbolize manifestation in the material world.

The Sun Glyph ☉

The sun is always shown by this powerful solar symbol, a circle with a point in the center. It is you, your spiritual center, your infinite personality incarnating the point into the finite cycles of birth and death.

This symbol was brought into common use in the 16th century, after a German occultist and scholar, Cornelius Agrippa (1486–1535) wrote a book called *Die Occulta*

Philosophia, which became accepted as the standard work in its field. Agrippa collected many medieval astrological and magical symbols in this book, which astrologers later copied and continued to use.

The Moon Glyph ☽

This is surely the easiest symbol to spot on a chart. The moon glyph is a left-facing arc stylized into the crescent moon, which perfectly captures the reactive, receptive, emotional nature of the moon. As part of a circle, the arc symbolizes the potential fulfillment of the entire circle. It is the life force that is still incomplete.

The Mercury Glyph ☿

This is the "Venus with a hat" glyph. With another stretch of the imagination, can't you see the winged cap of Mercury the messenger? The upturned crescent could be antennae that tune in and transmit messages from the sun, signifying that Mercury is the way you communicate, the way your mind works. The upturned arc is receiving energy into the spirit or solar circle, which will later be translated into action on the material plane, symbolized by the cross. All the elements are equally sized because Mercury is neutral—it doesn't play favorites! This planet symbolizes objective, detached, unemotional thinking.

The Venus Glyph ♀

Here the relationship is between two elements—the circle, or spirit, above the cross of matter. Spirit is elevated over matter, pulling it upward. Venus asks, "What is beautiful? What do you like best, what do you love to have done to you?" Venus determines both your ideal of beauty and what feels good sensually. It governs your own allure and power to attract, as well as what attracts and pleases you.

The Mars Glyph ♂

In this glyph, the cross of matter is stylized into an arrowhead pointed up and outward, propelled by the circle of spirit. You can deduce that Mars embodies your spiritual energy projected into the outer world. It's your assertiveness, your initiative, your aggressive drive; it's what you like to do to others; it's your temper. If you know someone's Mars, you know whether they'll blow up when angry or do a slow burn. Your task is to use your outgoing Mars energy wisely and well.

The Jupiter Glyph ♃

Jupiter is the basic cross of the matter, with a large stylized crescent perched on the left side of the horizontal, temporal plane. You might think of the crescent as an open hand—one meaning of Jupiter is "luck," or what's handed to you. You don't work for what you get from Jupiter—it comes to you if you're open to it.

The Jupiter glyph might also remind you of a jumbo jet with a huge tail fin, about to take off. This is the planet of travel, mental and spiritual, and of expanding your horizons via new ideas, new spiritual dimensions, and new places. Jupiter embodies the optimism and enthusiasm of the traveler about to embark on an exciting adventure.

The Saturn Glyph ♄

Flip Jupiter over and you've got Saturn. (This might not be immediately apparent, because Saturn is usually stylized into an "h" form like the one shown here.) But the principle it expresses is the opposite of Jupiter's expansive tendencies. Saturn pulls you back to earth—the receptive arc is pushed down underneath the cross of matter. Before there are any rewards or expansion, the duties and obligations of the material world must be considered. Saturn says, "Stop, wait, and finish your chores before you take off!"

Saturn's glyph also resembles the sickle of old Father Time. Saturn was first known as Chronos, the Greek god of time, for time brings all matter to an end. When it was thought to be the most distant planet (before the discovery of Uranus), Saturn was believed to be the place where time stopped. After the soul, having departed from earth, journeyed back to the outer reaches of the universe, it finally stopped at Saturn, at "the end of time."

The Uranus Glyph ♅

The glyph for Uranus is often stylized to form a capital "H" after Sir William Herschel, the planet's discoverer. But the more esoteric version curves the two pillars of the H into crescent antennae, or ears, or like satellite discs receiving signals from space. These are perched on the horizontal material line of the cross (matter) and pushed from below by the circle of the spirit. To many sci-fi fans, Uranus looks like an orbiting satellite.

Uranus channels the highest energy of all, the white electrical light of the universal spiritual sun, the force that holds the cosmos together. This pure electrical energy is gathered from all over the universe. Because it doesn't follow an ordinary celestial drumbeat, it can't be controlled or predicted, which is also true of those who are strongly influenced by this eccentric planet. In the symbol, this energy is manifested through the balance of polarities (the two opposite arms of the glyph) like the two polarized wires of a lightbulb.

The Neptune Glyph ♆

Neptune's glyph is usually stylized to look like a trident, the weapon of the Roman god Neptune. However, on a more esoteric level, it shows the large upturned crescent of the soul pierced through by the cross of matter. Neptune nails down, or materializes, soul energy, bringing impulses from the soul level into manifestation. That is why Neptune is associated with imagination or "imagining in," making an image of the soul. Neptune works through feeling, sensitivity, and mystical capacity to bring the divine into the earthly realm.

The Pluto Glyph ♇

Pluto is written two ways. One is a composite of the letters "PL," the first two letters of the word Pluto and coincidentally the initials of Percival Lowell, one of the planet's discoverers. The other, more esoteric symbol is a small circle above a large open crescent that surmounts the cross of matter. This depicts Pluto's power to regenerate—you might imagine from this glyph a new little spirit emerging from the sheltering cup of the soul. Pluto rules the forces of life and death—after a Pluto experience, you are transformed or reborn in some way.

Sci-fi fans might visualize this glyph as a small satellite (the circle) being launched. It was shortly after Pluto's discovery that we learned how to harness the nuclear forces that made space exploration possible. Pluto rules the transformative power of atomic energy, which totally changed our lives and from which there was no turning back.

The Glyphs for the Signs

On an astrological chart, the glyph for the sign will appear after that of the planet. When you see the moon glyph followed by a number and the glyph for the sign, this means that the moon was passing over a certain degree of an astrological sign at the time of the chart. On the dividing points between the segments, or "houses," on your chart, you'll find the symbol for the sign that rules the house.

Since sun-sign symbols do not always bring together the same basic components of the planetary glyphs, where do their meanings come from? Many have been passed down from ancient Egyptian and Chaldean civilizations with few modifications. Others have been adapted over the centuries. In deciphering many of the glyphs, you'll often find that many symbols reveal a dual nature of the sign, which is not always apparent in sun-sign descriptions. For instance, the Gemini glyph is similar to the Roman numeral for two, and reveals this sign's longing to discover a twin soul. The Cancer glyph may be interpreted as resembling either nurturing breasts or the self-protective claws of the crab. Libra's glyph embodies the duality of the spirit balanced with material reality. The Sagittarius glyph shows that the aspirant must also carry along the earthly animal nature in his quest. The Capricorn sea goat is another symbol with dual emphasis. The goat climbs high yet is always pulled back by the deep waters of the unconscious. Aquarius embodies the double waves of mental detachment, balanced by the desire for connection with others in a friendly way. And finally, the two fishes of Pisces, which are forever tied together, show the duality of the soul and the spirit that must be reconciled.

The Aries Glyph ♈

Since the symbol for Aries is the ram, this glyph's most obvious association is with a ram's horns, which characterize one aspect of the Aries personality—an aggressive, me-first, leaping-head-first attitude. But the symbol may have other meanings for you, too. Some astrologers liken it to a fountain of energy, which Aries people also embody. The first sign of the zodiac bursts on the scene eagerly, ready to go. Another analogy is to the eyebrows and nose of the human head, which Aries rules, and the thinking power that is initiated in the brain. Another interesting theory is that the symbol represents spirit descending from a higher realm into the mind of man, which would be the point of the V shape in the Aries glyph.

The origin of this symbol links it to the Egyptian god Amun, represented by a ram. As Amon-Ra, this god was believed to embody the creator of the universe, the leader of all the other gods. This relates easily to the position of Aries as the leader (or first sign) of the zodiac, which begins at the spring equinox, a time of the year when nature is renewed.

The Taurus Glyph ♉

This is another easy glyph to draw and identify. It takes little imagination to decipher the bull's head with long, curving horns. Like the bull, the archetypal Taurus is slow to anger but ferocious when provoked, as well as stubborn, steady, and sensual. Another association is the Taurus-ruled larynx (and thyroid) of the throat area and the Eustachian tubes (the "horns" of the glyph) running up to the ears, which coincide with the relationship of Taurus to the voice, song, and music. Many famous singers, musicians, and composers have prominent Taurus influences.

Many ancient religions involved a bull as the central figure in fertility rites or initiations, usually symbolizing the victory of man over his animal nature. Another possible origin is in the sacred bull of Egypt, who embodied the incarnate form of Osiris, god of death and resurrection. In early Christian imagery, the Taurean bull, representing St. Luke, appears in many art forms along with the Lion (Leo and St. Mark), the Man (Aquarius and St. Matthew) and the Eagle (Scorpio and St. John).

The Gemini Glyph ♊

The standard glyph immediately calls to mind the Roman numeral for two and the symbol for Gemini, the "twins." In almost all images for this sign, the relationship between two persons is emphasized. This is the sign of communication and human contact, and it manifests the desire to share. Many of the figurative images for Gemini show twins with their arms around each other, emphasizing that they are sharing the same ideas and the same ground. In the glyph, the top line indicates mental communication, while the bottom line indicates shared physical space.

The most famous Gemini legend is that of the twin sons, Castor and Pollux, one of whom had a mortal father, while the other was the son of Zeus, king of the gods. When it came time for the mortal twin to die, his grief-stricken brother pleaded with Zeus, who agreed to let them spend half the year on earth, in mortal form, and half in immortal life, with the gods on Mt. Olympus. This reflects a basic concept of humankind, which possesses an immortal soul yet is also subject to the limits of mortality.

The Cancer Glyph ♋

Two convenient images relate to the Cancer glyph. The easiest to picture is the curving claws of the Cancer symbol, the crab. Like the crab, Cancer's element is water. This sensitive sign also has a hard protective shell to protect its tender interior. It must be wily to escape predators, scampering sideways and hiding shyly under the rocks. The crab also responds to the cycles of the moon, as do all shellfish. The other image is that of two female breasts, which Cancer rules, showing that this is a sign that nurtures and protects others as well as itself. In ancient Egypt, Cancer was also represented by the scarab beetle, a symbol of regeneration and eternal life.

The Leo Glyph ♌

Lions have belonged to the sign of Leo since earliest times and it is not difficult to imagine the king of beasts with his sweeping mane and curling tail from this glyph. The upward sweep of the glyph easily describes the positive energy of Leos—the flourishing tail and the flamboyant qualities. Another analogy, which is a stretch, is that of a heart leaping up with joy and enthusiasm, also very typical of Leo. Notice that the Leo glyph seems to be an extension of Cancer's glyph, with a significant difference. In the Cancer glyph, the figures are folding inward, protectively, while the Leo glyph expresses energy outwardly, with no duality in the symbol (or in

Leo). In early Christian imagery, the Leo lion represented St. Mark.

The Virgo Glyph ♍

You can read much into this mysterious glyph. For instance, it could represent the initials of "Mary Virgin," or a young woman holding a staff of wheat, or stylized female genitalia, all common interpretations. The "M" shape might also remind you that Virgo is ruled by Mercury. The cross beneath the symbol could indicate the grounded, practical nature of this earth sign.

The earliest zodiacs link Virgo with the Egyptian goddess Isis, who gave birth to the god Horus after her husband Osiris had been killed, in the archetype of a miraculous conception. There are many statues of Isis nursing her baby son, which are reminiscent of medieval Virgin and Child motifs. This sign has also been associated with the image of the Holy Grail, where the Virgo symbol was substituted with a chalice.

The Libra Glyph ♎

It is not difficult to read the standard image for Libra, the scales, into this glyph. There is another meaning, however, that is equally relevant: the setting sun as it descends over the horizon. Libra's natural position on the zodiac wheel is the descendent or sunset position (as Aries' natural position is the ascendant, or rising sign). Both images relate to Libra's personality. Libra is always weighing pros and cons for a balanced decision. In the sunset image, the sun (male) hovers over the horizontal Earth (female) before setting. Libra is the space between these lines, harmonizing yin and yang, spiritual and material, the ideal and real worlds. The glyph has also been linked to the kidneys, which are ruled by Libra.

The Scorpio Glyph ♏

With its barbed tail, this glyph is easy to identify with the sign of the Scorpion. It also represents the male sexual parts, over which the sign rules. However, some earlier symbols for Scorpio, such as the Egyptian, represent it as an erect serpent. You can also draw the conclusion that Mars is ruled by the arrowhead.

Another image for Scorpio, not identifiable in this glyph, is the eagle. Scorpios can go to extremes, soaring like the eagle or self-destructing like the Scorpion. In early Christian imagery, which often used zodiacal symbols, the Scorpio eagle was chosen to symbolize the intense apostle St. John the Evangelist.

The Sagittarius Glyph ♐

This glyph is one of the easiest to spot and draw—an upward pointing arrow lifting up a cross. The arrow is pointing skyward, while the cross represents the four elements of the material world, which the arrow must convey. Elevating materiality into spirituality is an important Sagittarius quality, which explains why this sign is associated with higher learning, religion, philosophy, and travel—the aspiring professions. Sagittarius can also send barbed arrows of frankness in the pursuit of truth. (This is also the sign of the super-salesman.)

Sagittarius is symbolically represented by the centaur, a mythological creature who is half-man, half horse, aiming his arrow toward the skies. Though Sagittarius is motivated by spiritual aspiration, it also must balance the powerful appetites of the animal nature. The centaur Chiron, a figure in Greek mythology, became a wise teacher after many adventures and world travels.

The Capricorn Glyph ♑

One of the most difficult symbols to draw, this glyph may take some practice. It is a representation of the seagoat: a mythical animal that is a goat with a curving fish's tail. The goat part of Capricorn wants to leave the waters of the emotions and climb to the elevated areas of life. But the first part is the unconscious, the deep chaotic psychic level that draws the goat back. Capricorn is often trying to escape the deep, feeling part of life by submerging himself in work, steadily climbing to the top. To some people, the glyph represents a seated figure with a bent knee, a reminder that Capricorn governs the knee area of the body.

An interesting aspect of this figure is how the sharp pointed horns of the symbol, which represent the penetrating, shrewd, conscious side of Capricorn, contrast with the swishing tail, which represents its serpentine, unconscious, emotional force. One Capricorn legend, which dates from Roman times, tells of the earthy fertility god, Pan, who tried to save himself from uncontrollable sexual desires by jumping into the Nile. His upper body then turned into a goat, while the lower part became a fish. Later, Jupiter gave him a safe haven in the skies, as a constellation.

The Aquarius Glyph ≈

This ancient water symbol can be traced back to an Egyptian hieroglyph representing streams of life force. Symbolized by the water bearer, Aquarius is distributor of the waters of life—the magic liquid of regeneration. The two waves can also be linked to the positive and negative charges of the electrical energy that Aquarius rules, a sort of universal wavelength. Aquarius is tuned in intuitively to higher forces via this electrical force. The duality of the glyph could also refer to the dual nature of Aquarius, a sign that runs hot and cold, is friendly but also detached in the mental world of air signs.

In Greek legends, Aquarius is represented by Ganymede, who was carried to heaven by an eagle in order to become the cup bearer of Zeus, and to supervise the annual flooding of the Nile. The sign became associated with aviation and notions of flight.

The Pisces Glyph ⊬

Here is an abstraction of the familiar image of Pisces, two fishes swimming in opposite directions, bound together by a cord. The fishes represent spirit, which yearns for the freedom of heaven, while the soul remains attached to the desires of the temporal world. During life on earth, the spirit and the soul are bound together and when they complement each other, instead of pulling in opposite directions, this facilitates the creative expression for which Pisceans are known. The ancient version of this glyph, taken from the Egyptians, had no connecting line, which was added in the fourteenth century.

Another interpretation is that the left fish indicates the direction of involution or the beginning of the cycle; the right-hand fish, the direction of evolution, the way to completion of a cycle. It's an appropriate meaning for Pisces, the last sign of the zodiac.

CHAPTER 6

Answers to Your Questions

Here are the answers to some questions frequently asked by regular readers of this book. You may have been wondering about them, too.

QUESTION: *Why don't other stars in the cosmos influence our horoscopes?*

Most astrologers find that ten planets—considering the sun and moon as "planets"—give us quite enough information to delineate a horoscope. However, a growing number of astrologers are finding that other celestial bodies, such as asteroids and certain fixed stars, add an extra dimension and special nuances to the horoscope. Certain stars are said to bring specific lessons on life's journey when they are also linked with one of the key planets in a horoscope. These lessons are expressed by the mythology the star represents.

The fixed stars were used by the ancient astrologers and now are enjoying a renaissance thanks to a group of scholars dedicated to reinterpreting their mythology and adapting ancient techniques for modern times. Those interested in fixed stars will find much fascinating information in *Brady's Book of Fixed Stars* by Bernadette Brady (Samuel Weiser, 1998).

QUESTION: *If I was born on a Mercury retrograde, does it make a difference?*

Many highly original and creative thinkers were born with Mercury in retrograde, or apparent backward motion, such as Oscar Wilde, Norman Mailer, Dylan

Thomas, Bruce Springsteen, Hillary Clinton, Harry S. Truman, and Mae West. You might find the three Mercury retrograde periods each year easier to cope with than other people. However, it is the whole chart and the aspects to your natal Mercury that must be considered before drawing any conclusions.

QUESTION: *I'm very different from my twin brother. Since we were born only twenty minutes apart, how do you account for that?*
If you have your exact time of birth, you might be able to find out for yourself by having an accurate horoscope chart made. Even a few minutes difference in time of birth can change the emphasis in a chart because of the movement of the earth. A different rising sign, which sets up the "houses" of your chart, moves over the horizon every two hours. And the moon moves about 13 degrees in a day. A change of degree or a rising sign can make a big difference.

If you have the exact degree of your moon and rising sign and your brother's moon and rising sign, you might be interested in comparing Sabian Symbols, which are symbolic meanings for each degree; they can be quite enlightening. There are several books on the Sabian Symbols, such as *The Sabian Symbols as an Oracle* by Lynda and Richard Hill (White Horse Books, 1995), a very readable recent addition to these interpretations.

Another possible reason for your differences is that you may each operate on a different level of your similar horoscopes. Or because you react to each other, you may each choose to manifest other facets of your charts. For example, one twin with a Cancer sun sign may manifest the creative, perceptive facets of her chart and become a child psychologist. Her sister may become a sharp businesswoman, running a hotel or real estate business, choosing the more practical side of her chart.

QUESTION: *If you were born on a day when the sun was changing signs, does that mean that you have characteristics of the preceding or following sign?*

If you were born on a day when the Sun or moon was changing signs, then it is very important to get your exact time of birth and to have an accurate horoscope chart cast. When there is a sign change, there are many shifts in energy. Between one sign and the next, there is a difference in element, modality, and polarity. Therefore, you are not likely to be partly one sign and partly another. If you do manifest characteristics of the adjacent sign, it may be due to other planets in that sign or to your rising sign.

QUESTION: *How do I answer my religious friends and family who disapprove of my interest in astrology?*

Astrology has a long history of being attacked by religious and scientific skeptics, most of whom know little about real astrology. (There's even an Internet mailing list especially for those who wish to ventilate their anti-astrology feelings.) Point out that there has never been any conflict between astrology and religion; there are no anti-astrology writings in the Bible. In fact, the three Wise Men or Magi were astrologers. In medieval times, astrology was integrated with religion. Many famous European cathedrals, such as Chartres and Canterbury, have astrology motifs, and there's a very ancient zodiac from the floor of a synagogue in New York's Jewish Museum. There is no dogma to astrology that might counter religious beliefs—astrology is not a belief system, it is a technique. In other words, you are not getting into anything dangerous with astrology, which may be what your friends fear.

Many religious people feel threatened by astrologers because they confuse modern-day astrology with that practiced by charlatans of the past or because they feel that someone interested in astrology will turn away from religion. However, as anyone who has delved seriously into astrology can attest, the study of astrology tends to bring one closer to a spiritual understanding of the interchange between a universal design, the material world, and man's place in it. Astrology can, in a very practical way, help man keep in balance with the forces of the universe.

QUESTION: *Can I find the answer to a question based on a horoscope for the time it is asked?*
This belongs to a specific discipline within astrology called *horary astrology*. It works according to specific rules and is practiced by specialists within the field. If you would like to find an answer this way, be sure to consult an astrologer who specializes in horary techniques. There is also an astrology program called "Nostradamus" (by Air Software; see our resource list in the Internet chapter), which was created for horary work.

CHAPTER 7

Your Daily Agenda:

Make the Most of the Millennium!

Set your schedule on a successful course by letting astrology help you coordinate your activities with the most beneficial times. For instance, if you know the dates that the tricky planet Mercury will be creating havoc with communications, you'll be sure to back up the hard drive on your computer, keep duplicates of your correspondence, record those messages, and read between the lines of contracts. When Venus is in your sign, you'll get a new hairstyle, entertain a VIP client, and circulate where you'll be seen and admired.

To find out for yourself if there's truth to the saying "timing is everything," mark your own calendar for love, career moves, vacations, and important events by using the following information and the tables in this chapter and the one titled "Look Up Your Planets," as well as the moon sign listings under your daily forecast. Here are the happenings to note on your agenda:

- Dates of your sun sign (high-energy period)
- The month previous to your sun sign (love energy period)
- Dates of planets in your sign this year
- Full and new moons (pay special attention when these fall in your sun sign)
- Eclipses

- Moon in your sun sign every month, as well as moon in the opposite sign (listed in daily forecast)
- Mercury retrogrades
- Other retrograde periods

When to Switch on the Power!

Every birthday starts a cycle of solar energy for you. You should feel a new surge of vitality as the powerful sun enters your sign. This is the time when predominant energies are most favorable to you—so go for it! Start new projects, make your big moves. You'll get the recognition you deserve now, because your sun sign is most prominent. Look in the tables in this book to see if other planets will also be passing through your sun sign at this time. Venus (love, beauty), Mars (energy, drive), or Mercury (communication, mental sharpness) reinforce the sun and give an extra boost to your life in the areas they affect. Venus will rev up your social and love life, making you seem especially attractive. Mars gives you extra energy and drive, while Mercury fuels your brain power and helps you communicate. Jupiter signals an especially lucky period of expansion.

There are two "down" times related to the sun. During the month before your birthday period, when you are winding up your annual cycle, you could be feeling especially vulnerable and depleted, so get extra rest, watch your diet, and don't overstress yourself. Use this time to gear up for a big "push" when the sun enters your sign.

Another "down" time is when the sun is the opposite sign (six months from your birthday) and the prevailing energies are very different from yours. You may feel at odds with the world and things might not come easily. You'll have to work harder for recognition, because people are not on your wavelength. However, this could be a good time to work on a team, in cooperation with others, or behind the scenes.

Phase in and Phase out with the Moon

Working with the phases of the moon is as easy as looking up at the night sky. At the new moon, when both sun and moon are in the same sign, it's the best time to begin new ventures, especially the activities that are favored by that sign. You'll have powerful energies pulling you in the same direction. You'll be focused outward, toward action. Postpone breaking off, terminating, deliberating, or reflecting, activities that require introspection and passive work.

Get your project under way during the first quarter, then go public at the full moon, a time of high intensity, when feelings come out into the open. This is your time to shine—to express yourself. Be aware, however, that because pressures are being released, other people are also letting off steam and confrontations are possible. So try to avoid arguments. Traditionally, astrologers often advise against surgery at this time, for it could produce heavier bleeding.

From the last quarter to the new moon is a winding-down phase, a time to cut off unproductive relationships, do serious thinking, and perform inwardly directed activities.

You'll feel some new and full moons more strongly than others, especially the new moons that fall in your sun sign and the full moons in your opposite sign. Because that particular full moon happens at your low-energy time of year, it is likely to be an especially stressful time in a relationship, when hidden problems or unexpressed emotions could surface.

The Year 2000 Full and New Moons

New Moon in Capricorn—January 6
Full Moon in Leo—January 20 (eclipse 11:45 p.m. EST)
New Moon in Aquarius—February 5 (eclipse 8:03 a.m. EST)
Full Moon in Virgo—February 19

New Moon in Pisces—March 6
Full Moon in Virgo—March 20
New Moon in Aries—April 4
Full Moon in Libra—April 18
New Moon in Taurus—May 4
Full Moon in Scorpio—May 18
New Moon in Gemini—June 2
Full Moon in Sagittarius—June 16
New Moon in Cancer—July 1 (eclipse 3:34 p.m. EDT)
Full Moon in Capricorn—July 16 (eclipse 9:55 a.m. EDT)
New Moon in Leo—July 30 (eclipse 10:25 p.m. EDT)
Full Moon in Aquarius—August 15
New Moon in Virgo—August 29
Full Moon in Pisces—September 13
New Moon in Libra—September 27
Full Moon in Aries—October 13
New Moon in Scorpio—October 27
Full Moon in Taurus—November 11
New Moon in Sagittarius—November 25
Full Moon in Gemini—December 11
New Moon in Capricorn—December 25 (eclipse 12:22 p.m. EST)

Six Eclipses this Year!

There are six eclipses this year (last year, there were only four), which means you can expect changes that will be sure to influence your life, especially if you are a Capricorn, Cancer, Leo, or Aquarius. Both solar and lunar eclipses are times when our natural rhythms are altered, depending on where the eclipse falls in your horoscope and how many planets you have in the sign of the eclipse. If it falls on or close to your birthday, you're going to have important changes in your life, perhaps a turning point.

Lunar eclipses happen when the earth is on a level plane with the sun and moon and moves exactly between them during the time of the full moon, breaking the powerful monthly cycle of opposition of these two forces. We might say the earth "short circuits" the connection between them. The effect can be either confusion or clarity, as our subconscious energies, which normally react to the pull of opposing sun and moon, are turned off. As we are temporarily freed from the subconscious attachments, we might have objective insights that could help us change any destructive emotional patterns, such as addictions, which normally occur at this time. This momentary "turn off" could help us turn our lives around. On the other hand, this break in the normal cycle could cause a bewildering disorientation that intensifies our insecurities.

The solar eclipse occurs at the new moon and this time the moon blocks the sun's energies as it passes exactly between the sun and the earth. This means the objective, conscious force, represented by the sun, will be temporarily darkened. Subconscious lunar forces, activating our deepest emotions, will now dominate, putting us in a highly subjective state. Emotional truths can be revealed or emotions can run wild, as our objectivity is cut off and hidden patterns surface. If your sign is affected, you may find yourself beginning a period of work on a deep inner level; you may have psychic experiences or a surfacing of deep feelings.

You'll start feeling the energies of an upcoming eclipse a few days after the previous new or full moon. The energy continues to intensify until the actual eclipse, then disperses for three or four days. So plan ahead at least a week or more before an eclipse and allow several days afterward for the natural rhythms to return. Try not to make major moves during this period (it's not a great time to get married, change jobs, or buy a home).

Eclipses in 2000

Lunar Eclipse in Leo—January 20 (11:45 p.m. EST)
Solar Eclipse in Aquarius—February 5 (8:03 a.m. EST)
Solar Eclipse in Cancer—July 1 (3:34 p.m. EDT)

Lunar Eclipse in Capricorn—July 16 (9:55 a.m. EDT)
Solar Eclipse in Leo—July 30 (10:25 p.m. EDT)
Solar Eclipse in Capricorn—December 25 (12:22 p.m. EST)

Moon Sign Timing

You can forecast the daily emotional "weather" to determine your monthly high and low days, or to synchronize your activities with the cycles and the sign of the moon. Take note of the moon's daily sign under your daily forecast at the end of the book. Here are some of the activities favored and moods you are likely to encounter under each sign.

Moon in Aries

Get moving! The new moon in Aries is an ideal time to start new projects. Everyone is pushy and raring to go, rather impatient and short tempered. Leave details and follow-up for later. Competitive sports or martial arts are great ways to let off steam. Quiet types could use some assertiveness, but it's a great day for dynamos. Be careful not to step on too many toes.

Moon in Taurus

It's time to do solid, methodical tasks. This is the time to tackle follow-through or backup work, laying the foundations for success. Make investments, buy real estate, do appraisals, make some hard bargains. Attend to your property—get out in the country or spend some time in your garden. Enjoy creature comforts, music, a good dinner, and sensual lovemaking. Forget about starting a diet.

Moon in Gemini

Talk means action today. Telephone, write letters, fax! Make new contacts, and be sure to stay in touch with steady customers as well. You can handle lots of tasks at once. It's a great day for mental activity of any kind. Don't try to pin people down—they too are feeling restless, so keep it light. Flirtations and socializing are good. Watch gossip—and don't give away secrets.

Moon in Cancer

This is a moody, sensitive, emotional time. People respond to personal attention and mothering. Stay at home, have a family dinner, call your mother. Nostalgia, memories, and psychic powers are heightened. You'll want to hang on to people and things—don't clean out your closets now. You could have some shrewd insights into what others really need and want, so pay attention to dreams, intuition, and gut reactions.

Moon in Leo

Everybody is in a much more confident, enthusiastic, generous mood. It's a good day to ask for a raise, show what you can do, and dress like a star. People will respond to flattery, and are sure to enjoy a bit of drama and theater. You may be feeling extravagant, so treat yourself royally and show off a bit—but don't break the bank! Be careful that you don't promise more than you can deliver!

Moon in Virgo

Do practical, down-to-earth chores, such as reviewing your budget and making repairs. Be an efficiency expert. This is not a day to ask for a raise. Have a health checkup, revamp your diet, buy vitamins or health food. Make your home spotless, taking care of details and piled-up chores. Reorganize your work and life so they run more smoothly, efficiently, and inexpensively. Be prepared for others to be in a critical, fault-finding mood.

Moon in Libra

Relationships of all kinds are favored. Attend to legal matters, negotiate contracts, and arbitrate. Do things with your favorite partner—socialize, be romantic, or buy a special gift or a beautiful object. Decorate yourself or your surroundings, buying new clothes, throwing a party, or having an elegant, romantic evening. Smooth over any ruffled feathers as you avoid confrontations and stick to civilized discussions.

Moon in Scorpio

This is a day to do things with passion. You'll have excellent concentration and focus, but try not to get too intense emotionally, and avoid sharp exchanges with loved ones. Others may tend to go to extremes, get jealous, and overreact. Today is great for troubleshooting, problem-solving, research, scientific work—and making love. Pay attention to psychic vibes.

Moon in Sagittarius

It's a great time for travel and for having philosophical discussions. Set long-range career goals, work out, do sports, or buy athletic equipment. Others will be feeling upbeat, exuberant, and adventurous. Risk taking is favored today—you may feel like taking a gamble, betting on the horses, visiting a local casino, or buying a lottery ticket. Teaching, writing, and spiritual activities also get the green light. Relax outdoors; take care of animals.

Moon in Capricorn

You can accomplish a lot today, so get on the ball! Issues concerning your basic responsibilities, duties, family, and parents could crop up. You'll be expected to deliver on your promises and stick to your schedule now, so weed out the deadwood from your life and attack chores systematically. Get a dental checkup or attend to your aching knees.

Moon in Aquarius

It's a great day for doing things in groups—so take part in clubs, meetings, outings, politics, or parties. Campaign for your candidate, work for a worthy cause, or deal with larger issues that affect the welfare of humanity. Buy a computer or electronic gadget. Watch TV. Wear something outrageous or try something you've never done before. Present an original idea. Don't stick to a rigid schedule—go with the flow. Take a class in meditation, mind control, or yoga.

Moon in Pisces

This can be a very creative day, so let your imagination work overtime. Film, theater, music, or ballet could inspire you. Spend some time alone, resting and reflecting, reading, watching a favorite film, or writing poetry. Daydreams can also be profitable. Help those less fortunate or lend a listening ear to someone who may be feeling blue. Don't overindulge in self-pity or escapism via alcohol, however, for people are especially vulnerable to substance abuse now. Turn your thoughts to romance and someone special.

When the Planets Go Backward

All the planets, except for the sun and moon, have times when they appear to move backward—or retrograde—in the sky, or so it seems from our point of view on earth. At these times, planets do not work as they usu-

ally do, so it's best to take a break from that planet's
energies in our life and do some work on an inner level.

How to Outwit Mercury Mischief

Mercury goes retrograde most often, and its effects can
be especially irritating. When it reaches a short distance
ahead of the sun three times a year, it seems to move
backward from our point of view. Astrologers often
compare retrograde motion to the optical illusion that
occurs when we ride on a train that passes another train
traveling at a different speed—the second train appears
to be moving in reverse.

What this means to you is that the Mercury-ruled
areas of your life—analytical thought processes, communications, scheduling, and such—are subject to all kinds
of confusion. So be prepared as people change their
minds and renege on commitments. Communications
equipment can break down, schedules must be changed
on short notice, and people are late for appointments or
don't show up at all. Traffic is terrible, and major purchases malfunction, don't work out, or get delivered in
the wrong color. Letters don't arrive or are delivered to
the wrong address. Employees will make errors that
have to be corrected later. Contracts don't work out or
must be renegotiated.

Since most of us can't put our lives on hold for nine
weeks every year (three Mercury retrograde periods),
we should learn to tame the trickster and make it work
for us. The key is in the prefix "re." This is the time to
go back over things in your life. Reflect on what you've
done during the previous months, looking for deeper
insights, spotting errors you've missed, and taking time
to review and reevaluate what has happened. This time
is very good for inner spiritual work and meditations.
REst and REward yourself—it's a good time to take a
vacation, especially if you REvisit a favorite place. RE-
organize your work and finish up projects that are
backed up, or clean out your desk and closets, throwing
away what you can't REcycle. If you must sign contracts

or agreements, do so with a contingency clause that lets you REevaluate the terms later.

Postpone major purchases or commitments. Don't get married (unless you're remarrying the same person). Try not to rely on other people keeping appointments, contracts or agreements to the letter—it's best to have several alternatives. Double-check and read between the lines. Don't buy anything connected with communications or transportation—and if you must, be sure to cover yourself. Mercury retrograding through your sun sign will intensify its effect on your life.

If Mercury was retrograde when you were born, you may be one of the lucky people who don't suffer the frustrations of this period. If so, your mind probably works in a very intuitive, insightful way.

The sign Mercury is retrograding through can give you an idea of what's in store—as well as the sun signs that will be especially challenged.

Mercury Retrograde Periods in 2000
February 21–March 14
June 23–July 17
October 18–November 8
Fortunately, there are no Venus or Mars retrograde periods this year; however, both planes were retrograde in 1999, so it might be useful to reexamine what to do during these times.

Venus Retrograde—Make Peace!

Retrograding Venus can cause relationships to take a backward step or it can make you extravagant and impractical. It's *not* a good time to redecorate—you'll hate the color of the walls later. Postpone getting a new hairstyle and try not to fall in love either. But if you wish to make amends in an already-troubled relationship, make peaceful overtures then.

There is no Venus retrograde period in the year 2000.

Mars Tips—When to Push and When to Hold Back!

Mars shows how and when to get where you want to go, so timing your moves with Mars on your side can give you a big push. On the other hand, pushing Mars the wrong way can guarantee that you'll run into frustrations in every corner. Your best times to forge ahead are during the weeks when Mars is traveling through your sun sign or your Mars sign (look these up in the chapter on how to find your planets). Also consider times when Mars is in a compatible sign (fire with air signs, or earth with water signs). You'll be sure to have planetary power on your side.

Hold your fire when Mars retrogrades (fortunately this is a "go-ahead" year, when Mars moves forward all year long). This is the time to exercise patience, so let someone else run with the ball, especially if it's the opposing team. You may feel that you're not accomplishing much, but that's the right idea. Slow down and work off any frustrations at the gym. It's also best to postpone buying mechanical devices, which are Mars ruled, and to take extra care when handling sharp objects. Sports, especially those requiring excellent balance, should be played with care—be sure to use the appropriate protective gear and don't take unnecessary chances. This is not the time for daredevil moves! Pace yourself and pay extra attention to your health, since you may be especially vulnerable at this time.

When Other Planets Retrograde

The slower-moving planets, (Saturn, Jupiter, Neptune, Uranus, and Pluto) stay retrograde for months at a time. When Saturn is retrograde, you may feel more like hanging out at the beach than getting things done—it's an uphill battle with self-discipline at this time. Neptune retrograde promotes a dreamy escapism from reality, whereas Uranus retrograde may mean setbacks in areas where there have been sudden changes. Think of this as an adjustment period, a time to think things over and allow new ideas to develop. Pluto retrograde is a time to work on establishing proportion and balance in areas where there have been recent dramatic transformations.

When the planets start moving forward again, there's a shift in the atmosphere. Activities connected with each planet start moving ahead; planets that were stalled get rolling. Make a special note of those days on your calendar and proceed accordingly.

Other Retrogrades in 2000

Pluto turns retrograde in Sagittarius—March 15
Neptune turns retrograde in Aquarius—May 8
Uranus turns retrograde in Aquarius—May 25
Pluto turns direct in Sagittarius—August 20
Saturn turns retrograde in Taurus—September 12
Jupiter turns retrograde in Taurus—September 29
Neptune turns direct in Aquarius—October 15
Uranus turns direct in Aquarius—October 26

CHAPTER 8

What Makes Your Horoscope Special—Your Rising Sign

At the moment you were born, when you assumed an independent physical body, one of the signs of the zodiac (that is, a 30-degree slice of the sky) was just passing over the eastern horizon. In astrology, this is called the rising sign or ascendant, and it is one of the most important factors in your horoscope because it determines the uniqueness of your chart. Other babies who were born later or earlier in the day, in the same hospital as you were born, might have planets in the same signs as you do, but would have a different rising sign because as the earth turns, a different sign rises over the horizon every two hours. Therefore the planets would be in a different place in their horoscopes, emphasizing different areas of their lives.

In a horoscope, the other signs follow the rising sings in sequence, rotating counterclockwise. Therefore, the rising sign sets up the pathway of your chart. It rules the first house, which is your physical body and your appearance, and it also influences your style, tastes, health, and physical environment—where you are most comfortable working and living. The rising sign is one of the most important factors in your chart because it not only shows how you appear outwardly, but it also sets up the path you are to follow through the horoscope. After the rising sign is determined, then each house or area of your chart will be influenced by the signs following in sequence.

When we know the rising sign of a chart, we know where to put each planet—in which area of life it will operate. Without a valid rising sign, your collection of planets would have no "homes." Once the rising sign is established, it becomes possible to analyze a chart accurately. That is why many astrologers insist on knowing the exact time of a client's birth before they analyze a chart.

Your rising sign has an important relationship with your sun sign. Some complement the sun sign; others hide the sun under a totally different mask, as if playing an entirely different role. So it is often difficult to guess the person's sun sign from outer appearances. For example, a Leo with a conservative Capricorn ascendant would come across as much less flamboyant than a Leo with an Aries or Sagittarius ascendant. If the sun sign is reinforced by other planets in the same sign, it can also assert its personality much more strongly. A Leo with Venus and Jupiter also in Leo might counteract the conservative image of the Capricorn ascendant, in the preceding example. However, it is usually the ascendant that is reflected in the first impression.

Rising signs change every two hours with the earth's rotation. Those born early in the morning when the sun was on the horizon, will be most likely to project the image of the sun sign. These people are often called a "double Aries" or a "double Virgo," because the same sun sign and ascendant reinforce each other.

Look up your rising sign on the chart at the end of this chapter. Since rising signs change rapidly, it is important to know your birth time as close to the minute as possible. Even a few minutes' difference could change the rising sign and the setup of your chart. If you are unsure about the exact time, but know within a few hours, check the following descriptions to see which is most like the personality you project.

Aries Rising—Fiery Emotions

You are the most aggressive version of your sun sign, with boundless energy that can be used productively. Watch a tendency to overreact emotionally and blow your top. You come across as openly competitive, a positive asset in business or sports, but be on guard against impatience, which could lead to head injuries. Your walk and bearing could have the telltale head-forward Aries posture. You may wear more bright colors, especially red, than others of your sign. You may also have a tendency to drive your car faster.

Taurus Rising—The Earth Mother

You'll exude a protective nurturing quality, even if you're male, which draws those in need of TLC and support. You're slow moving, with a beautiful (or distinctive) speaking or singing voice that can be especially soothing or melodious. You probably surround yourself with comfort, good food, luxurious surroundings, and sensual pleasures, and you prefer welcoming others into your home to gadding about. You may have a talent for business, especially in trading, appraising, or real estate. This ascendant gives a well-padded physique that gains weight easily.

Gemini Rising—Expressive Talents

You're naturally sociable, with a lighter, more ethereal look than others of your sign, especially if you're female. You love to be with people and you express your ideas and feelings easily; you may have writing or speaking talent. You thrive on variety and a constantly changing scenario, with many different characters, though you may relate at a deeper level than might be suspected and you will be far more sympathetic and caring than you might project. You will probably travel widely and change partners and jobs several times (or juggle two at once). Physically, you should try to cultivate tranquility and create a calmer atmosphere, because your nerves are quite sensitive.

Cancer Rising—Sensitive Antenna

You easily pick up others' needs and feelings—a great gift in business, the arts, and personal relationships—but guard against overreacting or taking things too personally, especially during full-moon periods. Find creative outlets for your natural nurturing gifts, such as helping the less fortunate, particularly children. Your insights would be useful in psychology; your desire to feed and care for others in the restaurant, hotel, or child-care industry. You may be especially fond of wearing romantic old clothes, collecting antiques, and, of course, good food. Since your body will retain fluids, you should pay attention to your diet. Escape to places near water for relaxation.

Leo Rising—Scene Player

You may come across as more poised than you really feel, but you play it to the hilt, projecting a proud royal presence. This ascendant gives you a natural flair for drama, as you project a much more outgoing, optimistic, sunny personality than others of your sign. You take care to please your public by always projecting your best star quality, probably tossing a luxuriant mane of hair or, if you're female, dazzling with a spectacular jewelry collection. Since you may have a strong parental nature, you could well be the regal family matriarch or patriarch.

Virgo Rising—Cool and Calculating

Virgo rising masks your inner nature with a practical, analytical outer image. You seem very neat, orderly, and more particular, than others of your sign. Others in your life may feel they must live up to your high standards. Though at times you may be openly critical, this masks a well-meaning desire to have only the best for your loved ones. Your sharp eye for details could be used in the financial world, or your literary skills could draw you to teaching or publishing. The healing arts, health care, and other service-oriented professions attract many with this Virgo emphasis in their chart. Physically, you may have a very sensitive digestive system.

Libra Rising—The Charmer

Libra rising makes you appear a charmer—a more social, public person than others of your sign. Your private life will extend beyond your home and family to include an active social life. You may tend to avoid confrontations in relationships, preferring to smooth the way or negotiate diplomatically than give in to an emotional reaction. Because you are interested in all aspects of a situation, you may be slow to reach decisions. Physically, you'll have good proportions and pleasing symmetry. You're likely to have pleasing, if not beautiful, facial features. You move gracefully, and you have a winning smile and good taste in your clothes and home decor. Legal, diplomatic, or public relations professions could draw your interest.

Scorpio Rising—Magnetic Power

You project an intriguing air of mystery when Scorpio's secretiveness and sense of underlying power combines with your sign. You can project the image of a master manipulator, always in control and moving comfortably in the world of power. Your physical look comes across as intense and many of you have remarkable eyes, with a direct, penetrating gaze. But you'll never reveal your private agenda and you tend to keep your true feelings under wraps (watch a tendency toward paranoia). You may have an interesting romantic history with secret love affairs. Many of you heighten your air of mystery by wearing black. You're happiest near water and should provide yourself with a seaside retreat.

Sagittarius Rising—The Wanderer

You travel with this ascendant. You may also be a more outdoor, sportive type, with an athletic, casual, outgoing air. Your moods are camouflaged with cheerful optimism or a philosophical attitude. Though you don't hesitate to speak your mind, you can also laugh at your troubles or crack a joke more easily than others of your sign. This ascendant can also draw you to the field of higher education or to a spiritual life. You'll seem to have less attachment to things and people and you may travel widely. Your strong, fast legs are a physical bonus.

Capricorn Rising—Serious Business

This rising sign makes you come across as serious, goal oriented, disciplined, and careful with cash. You are not one of the zodiac's big spenders, though you might splurge occasionally on items with good investment value. You're the traditional, conservative type in dress and environment, and you might come across as quite formal and businesslike. You'll function well in a structured or corporate environment where you can climb to the top (you are always aware of who's the boss). In your personal life, you could be a loner or a single parent who is "father and mother" to your children.

Aquarius Rising—One of a Kind

You come across as less concerned about what others think and could even be a bit eccentric. You're more at ease with groups of people than others in your sign, and you may be attracted to public life. Your appearance may be unique—either unconventional or unimportant to you. Those with the sun in a water sign (Cancer, Scorpio, Pisces) may exercise your nurturing qualities with a large group, an extended family, or a day-care or community center.

Pisces Rising—Romantic Roles

Your creative, nurturing talents are heightened, and so is your ability to project emotional drama. And your dreamy eyes and poetic air bring out the protective instinct in others. You could be attracted to the arts, especially theater, dance, film, or photography, or to psychology or spiritual or charity work. Since you are vulnerable to up-and-down mood swings, it is especially important for you to find interesting, creative work where you can express your talents and boost your self-esteem. Accentuate the positive and be wary of escapist tendencies, particularly involving alcohol or drugs, to which you are supersensitive.

	1 AM	2 AM	3 AM	4 AM	5 AM	6 AM	7 AM	8 AM	9 AM	10 AM	11 AM	12 NOON
Jan 1	Lib	Sc	Sc	Sc	Sag	Sag	Cap	Cap	Aq	Aq	Pis	Ar
Jan 9	Lib	Sc	Sc	Sag	Sag	Sag	Cap	Cap	Aq	Pis	Ar	Tau
Jan 17	Sc	Sc	Sc	Sag	Sag	Cap	Cap	Aq	Aq	Pis	Ar	Tau
Jan 25	Sc	Sc	Sag	Sag	Sag	Cap	Cap	Aq	Pis	Ar	Tau	Tau
Feb 2	Sc	Sc	Sag	Sag	Cap	Cap	Aq	Pis	Pis	Ar	Tau	Gem
Feb 10	Sc	Sag	Sag	Sag	Cap	Cap	Aq	Pis	Ar	Tau	Tau	Gem
Feb 18	Sc	Sag	Sag	Cap	Cap	Aq	Pis	Pis	Ar	Tau	Gem	Gem
Feb 26	Sag	Sag	Sag	Cap	Aq	Aq	Pis	Ar	Tau	Tau	Gem	Gem
Mar 6	Sag	Sag	Cap	Cap	Aq	Pis	Pis	Ar	Tau	Tau	Gem	Gem
Mar 14	Sag	Cap	Cap	Aq	Aq	Pis	Ar	Tau	Tau	Gem	Gem	Can
Mar 22	Sag	Cap	Cap	Aq	Pis	Ar	Ar	Tau	Gem	Gem	Can	Can
Mar 30	Cap	Cap	Aq	Pis	Pis	Ar	Tau	Tau	Gem	Can	Can	Can
Apr 7	Cap	Cap	Aq	Pis	Ar	Ar	Tau	Gem	Gem	Can	Can	Leo
Apr 14	Cap	Aq	Aq	Pis	Ar	Tau	Tau	Gem	Gem	Can	Can	Leo
Apr 22	Cap	Aq	Pis	Ar	Ar	Tau	Gem	Gem	Gem	Can	Leo	Leo
Apr 30	Aq	Aq	Pis	Ar	Tau	Tau	Gem	Can	Can	Can	Leo	Leo
May 8	Aq	Pis	Ar	Ar	Tau	Gem	Gem	Can	Can	Leo	Leo	Leo
May 16	Aq	Pis	Ar	Tau	Gem	Gem	Can	Can	Can	Leo	Leo	Vir
May 24	Pis	Ar	Ar	Tau	Gem	Gem	Can	Can	Leo	Leo	Leo	Vir
June 1	Pis	Ar	Tau	Tau	Gem	Gem	Can	Can	Leo	Leo	Vir	Vir
June 9	Ar	Ar	Tau	Gem	Gem	Can	Can	Leo	Leo	Leo	Vir	Vir
June 17	Ar	Tau	Gem	Gem	Can	Can	Can	Leo	Leo	Vir	Vir	Vir
June 25	Tau	Tau	Gem	Gem	Can	Can	Leo	Leo	Leo	Vir	Vir	Lib
July 3	Tau	Gem	Gem	Can	Can	Can	Leo	Leo	Vir	Vir	Vir	Lib
July 11	Tau	Gem	Gem	Can	Can	Leo	Leo	Leo	Vir	Vir	Lib	Lib
July 18	Gem	Gem	Can	Can	Can	Leo	Leo	Vir	Vir	Vir	Lib	Lib
July 26	Gem	Gem	Can	Can	Leo	Leo	Vir	Vir	Vir	Lib	Lib	Lib
Aug 3	Gem	Can	Can	Can	Leo	Leo	Vir	Vir	Vir	Lib	Lib	Sc
Aug 11	Gem	Can	Can	Leo	Leo	Leo	Vir	Vir	Lib	Lib	Lib	Sc
Aug 18	Can	Can	Can	Leo	Leo	Vir	Vir	Vir	Lib	Lib	Sc	Sc
Aug 27	Can	Can	Leo	Leo	Leo	Vir	Vir	Lib	Lib	Lib	Sc	Sc
Sept 4	Can	Can	Leo	Leo	Leo	Vir	Vir	Vir	Lib	Lib	Sc	Sc
Sept 12	Can	Leo	Leo	Leo	Vir	Vir	Lib	Lib	Lib	Sc	Sc	Sag
Sept 20	Leo	Leo	Leo	Vir	Vir	Vir	Lib	Lib	Lib	Sc	Sc	Sag
Sept 28	Leo	Leo	Leo	Vir	Vir	Lib	Lib	Lib	Sc	Sc	Sag	Sag
Oct 6	Leo	Leo	Vir	Vir	Vir	Lib	Lib	Sc	Sc	Sc	Sag	Sag
Oct 14	Leo	Vir	Vir	Vir	Lib	Lib	Lib	Sc	Sc	Sag	Sag	Cap
Oct 22	Leo	Vir	Vir	Lib	Lib	Lib	Sc	Sc	Sc	Sag	Sag	Cap
Oct 30	Vir	Vir	Vir	Lib	Lib	Sc	Sc	Sc	Sag	Sag	Cap	Cap
Nov 7	Vir	Vir	Lib	Lib	Lib	Sc	Sc	Sc	Sag	Sag	Cap	Cap
Nov 15	Vir	Vir	Lib	Lib	Sc	Sc	Sc	Sag	Sag	Cap	Cap	Aq
Nov 23	Vir	Lib	Lib	Lib	Sc	Sc	Sag	Sag	Sag	Cap	Cap	Aq
Dec 1	Vir	Lib	Lib	Sc	Sc	Sc	Sag	Sag	Cap	Cap	Aq	Aq
Dec 9	Lib	Lib	Lib	Sc	Sc	Sag	Sag	Sag	Cap	Cap	Aq	Pis
Dec 18	Lib	Lib	Sc	Sc	Sc	Sag	Sag	Cap	Cap	Aq	Aq	Pis
Dec 28	Lib	Lib	Sc	Sc	Sag	Sag	Sag	Cap	Aq	Aq	Pis	Ar

	1 PM	2 PM	3 PM	4 PM	5 PM	6 PM	7 PM	8 PM	9 PM	10 PM	11 PM	12 MID-NIGHT
Jan 1	Tau	Gem	Gem	Can	Can	Can	Leo	Leo	Vir	Vir	Vir	Lib
Jan 9	Tau	Gem	Gem	Can	Can	Leo	Leo	Leo	Vir	Vir	Vir	Lib
Jan 17	Gem	Gem	Can	Can	Can	Leo	Leo	Vir	Vir	Vir	Lib	Lib
Jan 25	Gem	Gem	Can	Can	Leo	Leo	Leo	Vir	Vir	Lib	Lib	Lib
Feb 2	Gem	Can	Can	Can	Leo	Leo	Vir	Vir	Vir	Lib	Lib	Sc
Feb 10	Gem	Can	Can	Leo	Leo	Leo	Vir	Vir	Lib	Lib	Lib	Sc
Feb 18	Can	Can	Can	Leo	Leo	Vir	Vir	Vir	Lib	Lib	Sc	Sc
Feb 26	Can	Can	Leo	Leo	Leo	Vir	Vir	Lib	Lib	Lib	Sc	Sc
Mar 6	Can	Leo	Leo	Leo	Vir	Vir	Vir	Lib	Lib	Sc	Sc	Sc
Mar 14	Can	Leo	Leo	Vir	Vir	Vir	Lib	Lib	Lib	Sc	Sc	Sag
Mar 22	Leo	Leo	Leo	Vir	Vir	Lib	Lib	Lib	Sc	Sc	Sc	Sag
Mar 30	Leo	Leo	Vir	Vir	Vir	Lib	Lib	Sc	Sc	Sc	Sag	Sag
Apr 7	Leo	Leo	Vir	Vir	Lib	Lib	Lib	Sc	Sc	Sc	Sag	Sag
Apr 14	Leo	Vir	Vir	Vir	Lib	Lib	Sc	Sc	Sc	Sag	Sag	Cap
Apr 22	Leo	Vir	Vir	Lib	Lib	Lib	Sc	Sc	Sc	Sag	Sag	Cap
Apr 30	Vir	Vir	Vir	Lib	Lib	Sc	Sc	Sc	Sag	Sag	Cap	Cap
May 8	Vir	Vir	Lib	Lib	Lib	Sc	Sc	Sag	Sag	Sag	Cap	Cap
May 16	Vir	Vir	Lib	Lib	Sc	Sc	Sc	Sag	Sag	Cap	Cap	Aq
May 24	Vir	Lib	Lib	Lib	Sc	Sc	Sag	Sag	Sag	Cap	Cap	Aq
June 1	Vir	Lib	Lib	Sc	Sc	Sc	Sag	Sag	Cap	Cap	Aq	Aq
June 9	Lib	Lib	Lib	Sc	Sc	Sag	Sag	Sag	Cap	Cap	Aq	Pis
June 17	Lib	Lib	Sc	Sc	Sc	Sag	Sag	Sag	Cap	Cap	Aq	Pis
June 25	Lib	Lib	Sc	Sc	Sag	Sag	Sag	Cap	Cap	Aq	Pis	Ar
July 3	Lib	Sc	Sc	Sc	Sag	Sag	Cap	Cap	Aq	Aq	Pis	Ar
July 11	Lib	Sc	Sc	Sag	Sag	Sag	Cap	Cap	Aq	Pis	Ar	Tau
July 18	Sc	Sc	Sc	Sag	Sag	Cap	Cap	Aq	Aq	Pis	Ar	Tau
July 26	Sc	Sc	Sag	Sag	Sag	Cap	Cap	Aq	Pis	Ar	Tau	Tau
Aug 3	Sc	Sc	Sag	Sag	Cap	Cap	Aq	Aq	Pis	Ar	Tau	Gem
Aug 11	Sc	Sag	Sag	Sag	Cap	Cap	Aq	Pis	Ar	Tau	Tau	Gem
Aug 18	Sc	Sag	Sag	Cap	Cap	Aq	Pis	Pis	Ar	Tau	Gem	Gem
Aug 27	Sag	Sag	Sag	Cap	Cap	Aq	Pis	Ar	Tau	Tau	Gem	Gem
Sept 4	Sag	Sag	Cap	Cap	Aq	Pis	Pis	Ar	Tau	Gem	Gem	Can
Sept 12	Sag	Sag	Cap	Aq	Aq	Pis	Ar	Tau	Tau	Gem	Gem	Can
Sept 20	Sag	Cap	Cap	Aq	Pis	Pis	Ar	Tau	Gem	Gem	Can	Can
Sept 28	Cap	Cap	Aq	Aq	Pis	Ar	Tau	Tau	Gem	Gem	Can	Can
Oct 6	Cap	Cap	Aq	Pis	Ar	Ar	Tau	Gem	Gem	Can	Can	Leo
Oct 14	Cap	Aq	Aq	Pis	Ar	Tau	Tau	Gem	Gem	Can	Can	Leo
Oct 22	Cap	Aq	Pis	Ar	Ar	Tau	Gem	Gem	Can	Can	Leo	Leo
Oct 30	Aq	Aq	Pis	Ar	Tau	Tau	Gem	Can	Can	Can	Leo	Leo
Nov 7	Aq	Aq	Pis	Ar	Tau	Tau	Gem	Gem	Can	Can	Leo	Leo
Nov 15	Aq	Pis	Ar	Tau	Gem	Gem	Can	Can	Can	Leo	Leo	Vir
Nov 23	Pis	Ar	Ar	Tau	Gem	Gem	Can	Can	Leo	Leo	Vir	Vir
Dec 1	Pis	Ar	Tau	Gem	Gem	Can	Can	Can	Leo	Leo	Vir	Vir
Dec 9	Ar	Tau	Tau	Gem	Gem	Can	Can	Leo	Leo	Vir	Vir	Vir
Dec 18	Ar	Tau	Gem	Gem	Can	Can	Can	Leo	Leo	Vir	Vir	Vir
Dec 28	Tau	Tau	Gem	Gem	Can	Can	Leo	Leo	Vir	Vir	Vir	Lib

CHAPTER 9

Stay Healthy and Fit This Millennium Year

Of all the changes in the past few years, those involving our health care may have the most effect on our future well-being. Rather than depending on medical experts, we'll be taking on more and more responsibility for our own health, beginning with adopting a healthier lifestyle.

Astrology can help you sort out your health priorities and put your life on a healthier course. Since before the last millennium, different parts of the body and their potential illnesses have been associated with specific signs of the zodiac. Today's astrologers use these ancient associations not only to locate potential health problems, but also to help clients harmonize their activities with those favored by each sign.

Using the stars as a guide, you can create your own calendar for a healthier millennium, by focusing on the part of the body associated with each sun sign and the general health concerns related to that sign during the dates when each sign is predominant. By the end of the year, you should be healthier from head to toe.

Capricorn (December 22– January 19)

Capricorn, the sign of Father Time, brings up the subject of aging. If sags and wrinkles are keeping you from looking as young as you feel, you may want to investigate plastic surgery during this period. Many foods have anti-aging qualities and might be worth adding to your diet. Teeth are also ruled by this sign, a reminder to have regular cleanings and dental checkups.

Capricorn is also the sign of the workaholic, so be sure not to overdo in your quest for health. Plan for long-term gains and keep a steady, even pace for lasting results. Grim determination can be counterproductive if you're also trying to relieve tension, so remember to include pleasurable activities in your self-care program. Take up a sport for pure enjoyment, instead of pushing yourself to excel.

Here are some other health-producing things to do during Capricorn: Check your office environment for hidden health saboteurs, like poor air quality, poor lighting, and uncomfortable seating. Get an ergonomically designed chair to protect your back, or buy a specially designed back support cushion if your chair is uncomfortable. If you work at a computer, check your keyboard and the height of the computer screen for ergonomic comfort.

Capricorn rules the skeletal structure, which makes this a great time to look at the state of your posture and the condition of your bones and joints. It's never too early to counteract osteoporosis by adding weight-bearing exercise to your routine. If your joints (especially your knees) are showing early signs of arthritis, you may need to add calcium supplements to your diet. Check your posture, which affects your looks and your health. Remember to protect your knees when you work out or play sports, perhaps adding exercises to strengthen this area.

Aquarius (January 20–February 18)

Aquarius, the sign of high-tech gadgets and new ideas, should inspire you with new ways to get fit and healthy. This sign reminds us that we don't have to follow the crowd to keep fit. There are many ways to adapt your exercise routine to your individual needs. If your schedule makes it difficult to get to the gym or take regular exercise classes, look over the vast selection of exercise videos available and take class anytime you want. Or set up a gym at home with portable home exercise equipment.

New Age health treatments are favored by Aquarius, which makes this an ideal month to consider alternative approaches to health and fitness. Since Aquarius rules the circulatory system, you might benefit from a therapeutic massage, a relaxing whirlpool, or one of the new electronic massage machines. If your budget permits, this is an ideal month to visit one of the many wonderful health spas around the country for a spring tune-up.

Calves and ankles are Aquarius territory and should be emphasized in your exercise program. Be sure your ankles are well supported and protect yourself against sprains.

This is also a good time to consider the air quality around you. Aquarians are often vulnerable to airborne allergies and are highly sensitive to air pollution. Do some air quality control on your environment with an air purifier, ionizer, or humidifier. During flu season, read up on ways to strengthen your immune system.

Aquarius is a sign of reaching out to others, a cue to make your health regime more social—doing your exercises with friends could make staying fit more fun.

Pisces (February 19–March 20)

Perhaps it's no accident that we do spring cleaning during Pisces. The last sign of the zodiac, which rules the lymphatic system, is supersensitive to toxins. This is the ideal time to detox your system with a liquid diet or a supervised fast. This may also help you get rid of water retention, a common Pisces problem.

Feet are Pisces territory. Consider how often you take your feet for granted and how miserable life can be when your feet hurt. Since our feet reflect and affect the health of the entire body, devote some time this month to pampering them. Check your walking shoes or buy new ones tailored especially for your kind of exercise. Investigate orthotics, especially if you walk or run a lot. These custom-molded inserts could make a big difference in your comfort and performance.

The soles of our feet connect with all other parts of our body, just as the sign of Pisces embodies all the previous signs. This is the theory behind reflexology, a therapeutic foot massage technique that treats all areas of the body via the nerve endings on the soles of the feet. For the sake of your feet, as well as your entire body, consider treating yourself to a session with a local practitioner of this technique.

Pisces is the ideal time to start walking outdoors again, enjoying the first signs of Spring. Try doing local errands on foot, as much as possible.

Aries (March 21–April 19)

This Mars-ruled sign is a high-energy time of year. It's time to step up the intensity of your workouts, so you'll be in great shape for summer. Aerobics, competitive sports, and activities that burn calories are all favored. Try a new sport that has plenty of action and challenge, like soccer or bike racing. Be sure you have the proper headgear, since Aries rules the head.

Healthwise, if you've been burning the candle at both ends, or repressing anger, this may show up as head-aches. The way to work off steam under Aries is to schedule extra time at the gym, take up a racket sport or ping pong—anything that lets you hit an object hard! If there's a martial arts studio nearby, why not investigate this fascinating form of exercise—you too can do Kung Fu! Or get into spring training with your local baseball team!

Taurus (April 20–May 20)

Spring is in full bloom, and what better time to awaken your senses to the beauty of nature? Planting a garden can be a relaxing antidote to a stressful job. Long walks in the woods, listening to the sounds of returning birds, and smelling the spring flowers help you slow down and enjoy the pleasures of the Earth. If you've been longing for a pet, why not adopt one now from your local animal shelter? Walking your new dog could bring you a new circle of animal-loving friends.

This is a month to enjoy all your senses. Add more beautiful music to your library, try some new recipes, take up a musical instrument, or learn the art of massage. This pleasure-loving time can be one of the most sensual in your love life, so plan a weekend getaway to somewhere special with the one you love.

This is also a time to go to local farmers' markets and add more fresh vegetables to your diet. While we're on the subject of food, you may be tempted to overindulge during the Taurus period, so be sure there are plenty of low-calorie treats available. If you are feeling too lethargic, your thyroid might be sluggish. Taurus is associated with the neck and throat area, which includes the thyroid glands and vocal cords.

Since we often hold tension in our neck area, pause several times during the day for a few stretches and head rolls. If you wake up with a stiff neck, you may be using the wrong kind of pillow. Perhaps a smaller, more flexible pillow filled with flax seeds would make a difference.

Gemini (May 21–June 20)

One of the most social times of year, Gemini is related to the nerves, our body's lines of communication, so this would be a great time to combine socializing with exercise—include friends in your exercise routines. Join a friendly exercise class or jogging group. Or learn a Gemini-type sport, such as tennis or golf, which will develop your timing and manual dexterity, and improve your communication with others.

If your nerves are on edge, you may need more fun and laughter in your life. Getting together with friends, going to parties, and doing things in groups brings more perspective into your life.

Since Gemini is also associated with the lungs, this is an ideal time to quit smoking. Investigate natural ways to relieve tension, such as yoga or meditation. Doing things with your hands—playing the piano, typing, doing craftwork—are also helpful.

Those of you who run, race-walk, or jog may want to try hand weights during the Gemini month, or add upper-body exercises to your daily routine.

Cancer (June 21–July 22)

Good health begins at home, and Cancer is the perfect time to do some healthy housekeeping. Evaluate your home for potential toxins in the water or building material. Could you benefit from air and water purifiers, undyed sheets and towels, biodegradable cleaners? How about safer cooking utensils of stainless steel or glass?

This is also a good month for nurturing others and yourself, airing problems and providing the emotional support that should make your home a happier, more harmonious place to live.

Cancer rules digestive difficulties, especially gastric ulcers. Emotionally caused digestive problems—those stomach-knotting insecurities—can crop up under Cancer. Baby yourself with some extra pampering if you're feeling blue.

All boating and water sports are ideal Cancer-time activities. Sometimes just a walk by your local pond or sitting for a few moments by a fountain can do wonders to relieve stress and tension.

If you've been feeling emotionally insecure, these feelings may be sensitized now, especially near the full moon. Being with loved ones, old friends, and family could supply the kind of support you need. Plan some special family activities that bring everyone close together.

The breast area is ruled by Cancer, a reminder to have regular checkups, according to your age and family history of breast-related illness.

Leo (July 23–August 22)

We're now in the heart of summer, the time when you need to consider your relationship to Leo's ruler, the sun. Tans do look great, but in recent years we've all been warned about the permanent damage the sun can do. So don't leave home without a big hat or an umbrella, along with some sunblock formulated for your skin type.

If you've been faithful to your exercise program, you probably look great in your swimsuit. If not, now's the time to contemplate some spot-reducing exercises to zero in on problem areas. This is prime time for outdoor activity—biking, swimming, team sports—that can supplement your routine. Leos like Arnold Schwartzenegger and Madonna are models of the benefits of weight training. Since this is a time to glorify the body beautiful, why not consider what a body-building regime could do for you?

Leo rules the upper back and heart, so consider your cardiovascular fitness and make your diet healthier for your heart. Are you getting enough aerobic exercise? Also, step up exercises that strengthen the Leo-ruled upper back, such as swimming.

If you have planned a vacation for this month, make it a healthy one, a complete change of pace. Spend time playing with children, expressing the child within yourself. The Leo time is great for creative activities and doing whatever you enjoy most.

Virgo (August 23–September 22)

Virgo is associated with the care of the body in general and the maintenance of the abdomen, digestive system, lower liver, and intestines in particular. This is a trouble-shooting time of year, the perfect weeks to check your progress, schedule medical exams and diagnostic tests, and generally evaluate your health. If you need a change of diet, supplements, or special care, consult the appropriate advisers.

It's also a good time to make your life run more efficiently. It's a great comfort to know that you've got a smooth organization backing you up. Go through your files and closets to eliminate clutter; edit your drawers and toss out whatever is no longer relevant to your life.

In this back-to-school time, many of us are taking self-improvement courses. Consider a course to improve your health—nutrition, macrobiotic cooking, or massage, for example.

Libra (September 23–October 22)

Are your personal scales in balance? If you're overdoing in any area of your life, Libra is an excellent time to address the problem. If you have been working too hard or taking life too seriously, what you may need is a dose of culture, art, music, or perhaps some social activity.

If your body is off balance, consider yoga, spinal adjustments, or a detoxification program. Libra rules the kidneys and lower back, which respond to relaxation and tension-relieving exercises. Make time to entertain friends and to be romantic with the one you love. Harmonize your body with chiropractic work; cleanse your kidneys with plenty of liquids.

Since this is the sign of relationships, you may enjoy working out with a partner or with loved ones. Make morning walks or weekend hikes family affairs. Take a romantic bicycle tour and picnic in the autumn countryside, putting more beauty in all areas of your life.

Libra is also the sign of grace—and what's more graceful than dance? If ballet is not your thing, why not swing to a Latin or African beat? Dancing combines art, music, romance, relaxation, graceful movement, social contact, and exercise. What more can you ask?

Scorpio (October 23–November 21)

If you have been keeping an exercise program all year, you should see a real difference—if not a total transformation—now. Scorpio is the time to transform yourself with a new hair color, get a makeover, change your style. Eliminate what's been holding you back, including self-destructive habits. These weeks of Scorpio should enhance your willpower and determination.

The sign rules the regenerative and eliminative organs, so it's a great time to turn over a new leaf. Sexual activity comes under Scorpio, so this can be a passionate time for love. It's also a good time to examine your attitudes about sex and to put safe sexual practices into your life.

It's no accident that this passionate time is football season, which reminds us that sports are a very healthy way to express or diffuse emotions. If you enjoy winter sports, why not prepare for the ski slopes or ice skating? Scorpio loves intense, life-or-death competition, so be sure your muscles are warmed up before going all out.

Sagittarius (November 22– December 21)

Ruled by a jovial Jupiter, this is holiday time, a time to kick back, socialize with friends, and enjoy a whirl of parties and get togethers. High-calorie temptations abound, so you may want to add an extra workout or two after hitting the buffet table. Or better yet, head for the dance floor instead of the hors d'oeuvres. Most people tend to loosen up on resolve around this time of year . . . there's just too much fun to be had.

If you can, combine socializing with athletic activities. Local football games, bike riding, hikes, and long walks with your dog in tow are just as much fun in cooler weather. Let others know that you'd like a health-promoting gift—sports equipment, a gym membership, or an exercise video—for Christmas. Plan your holiday buffet to lessen temptation with plenty of low-calorie choices.

In your workouts, concentrate on Sagittarius-ruled areas with exercises for the hips, legs, and thighs. This is a sports-loving sign, ideal for downhill or cross-country skiing or roller blading and basketball.

You may find the more spiritual kinds of exercise, such as yoga or tai chi, which work on the mind as well as the body, more appealing now. Once learned, these exercises can be done anywhere. Yoga exercises are especially useful for those who travel, especially those designed to release tension in the neck and back. Isometric-type exercises, which work one muscle group against another, can be done in a car or plane seat. If you travel often, investigate equipment that fits easily in your suitcase, such as water-filled weights, home gym devices, or elastic bands.

This sign of expansiveness offers the ideal opportunity to set your goals for next year. Ask yourself what worked best for you this year and where you want to be at the end of 2001. Most important, in holiday-loving Sagittarius-time, go for the health-promoting activities and sports you truly enjoy. These are the best for you in the long run, for they're the ones you'll keep doing with pleasure.

CHAPTER 10

Astrology Adventures on the Internet:

What's New, What's Exciting, and What's Free!

Would you like a free copy of your chart, some sophisticated software to perform all the astrology calculations and give you a beautiful printout, or a screensaver custom designed for your sign? Then boot up your modem and get ready to tour the thousands of astrology websites lighting up cyberspace.

There's a global community of astrologers online with sites that offer everything from chart services to chat rooms to individual readings. Even better, many of the most exciting sites offer *free* software, *free* charts, and *free* articles to download. You can virtually get an education in astrology from your computer screen, sharing your insights with new astrology-minded pals in a chat room or on a mailing list and later meeting them in person at one of the hundreds of conferences around the world.

So if you're curious to see a copy of your chart (or someone else's), a mini-reading, even a personalized zodiac screen saver, or perhaps order a copy of your favorite astrology book, log on!

One caveat, however: Since the Internet is constantly changing, some of these sites may have changed addresses or content, even though this selection was chosen with an eye to longevity. If this happens, there is usually a referral to the new site at the old address.

Free Charts

Go to this Internet address: *http://www.alabe.com*. Astrolabe Software distributes some of the most creative and easy-to-use programs now available. Guests at this site are rewarded with a free chart of the moment you log on. They will also E-mail a copy of your chart, as well as a mini reading.

For an immediate chart printout, surf to this address: *http://www.astro.ch/*, and check into Astrodienst, home of a world atlas that will give you the accurate longitude and latitude worldwide. Once you have entered your birthday and place of birth, your chart will be displayed, ready to be downloaded to your printer. One handy feature of this particular chart is that the planetary placement is written out in an easy-to-read list alongside the chart (an important feature, if you haven't yet learned the astrology glyphs).

Free Software

Go right to this address: *http://www.alabe.com*. There you will find a demo preview of Astrolabe Software, programs that are favored by many professional astrologers. If you're serious about studying astrology, you'll want to check out the latest demo version of "Solar Fire," one of the most user-friendly astrology programs available. Try the program the pros use before you buy—you'll be impressed!

If you would like a totally functional astrology program, go to this address: *http://www.magitech.com/ ~cruiser1/astrolog.htm*.

Walter Pullen's amazingly complete ASTROLOG program is offered absolutely free at this site. Here is a program that is ultra-sophisticated, can be adapted for all formats—DOS, WINDOWS, MAC, UNIX—and has some very cool features such as a revolving globe and a constellation map. It's a must for those who want to get involved with astrology without paying the big bucks for a professional-caliber program, or for those who want to add ASTROLOG's unique features to their astrology software library. This program has it all!

Another great resource for software is Astro Computing Services. Their website has free demos of several excellent programs. Note especially their Electronic Astrologer, one of the most effective and reasonably priced programs on the market. Go to *http://www.astrocom.com* for software, books, readings, chart services, and software demos.

Free Social Life

Join a newsgroup or mailing list! You'll never feel lonely again, but you will be very busy reading the letters that overflow your mailbox every day, so be prepared! Of the many new groups, there are several devoted to astrology. The most popular is "alt.astrology." Here's your chance to connect with astrologers worldwide, exchange information, and answer some of the skeptics who frequent this newsgroup. Your mailbox will be jammed with letters from astrologers from everywhere on the planet, sharing charts of current events, special techniques, and personal problems. Check the "Web Fest" site below for astrologers on the Festival mailing list, a popular list for professional astrologers and beginners alike.

Free Screen Saver

Matrix New Age Voices offers a way to put your sign in view with a beautifully designed graphic screensaver, downloadable at this site. There are also many other diversions at this site, so spend some enjoyable hours here. Address: *http://thenewage.com/*.

Astrology Course

Schedule a long visit to *http://www.panplanet.com/*, where you will find the Canopus Academy of Astrology, a site loaded with goodies. For the experienced astrologer there are excellent articles from top astrologers. They've done the work for you when it comes to picking the best astrology links on the Web, so be sure to check out those bestowed with the Canopus Award of Excellence.

Astrologer Linda Reid, an accomplished astrology teacher and author, offers a complete online curriculum for all levels of astrology study, plus individual tutoring. To get your feet wet, Linda is offering a beginners' course at this site. A terrific way to get well grounded in astrology.

Visit an Astro-Mall

Surf to: America Online's Astronet at *http://www.astronet.com*. To cater to the thousands of astrology fans who belong to the America Online service, the Astronet area offers interactive fun for everyone. This site is also accessible to outside visitors at the above address. At this writing, there's a special area for teenage astrology fans, access to popular astrology magazines like *American Astrology* and *Planet Earth*, advice to the lovelorn, plus a grab bag of horoscopes, featured guests, a shopping area for books, reports, software, even jewelry.

Find an Astrologer Here

Metalog Directory of Astrology: *http://www.astrologer.com*

Looking for an astrologer in your local area? Perhaps you're planning a vacation in Australia or France and would like to meet astrologers or combine your activities with an astrology conference there? Go no further than this well-maintained resource. Here is an extensive worldwide list of astrologers and astrology sites. There is also an agenda of astrology conferences and seminars all over the world.

The A.F.A. Website:
http://www.astrologers.com

This is the interesting website of the prestigious American Federation of Astrologers. The A.F.A. has a very similar address to the Metalog Directory and also has a directory of astrologers, restricted to those who meet their stringent requirements. Check out their correspondence course if you would like to study astrology in depth.

Tools Every Astrologer Needs Are Online:

Internet Atlas:
http://www.astro.ch/atlas/

Find the geographic longitude and latitude and the correct time zone for any city worldwide. You'll need this information to calculate a chart.

The Zodiacal Zephyr:
http://www.zodiacal.com

A great place to start out your tour of the Astrology Internet. It has a wide selection of articles and tools for the astrologer, such as a U.S. and World Atlas, celebrity birth data, information on conferences, software, and tapes. The links at this site will send you off in the right direction.

Astrology World:
http://www.astrology-world.com

Astrologer Deborah Houlding has gathered some of the finest European astrologers for this terrific website. A great list of freebies at this site. A must!

Web Fest:
http://hudson.idt.net/~motive/

The imaginative graphics on this beautiful site are a treat. There's compilation of educational material, as well as biographies of top astrologers who contribute to the festival mailing list. Here is the place to look for an astrologer or an astrology teacher, or for information about joining the top-notch mailing list.

Astrology Alive:
http://www.astrologyalive.com/

Barbara Schermer has one of the most creative approaches to astrology. She's an innovator in the field and was one of the first astrologers to go online, so there's always a cutting edge to this site. Great list of links.

National Council for Geocosmic Research (NCGR):
http://www.geocosmic.org/

A key stop on any astrological tour of the Net. Here's where you can find out about local chapters in your area, or get information on their testing and certification programs. You can order lecture tapes from their nationwide conferences or get complete lists of conference topics. Good links to resources.

Charts of the Famous

This site has birthdays and charts of famous people to download: *http://www.astropro.com*

You can get the sun and moon sign, plus a biography of the hottest new stars, here: *http://www.celebsite. com*

Best General Search Engine: Yahoo
http://www.yahoo.com

You get the maximum search for your time at Yahoo. This search engine enters your input into other popular search engines.

Matrix Space Interactive:
http://thenewage.com

Browse this New-Age marketplace for free interactive astrology reports, an online astrology encyclopedia, lots of celebrity charts, and information about Matrix's excellent Winstar Plus and other astrology programs. A fun place to spend time.

For Astrology Books

National Clearinghouse for Astrology Books:
http://www.astroamerica.com

A wide selection of books on all aspects of astrology, from basics to advanced, as well as many hard-to-find books.

These addresses also have a good selection of astrology books, some of which are unique to the site.

http://www.panplanet.com
http://thenewage.com
http://www.astrocom.com

Browse the huge astrology list of online bookstore Amazon.com at *http:www.amazon.com/*

Your Astrology Questions Answered

Astrology FAQ (Frequently Asked Questions):
http://www.magitech.com/pub/astrology/ info/faq.txt

Questions that are on everyone's mind. Especially useful information when you're countering astrology-bashers.

History and Mythology of Astrology:
http://www.elore.com

Be sure to visit the astrology section of this gorgeous site, dedicated to the history and mythology of many traditions. One of the most beautifully designed sites we've seen.

The Mountain Astrologer:
http//www.mountainastrologer.com/ index.html

A favorite magazine of astrology fans, *The Mountain Astrologer,* has an interesting website featuring the latest news from an astrological point of view, plus feature articles from the magazine.

CHAPTER 11

The Sydney Omarr Yellow Pages

Ever wondered where to find astrologers in your area, where to get a basic astrology program for your new computer, or where to take a class with a professional astrologer? Look no further. In this chapter we'll give you the information you need to locate the latest products and services available.

There are very well-organized groups of astrologers all over the country who are dedicated to promoting the image of astrology in the most positive way. The National Council for Geocosmic Research (NCGR) is one nationwide group that is dedicated to bringing astrologers together, promoting fellowship and high-quality education. They have an accredited course system, with a systemized study of all the facets of astrology. Whether you'd like to know more about such specialties as financial astrology or the techniques for timing events, or if you'd prefer a psychological or mythological approach, you'll find the leading experts at NCGR conferences.

Your computer can be a terrific tool for connecting with other astrology fans at all levels of expertise. Even if you are using a "dinosaur" from the 1980s, there are still calculation and interpretation programs available for DOS and MAC formats. They may not have all the bells and whistles or exciting graphics, but they'll get the job done!

If you are a newcomer to astrology, it is a good idea to

learn the glyphs (astrology's special shorthand language) before you purchase a computer program. Use the chapter in this book to help you learn the symbols easily, so you'll be able to read the charts without consulting a book. Several programs, such as Astrolabe's "Solar Fire" for Windows, have pop-up definitions. Just click your mouse on a glyph or an icon on the screen and a window with an instant definition appears.

Astrology software is available at all price levels, from a sophisticated free application like "Astrolog," which you can download from the Internet, to inexpensive programs for under $100, to the more expensive astrology programs such as "Winstar," "Solar Fire," or "Io" (for the Mac), used by serious students and professionals. These are available from specialized dealers and cost approximately $200–$350. Before you make an investment, it's a good idea to download a sample from the company's website or order a demo disk from the company. If you just want to have fun, investigate an inexpensive program such as Matrix Software's "Kaleidoscope," an interactive application with lots of fun graphics. If you're baffled by the variety of software available, most of the companies on our list will be happy to help you find the right application for you needs.

If you live in an out-of-the-way place or are unable to fit classes into your schedule, correspondence courses are available. There are also online courses being offered at astrology websites. Some courses will send you a series of tapes; others use workbooks or computer printouts.

The Yellow Pages:

Nationwide Astrology Organizations and Conferences:

Contact these organizations for information on conferences, workshops, local meetings, conference tapes, or referrals:

National Council for Geocosmic Research

Educational workshops, tapes, conferences, and a directory of professional astrologers are available. For a $35 annual membership fee, you get their excellent educational publications and newsletters plus the opportunity to meet other astrology buffs at local chapter events in cities nationwide. For further information, contact:

Beverly Annen
9307 Thornewood Drive
Baltimore, MD 21234
Phone: 410-882-2856

Or visit their web page: http://www.geocosmic.org

American Federation of Astrologers (A.F.A.)

One of the oldest astrological organizations in the U.S., established 1938, it offers conferences, conventions, and a correspondence course. It will refer you to an accredited A.F.A. astrologer.

P.O. Box 22040
Tempe, AZ 85382
Phone: 602-838-1751
FAX: 602-838-8293

A.F.A.N. (Association for Astrological Networking)

Did you know that astrologers are still being arrested for practicing in some states? AFAN provides support and legal information, working toward improving the public image of astrology. Here are the people who will go to bat for astrology when it is attacked in the media. Everyone who cares about astrology should join!

A.F.A.N.
8306 Wilshire Blvd.
Berkeley Hills, CA 90211

ARC Directory

(Listing of Astrologers Worldwide)
2920 E. Monte Vista
Tucson, AZ 85716
602-321-1114

Pegasus Tapes

(Lectures, Conference tapes)
P.O. Box 419
Santa Ysabel, CA 92070

International Society for Astrological Research

(Lectures, Workshops, Seminars)
P.O. Box 38613
Los Angeles, CA 90038

ISIS Institute

(Newsletter, Conferences, Astrology tapes, Catalog)
P.O. Box 21222
El Sobrante, CA 94820-1222
Phone: 800-924-4747 or 510-222-9436
FAX: 510-222-2202

Computer Software

Astrolabe

Check out the latest version of their powerful "Solar Fire Windows" software, a breeze to use. This company also markets a variety of programs for all levels of expertise, a wide selection of computer astrology readings, and MAC programs. It's a good resource for innovative software as well as applications for older computers.

Box 1750–R
Brewster, MA 02631
800-843-6682

Matrix Software

You'll find a wide variety of software in all price ranges, demo disks at student and advanced level, and lots of interesting readings. Check out "Kaleidoscope," an inexpensive program with beautiful graphics, and "Winstar Plus," their powerful professional software, if you're planning to study astrology seriously.

315 Marion Ave.
Big Rapids, MI 49307
800-PLANETS

Astro Communications Services

Find books, software for MAC and IBM compatibles, individual charts, and telephone readings. Find technical astrology materials here, such as "The American Ephemeris." A good resource for those who do not have computers—they will calculate charts for you.

Dept. AF693, PO Box 34487
San Diego, CA 92163-4487
800-888-9983

Air Software

This is powerful, creative astrology software. For beginners, check out the "Father Time" program, which finds your best days, or "Nostradamus," which answers all your questions. There's also the "Airhead" astrology game, a fun way to test your knowledge.

115 Caya Avenue
West Hartford, CT 06110
800-659-1247

Time Cycles Research

(Beautiful graphic IO Series programs for the MAC)

375 Willets Avenue
Waterford, CT 06385
FAX: 869-442-0625
E-mail: astrology@timecycles.com
Internet: http://www.timecycles.com

Astro-Cartography

(Charts for location changes)

Astro-Numeric Service Box 336-B
Ashland, OR 97520
800-MAPPING

Microcycles

Which software is right for you? The "world's largest astrological software dealer" can help you get up and running. Call for catalogs or demo diskettes:

PO Box 2175
Culver City, CA 90231
800-829-2537

Astrology Magazines

In addition to articles by top astrologers, most have listings of astrology conferences, events, and local happenings.

AMERICAN ASTROLOGY
475 Park Avenue South
New York, NY 10016

DELL HOROSCOPE
P.O. Box 53352
Boulder, CO 89321-3342

PLANET EARTH
The Great Bear
P.O. Box 5164
Eugene, OR 97405

MOUNTAIN ASTROLOGER
P.O. Box 11292
Berkeley, CA 94701

ASPECTS
Aquarius Workshops
P.O. Box 260556
Encino, CA 91426

Astrology Schools:

Though there are many correspondence courses available through private teachers and astrological organizations, up until now there has never been an accredited college of astrology. That is why the following address is so important.

The Kepler College of Astrological Arts and Sciences

By the time this book is published, Kepler College, the first institution of its kind to combine an accredited liberal arts education with extensive astrological studies, should be in operation. A degree-granting college that is also a center of astrology, has long been the dream of the astrological community and will be a giant step forward in providing credibility to the profession.
For more information:

The Kepler College of Astrological Arts and Sciences
P.O. Box 77511
Seattle, WA 98177-0511
Phone: 206-706-0658
or http://www.keplercollege.org

CHAPTER 12

Is Your Life at a Crossroads?
Consider a Personal Reading

Now that the millennium is here, you may wonder if, at this important crossroads, now is the time for you to get a personal reading to plot your future course or help clarify issues in your personal life. Here is some guidance to help you sort through the variety of readings available.

The first thing you'll discover is that there seem to be as many different kinds of readings as there are astrologers. Besides face-to-face readings with a professional astrologer, there are mini-readings at psychic fairs, pay-by-the minute phone readings that can either be tape recorded or a live exchange with an "astrologer," offerings of beautiful computer-generated readings and many pages of "personal" interpretation. If you have access to the Internet, a simple search under "Astrology" will produce a mind-boggling array of websites. Online chat rooms and mailing lists dedicated to astrology are other resources frequented by professional astrologers as well as interested amateurs.

To confuse the matter further, astrologers themselves have specialties. Some are skilled in the technique of horary astrology, which involves answering questions based on the time the question is asked. Some astrologers are psychologically oriented; others are more practical. Some use traditional methods; others use more exotic techniques from India or China.

Though you can learn much about astrology from

books such as this one, nothing compares to a one-on-one consultation with a professional who has analyzed thousands of charts and can pinpoint the potential in yours. With your astrologer, you can address specific immediate problems in your life that may be holding you back. For instance, if you are not getting along with your mate or coworker, you could leave the reading with some new insights and some constructive ways to handle the situation. If you are going through a crisis in your life, an astrologer who is also a trained counselor might help you examine your options . . . and there are many astrologers who now combine their skills with training in psychology.

Before your reading, a reputable astrologer will ask for the date, time (as accurately as possible), and place of birth of the subject of the reading. (A horoscope can be cast about anything that has a specific time and place.) Most astrologers will then enter this information into a computer, which will calculate your chart (perhaps several types of charts related to your situation) in seconds. From the resulting chart or charts, the astrologer will do an interpretation.

If you don't know your exact birth time, you can usually find it filed at the Bureau of Vital Statistics at the city hall or county seat of the state where you were born. If you still have no success in getting your time of birth, some astrologers can estimate an approximate birth time by using past events in your life to determine the chart.

How to Find a Good Astrologer

Your first priority should be to choose a qualified astrologer. Rather than relying on word of mouth or grandiose advertising claims, do this with the same care you would choose any trusted adviser such as a doctor, lawyer, or banker. Unfortunately, anyone can claim to be an astrologer—to date, there is no licensing of astrologers or established professional criteria. However, there are nationwide organizations of serious, committed astrologers that can help you in your search.

Good places to start your investigation are organizations such as the American Federation of Astrologers or the National Council for Geocosmic Research (NCGR), which offers a program of study and certification. If you live near a major city, there is sure to be an active NCGR chapter or astrology club in your area—many are listed in astrology magazines available at your local newsstand. In response to many requests for referrals, the NCGR has compiled a directory of professional astrologers, which includes a glossary of terms and an explanation of specialties within the astrological field. Contact the NCGR headquarters (see the resource list in this book) for information.

As a potentially lucrative freelance business, astrology has always attracted self-styled experts who may not have the knowledge or the counseling experience to give a helpful reading. These astrologers can range from the well-meaning amateur to the charlatan or street-corner gypsy who has for many years given astrology a bad name. Be very wary of astrologers who claim to have occult powers or who make pretentious claims of celebrated clients or miraculous achievements. You can often tell from the initial phone conversation if the astrologer is legitimate. He or she should ask for your birthday time and place and conduct the conversation in a professional manner. Any astrologer who gives a reading based only on your sun sign is highly suspect. Be especially wary of fly-by-night corner gypsies, who claim to be astrologers.

When you arrive at the reading, the astrologer should be prepared. The consultation should be conducted in a private, quiet place. The astrologer should be interested in your problems of the moment. A good reading involves feedback on your part, so if the reading is not relating to your concerns, you should let the astrologer know. Feel free to ask questions and get clarifications of technical terms. The reading should be an interaction between two people, rather than a solo performance. The more you actively participate, rather than expecting the astrologer to carry the reading or come forth with oracular predictions, the more meaningful your experience will be. An astrologer should help you validate your current experience and be frank about possible negative happenings, but suggest a positive course of action.

In their approach to a reading, some astrologers may be more literal, others more intuitive. Those who have had counseling training may take a more psychological approach. Though some astrologers may seem to have an almost psychic ability, extrasensory perception or any other parapsychological talent is not essential. A very accurate picture can be drawn from the data in your horoscope chart.

An astrologer may do several charts for each client, including one for the time of birth and a "progressed chart," showing the evolution from birth to the present time. According to your individual needs, there are many other possibilities, such as a chart for a different location, if you are contemplating a change of place. Relationships between any two people, things, or events can be interpreted with a chart that compares the two horoscopes. Another commonly used device is a composite chart, which uses the midpoint between planets in two individual charts to describe the relationship.

An astrologer will be particularly interested in transits—times when planets will pass over the planets or sensitive points in your chart, which can signal important events in your life.

Many astrologers offer tape-recorded readings, another option to consider. In this case, you'll be mailed a tape of a reading based on your birth chart. Though this reading is more personal than a computer printout and can give you valuable insights, it is not equivalent to a live dialogue with an astrologer, where you can discuss your specific interests and issues of the moment.

About Telephone Readings

Telephone readings come in two varieties. One is a dial-in taped reading, usually by a well-known astrologer.

The other is a live consultation with an "astrologer" on the other end of the line. The taped readings are general daily or weekly forecasts, applied to all members of your sign and charged by the minute. The quality depends on the astrologer. One caution: Be aware that these readings can run up quite a telephone bill, especially if you get into the habit of calling every day. Be sure that you are aware of the per-minute cost of each call beforehand. (It might be wise to keep a timer next to the phone, to limit your calls beforehand.)

Live telephone readings also vary with the expertise of the astrologer. The advantage of a live telephone reading is that your individual chart is used and you can ask about a specific problem. Usually the astrologer on the other end of the line will enter your birth data into a computer and use the chart it generates during the reading. However, before you invest in any reading, be sure that your astrologer is qualified and that you fully understand in advance how much you will be charged.

About Computer Readings

Most of the companies that offer computer programs (such as ACS, Matrix, ASTROLABE) also offer computer-generated horoscope interpretations. These can be quite comprehensive, offering a beautiful printout of the chart plus many pages of information. A big plus is that you'll receive an accurate copy of your chart, which can be used for future reference. The accompanying natal chart interpretation can be a good way to learn about your own chart at your convenience, since most readings interpret the details of the chart in a very understandable way. However, since there is no input from you, the interpretations will be general and may not address your immediate issues.

This is still a good option for a first reading, to get your feet wet, especially since these printouts are much lower in cost than live consultations. You might consider them as either a supplement or preparation for a live reading (study one before you have a live reading to get familiar with your chart and plan specific questions). They also make a terrific gift for someone interested in astrology. If you are considering this type of reading, look into one of the companies on our astrology resource list.

CHAPTER 13

Your Sagittarius Star Quality

All About Your
Sagittarius Sun Sign

As a Sagittarius sun sign, you'll find that the qualities associated with this sign resonate through the many roles you play in life. And if there are other Sagittarius planets in your horoscope, or if your rising sign is Sagittarius, these conditions will intensify your Sagittarius-type personality. There'll be no mistaking you for another sun sign! For example, someone with a Sagittarius sun, Mars, and rising sign (ascendant) is likely to be much more obviously a "Sagittarius" type than someone with a Sagittarius sun combined with a less talkative Cancer ascendant and a slower moving Mars in Taurus. However, even if you have a different personality than the typical Sagittarius, you'll find that many of the traits and preferences described on the following pages will still apply to you.

The Sagittarius Man:
The Wheeler-Dealer Wizard

"Nothing ventured, nothing gained" could be the motto of the Sagittarius man, a gambler who understands that life's potentialities are unlimited. You'll go for broke when the occasion demands, with touching faith that luck (or the force of the universe) is on your side. Luck is a lady for you and you can conjure up dreams that keep you going for the next big deal.

More often than not, your enthusiasm for all that inspires you is contagious and your dreams catch on. Like filmmaker Steven Spielberg, you can spin fantasies that touch us deeply and that bring you fame and fortune.

Free-wheeling Sagittarius has great faith in yourself, knowing your attitude is likely to save the day, for you can always sell your idea. Although your main interest is moving ahead, sometimes you don't know quite where you're going. Or you may know your destination, but not how to get there; you'll trust to luck (or higher forces) to put you on the fast track, rather than stick to a pre-planned strategy. Somehow, planning ahead seems to take the fun out of it for you.

Physical and mental risks are challenges to you; most Sagittarians are superb athletes, and some have a dare-devil streak. You can also be the clown, full of practical jokes, with a boyish sense of humor and a love of games that endears you to others. You're the upbeat, fun companion, the jovial daddy, the good sportsman and great buddy, who has personal friends from all walks of life. You tend to be very male-oriented, taking love lightly and making a fast getaway if someone tries to tie you down, like Frank Sinatra in his Rat Pack days.

To reach your Sagittarius potential, you must find a way to help others reach theirs, imparting high ideals of honesty, fairness, and love of truth. Teach others to roll with the punches (by the way, you've probably thrown a few yourself) and take a philosophical view of life's ups and downs. As Frank Sinatra would have sung, "That's life."

Your style is charming but confrontational, as Phil Donohue, William F. Buckley, and Winston Churchill have demonstrated. You thoroughly enjoy a good debate and are very articulate when challenged, though sometimes you may be overly direct when you say exactly what you think, regardless of timing. Confrontations can be fiery, especially when you don't consider the consequences of your words. However, you rarely hold a grudge.

Since it can be difficult for Sagittarius to take direction, you'll do best operating freelance, where you can express your visionary views and where your wise and honest words are sure to be heard.

In a Relationship

You tend to be very idealistic and optimistic about marriage, looking for a fun-loving cheerful companion (with great legs), who shares your basic philosophy of life. But marital realities can bog you down or cause you to bolt when you discover that marriage involves more intense commitment and heavier responsibility than you anticipated. It is not easy to establish a solid stable home, when it is merely a base of operations for outside activities, a clubhouse, or a comfortable place to relax between trips. You can surmount the sense of restriction that marriage can entail if you establish good, honest communication with your mate, set common goals to hold your relationship together, and include your mate in trips, work, and outside interests. Though not known for fidelity, you'll come home to someone who accepts you as you are and gives you plenty of rope.

The Sagittarius Woman: The Born Leader

The Sagittarius woman is a live wire, an enthusiastic, dynamic companion. This is a woman who tells it like it is—like it or not. But like the "Divine Miss M" Bette Midler, you're likely to lace your truth telling with side-splitting humor and always leave 'em in an upbeat mood—if not rolling on the floor.

Sagittarius is the natural cheerleader of the zodiac, spurring others on to make the most of themselves. Like

Jane Fonda, you're at your best and are most successful when you're inspiring others. You'd much rather give orders than take them and often run your own business with flair and style. You have the ability to sell others on your schemes and dreams, whether it's an exciting promotional campaign, an all-female wrestling team, or buying up a whole town, as actress Kim Basinger once did. Many Sagittarius women become professional athletes who enjoy the competition and the chance to stretch themselves, like Chris Evert, Suzy Chaffee, and Tracy Austin.

Once an idea appeals to you, you can elevate it to sell to a big market. With contagious optimism and enthusiasm, you get out and spread the word. These qualities are naturally suited to politics, sales, public relations, or teaching, where your articulate qualities are appreciated. You're better off delegating routine chores; otherwise, you might neglect the repetitious but important day-to-day responsibilities, leaving others holding the bag. A good support system is the key to your success!

Though generally blessed with good fortune (your breezy positive mental attitude attracts it!), you can get into trouble if you make promises you can't deliver, or if you run rampant over the feelings of others.

In a Relationship

The Sagittarius woman usually has no problem juggling her career and home life, providing you find a good backup staff to handle finances and routine chores, while you pursue outside interests. This also assumes you have found a liberated partner who is unthreatened by your public personality and enjoys gadding about with you (or has a demanding career of his own). He should appreciate a woman with a fine mind, well-toned body, boundless energy, and strong opinions. You'll be sure to pull your own weight in the marriage, cope with constant changes, and manage a large, active family.

The Sagittarius Family

The Sagittarius Parent

Children bring out the jovial, fun-loving child within Sagittarius, and you welcome the challenge of raising them. But sometimes the realities and responsibilities of parenting are more than you bargained for. Sagittarius is not a sign that welcomes dependency of any sort and may resent the obligation to be there for your child, which cuts into free-wheeling career time, travel, sports, or community activities. Though very young children can tie you to the home, you'll think of some ingenious ways to get out and about to stay involved in community activities. A large family car or van, equipped with child seats, offers one way to take them along with you.

Sagittarians often discover that helping young minds to grow and explore life's adventures can be more interesting than gadding about. You'll discover that you're a born coach who can make learning fun. You know when to lighten up with a joke and understand children's restless antics. Once your children get past the dependent stage, you're one of the most enthusiastic parents.

The Sagittarius Stepparent

With your breezy, casual attitude, you find it easier to adjust to being a stepparent than many other signs. Your sense of humor will stand you in good stead when awkward situations crop up, and your honest, direct approach will help get problems out in the open. Since you allow your mate plenty of space, there will be little rivalry with the children. You'll enjoy planning outdoor activities for everyone to share. In time, you'll be a good friend to the children, one who encourages any effort to expand their horizons and supports their growth toward independence.

The Sagittarius Grandparent

Sagittarius stays young at heart right through the senior years. You'll enjoy the independence you now have, which gives you the chance to travel and pursue your interests. You may continue to work in some capacity, as a writer or teacher. You'll be well informed of global happenings, or at least what's happening outside of the home. This may be a time when you offer spiritual support and leadership in religious life. You'll enjoy the company of your grandchildren, and you'll have the energy to play right along with them. You'll encourage their educational progress, and perhaps even finance higher studies. You'll pass on your hard-won wisdom, thrilling them with tales of youthful adventures and inspiring them to follow their dreams. Best of all, you're a grandparent who laughs with them and teaches them to look on the bright side of life.

CHAPTER 14

Show Off the Sagittarius in You

Sagittarius Self-Expression

Everyone's intrigued by their sun sign personality. But did you know that it also influences the styles that present you at your best, the colors and sounds that lift your mood, even the best places to take a vacation? Why not try putting more Sagittarius style in every area of your life and see if it doesn't make a happier difference!

Sagittarius at Home

Many Sagittarians have great decorating flair and dress a room with drama, highlighting exotic souvenirs. Even if you are the rare Sagittarian who has never traveled, you are sure to collect some form of exotica, books, athletic trophies, or sporting pictures. Since many Sagittarians get involved with horses, you might like a western or equestrian theme, with hunter-green walls, plaid upholstery, and horse prints. Or yours may be a relaxed, casual hangout to rest between trips and entertain chums. You'll be unhappy in any room with a closed-in feeling. You need plenty of space and a fireplace, and you may need dog- and cat-proof furniture to accommodate your pets!

The Sagittarius Beat

Your musical tastes can be as exotic and varied as your travels! Your gypsy soul soars to Latin rhythms, flamenco guitar, and tango. Your spiritual side is uplifted by all sorts of religious music. Frank Sinatra, Noël Coward, Puccini, and George Gershwin speak your musical language. Sagittarius singers Sinead O'Connor, Tina turner, Bette Midler, and Dionne Warwick are on your wavelength.

Great Vacation Adventures for Sagittarius

Almost anyplace is a Sagittarius place, but not for long! Sagittarians are born globe-trotters, always on the move. You may want to settle down for a while in a place with great sports facilities, or attend a horse show in Ireland or the grand prix in Monaco. There's always the Olympics somewhere! Sagittarians like the challenge of outward-bound expeditions, wilderness camping trips, or exploring remote places such as Antarctica or Finland, Spain, Chile, Thailand, and Hungary, countries that resonate to your Sagittarius frequency.

Keep a bag packed with items you can't live without (that Swiss Army knife, copies of your favorite tapes, video workouts, portable exercise equipment, rollerblades). Choose hotels that have fitness equipment, pools, or jogging tracks, so you won't miss a workout. Keep a separate notebook for your contacts and favorite haunts in each city, so all your relevant numbers will be instantly available.

Your Sagittarius Colors

Purple, red, and royal blue with white are associated with Sagittarius. You are known for dramatic color combinations, combining vivid shades with flair. For inspiration, look at the vibrant homes and fashion designs of the late great Sagittarius designer Gianni Versace, whose artistic work has been featured in museums. Some of you love bright orange (the color Buddhist monks wear); it was Frank Sinatra's favorite color.

Sagittarius Fashion Tips

You need clothes that travel well, move with your body, and yet have flair and style. You love to look dashing and you're usually up to the minute on the latest trends. Stay away from fussy ruffles or demure patterns! You're naturally better suited to well-cut sports clothes and short skirts that show off your fabulous legs. Go all-out for the most sensational jogging suits and workout wear, especially if you're in great shape like Jane Fonda or *Sports Illustrated* cover girl Carol Alt. Stock up on great stockings and beautiful shoes (from Sagittarius designer Monolo Blahnik). Versatile, packable knits in bold colors are made especially for you!

Sagittarius Fashion Leaders

Your Sagittarius designers, including Donatella Versace and Thierry Mugler, understand how to use bright colors, bold jewelry, and dramatic lines. Your look is attention-getting, sometimes a bit shocking, and always full of interesting ideas. You'll be hip to the latest trends and know how to adapt them to your lifestyle. Because sports are usually a big part of your life, active sportswear often goes from the playing field to your working life. Sagittarius men are often fashion trendsetters, such as Don Johnson, who redefined menswear fashion with his combination of T-shirts and pastel Versace suits in the 1980s hit TV show *Miami Vice*. And who can forget Frank Sinatra's hats or the spiffy Rat Pack tailoring that exemplified the swinger of the fifties. With many of the looks of that decade now being revived, expect menswear to show new versions of the "Sinatra" look.

Sagittarius Edibles

Travel via your dinner, by choosing an exotic restaurant that serves Latin American, Thai, or Middle Eastern food. You'll enjoy the spicier forms of Chinese food from Szechwan or Hunan. Italian food is a perennial Sagittarius favorite. Or pick a restaurant with flair, a new hot spot with plenty of social action and lots of good-looking people. Even better, pack a tailgate picnic and head for a football or baseball game, a polo match, or a triathlon event. Combining food and sports events is a Sagittarius specialty.

CHAPTER 15

Unleash Your Sagittarius Potential—Find the Work You Love!

Sagittarius Careers

Sagittarius needs a job with scope for your soaring ambitions. Avoid stodgy offices and tradition-bound businesses. Instead, head straight for a field where your ideas will be recognized and appreciated, where you'll have plenty of room to explore new territory and expand your mind. You are very ambitious and motivated when you find a job that inspires you. Consider anything in sales, travel, and tourism, or make your athletic skills a profession in the sports or fitness fields. Your philosophical ideals can be expressed in the education, politics, or publishing field. You might also be drawn to New Age spiritual work. Any profession involving animals, especially horses, or the outdoors, is very appealing. Don't even think about a desk job or any work that gets bogged down in details or requires great patience. Go for a fast-paced job with lots of challenge and a constant change of scenery.

Sagittarius in Charge

You're a breezy, informal boss who covers a wide territory. You may be hard to pin down, but you stay on friendly terms with everybody and rarely stay around long enough to get into office politics. Unless, of course, someone challenges your territory—then you'll send them packing fast. You tell it like it is and expect others to change their tune accordingly and quickly. Even though you may step on some toes occasionally, subordinates know where they stand with you. You need a solid, well-organized backup team to make your high-flying ideas happen. Since organization is not your strong point, however, your business structure may be unconventional and sometimes nonexistent. You may have to learn the hard way not to trust to luck when you really need solid, practical support.

Sagittarius Teamwork

You are a born optimist whose energy and cheerful, positive attitude wins you a top place on the team. However, you'll get ahead faster if you run your own show. You work best when you have plenty of freedom and very loose reins. You'd rather give orders than follow them any day, and you might sound off rather than take strong direction. Diplomacy is not one of your strong points. You do respond to a challenge, be it intellectual or physical; when you're inspired, you don't need to be coddled on the job. You'll go off on an adventure for its own sake, but you'll crash down to earth if you make promises you can't deliver or go off on a tangent too often.

To Get Ahead Fast

Look for a job that inspires you and gives you lots of freedom. Then play up your strong points:
- Sales ability
- Personal flair and humor
- Energy and good physical condition
- Honesty
- Enthusiasm and positive attitude
- Decisiveness

Sagittarius Success Stories

Study the careers of these famous Sagittarius million-
aires for tips on how to make the most of your potential:

Steven Spielberg (film director)
Mike Ovitz (show-business entrepreneur)
Jean Paul Getty (oil tycoon)
Gordon Getty
Meshulam Riklis
William F. Buckley
Andrew Carnegie
Doris Duke
Don King (boxing promoter)
Alexis Lichine (the "Pope of Wine")
Walt Disney

CHAPTER 16

Sagittarius Celebrities— From Hollywood to the Halls of Power

Sagittarius Celebrities

Here's a list of the current crop of celebrities born under your Sagittarius sun sign. Though it's fun to see who shares your birthday, this list can also be a useful tool to practice what you've learned so far about astrology. Use it to compare similarities and differences between the stars who embody Sagittarius traits and those who don't. Look up the other planets in the horoscope of your favorites to see how their influence might color your sun sign emphasis.

William F. Buckley (11/24/25)
John F. Kennedy, Jr. (11/25/60)
John Larroquette (11/25/47)
Ricardo Montalban (11/25/30)
Kathryn Crosby (11/25/33)
Joe DiMaggio (11/25/14)
Little Richard (11/26/38)
Tina Turner (11/26/39)
Caroline Kennedy (11/27/57)
Jimi Hendrix (11/27/42)
Robin Givens (11/27/64)
Anna Nicole Smith (11/28/67)
Alexander Godunov (11/28/49)
Randy Newman (11/28/43)

Suzy Chaffee (11/29/46)
G. Gordon Liddy (11/30/30)
Winston Churchill (11/30/1874)
Mark Twain (11/30/1835)
Judd Nelson (12/1/60)
Carol Alt (12/1/60)
Woody Allen (12/1/35)
Bette Midler (12/1/45)
Julie Harris (12/2/25)
Andy Williams (12/3/30)
Katarina Witt (12/3/66)
Marisa Tomei (12/4/64)
Jeff Bridges (12/4/49)
Chelsea Noble (12/4/64)
Tyra Banks (12/4/73)
Walt Disney (12/5/01)
Janine Turner (12/6/62)
Don King (12/6/21)
Ellyn Burstyn (12/7/31)
Harry Chapin (12/7/42)
Jim Morrison (12/8/43)
Kim Basinger (12/8/53)
Sinead O'Connor (12/8/66)
Denzel Washington (12/8/54)
Dina Merrill (12/9/25)
Morton Downey, Jr. (12/9/33)
Beau Bridges (12/9/41)
Kirk Douglas (12/9/16)
Kenneth Branagh (12/10/67)
Susan Dey (12/10/52)
Dorothy Lamour (12/10/14)
Carlo Ponti (12/11/13)
Teri Garr (12/11/49)
Tom Hayden (12/11/39)
Mayim Bialik (12/12/75)
Cathy Rigby (12/12/52)
Dionne Warwick (12/12/41)
Frank Sinatra (12/12/15)
Ted Nugent (12/13/48)
Dick Van Dyke (12/13/25)

Charlie Rich (12/14/32)
Patty Duke (12/14/46)
Don Johnson (12/15/49)
Noël Coward (12/16/1899)
Lesley Stahl (12/16/41)
Steven Bochco (12/16/43)
Bob Guccione (12/17/30)
Keifer Sutherland (12/18/67)
Keith Richards (12/18/43)
Steven Spielberg (12/18/47)
Brad Pitt (12/18/63)
Jennifer Beals (12/19/63)
Alyssa Milano (12/19/72)
Robert Urich (12/19/47)
John Hillerman (12/20/32)
Uri Geller (12/20/46)
Chris Evert (12/21/54)
Phil Donohue (12/21/35)
Jane Fonda (12/21/37)

CHAPTER 17

Astrological Outlook for Sagittarius in 2000

During the year 2000 much that escaped you previously will be recaptured. This applies to your career, business, and romance. If single, the emphasis is on partnership and marriage. Married or single, you will be more in control of your own destiny.

During this year, people born under Cancer and Capricorn will pop up during various junctures of your life. Much emphasis is also on financial security, learning more about accounting procedures, the stock market, trends dictated by Madison Avenue. Your services will be sought; people will say to you, "You know plenty about this and I would very much appreciate if you would look at my accounts." You will be involved with campaigns relating to charity and politics. You will be pressured to sign documents which, if signed, will sap your energies and finances.

People born under Cancer this year relate to your eighth house; translated, the relationship will blend business with pleasure. With Cancer, you'll develop your interest in subjects associated with the occult.

It will be money, money, money in your connection with Capricorn. Once again you will learn more about accounting and finance. Partnership and marriage figure prominently. You will come across documents that could reveal the location of hidden wealth.

You will be fascinated by elements of timing and luck. You will also be drawn to the mystery of numbers. On that subject, the numbers 2 and 3 will figure prominently and you should pay attention to them when participating in matters of speculation.

During the first month of the year, you will obtain needed material at bargain prices. Solid investment opportunities present themselves—you could be on the way to becoming a fat cat.

Let us begin now with your diary in advance. Pay close attention to your daily forecasts, which include luck at the racetrack, good fortune in romance, ways of becoming a successful business executive, and many more valuable hints for making your life a song without too many false notes.

Ready, get set, go!

CHAPTER 18

Eighteen Months of Day-by-Day Predictions—July 1999 to December 2000

All times are calculated for EST and EDT.

JULY 1999

Thursday, July 1 (Moon in Aquarius) Changes and improvements continue to be sluggish, with both Uranus and Neptune retrograding in your third house of studies, neighborhood, and transportation matters. It's easy to be misinterpreted by younger people. Beware of the fast-talking con artists. Cerulean blue and reddish-purple are your colors; your lucky number is 4.

Friday, July 2 (Moon in Aquarius) Take care of local, small, and intangible matters. Consult relatives and neighbors when things in which you aren't interested suddenly demand your attention. There's a lot of gossip and some wishful thinking connected with these trends. Hot combination numbers: 6 and 1.

Saturday, July 3 (Moon in Aquarius to Pisces 12:24 a.m.) Domestic interests top your agenda. Children may require help in finding summer employment, but be cautious if a teenager with a new driver's license wants to borrow your car. There are mysteries coming to light that could concern your loved ones. Flame is your color. Lucky lottery: 8, 17, 26, 35, 44, 2.

Sunday, July 4 (Moon in Pisces)   You feel that you are not being told everything, and that loved ones are not leveling with you. This uncertainty can detract from the general excitement of this special national holiday. Even if you ask questions, you may not get the right answers. Your colors are pearl gray and off-white; your number is 1.

Monday, July 5 (Moon in Pisces to Aries 7:21 a.m.)   Now you are in the cycle of love, surrounded by people well disposed toward you. Today is excellent for lovemaking, partying, entertaining, and bonding more closely with children. Aries and Leo have key roles. Navy is your color; your lucky number is 5.

Tuesday, July 6 (Moon in Aries)   Aries, Leo, and another Sagittarius are taking the lead. You feel in your own element and these hours respond to your desires and wishes. Ambitions and aspirations can be realized if you push your special assets: intelligence, sophistication, and a far-roving mind. Hot combination numbers: 7 and 3.

Wednesday, July 7 (Moon in Aries to Taurus 11:22 a.m.)   The Pluto keynote in your horoscope indicates your wide use of intuitive processes. Mars is stirring up matters rooted in the past, and there are indications that you can profit greatly by remembering the teaching experiences of last year. Your color is apricot. Lucky lottery: 9, 18, 27, 36, 45, 3.

Thursday, July 8 (Moon in Taurus)   For racing luck, try these selections at all tracks. Post position special: number 2 p.p. in the second race. Pick six: 2, 3, 2, 1, 11, 12. Stay alert to the letters H, Q, and Z in the names of jockeys and horses. Hot daily doubles: 1 and 1, 1 and 2, 2 and 2. Good trends exist in health maintenance and job stability.

Friday, July 9 (Moon in Taurus to Gemini 1:00 p.m.)   This is one of your memorable days, with special lunar emphasis on sixth-house matters—your health and labor, an improved sense of fashion, and a lowering of your blood pressure if necessary. Taurus and Scorpio are your helpers. Hot combination numbers: 4 and 7.

Saturday, July 10 (Moon in Gemini)   Partnerships, including marriage, deserve your best shot under the prevailing aspects. It's a day for sharing, cooperating, giving, and showing special consideration for those who love you. The dialogue is especially good with Gemini on deck. Your color is lemon. Lucky lottery: 6, 15, 24, 33, 42, 51.

Sunday, July 11 (Moon in Gemini to Cancer 1:27 p.m.)   Good teamwork with your beloved can make this a special day. Don't try to go it alone, but seek consensus and reconciliation; be willing to compromise. It's an airy day, when you feel liberated but conscious of your partner's needs. Your lucky number is 8.

Monday, July 12 (Moon in Cancer)   Excellent trends exist in security matters, savings, investments, insurance, and home and office security. Discuss personal security with youngsters, who look to you for direction in life, and be sure you know what is taking place at their schools. Your lucky number is 3.

Tuesday, July 13 (Moon in Cancer to Leo 2:26 p.m.)   The new moon in your eighth house illuminates new security worries and uncertainties. Take responsibility within the family for keeping your loved ones aware of dangers in the streets, at school, and elsewhere. Remain alert to the character of your offspring's friends. Your number is 5.

Wednesday, July 14 (Moon in Leo)   Venus and Mercury keynotes in your horoscope indicate a warming up to your career potential and advantages, and a slowing down of transportation schedules. You may feel obliged to cancel some travel plans due to rising expenses and less certain arrangements. Lucky lottery: 7, 16, 25, 34, 43, 3.

Thursday, July 15 (Moon in Leo to Virgo 5:39 p.m.) There's strong emphasis on the problems connected with travel plans, the feelings of companions about your plans, and the need to rethink when and where you want to go. Leo and Aries are in this picture. Your winning colors are strawberry and gold. Hot combination numbers: 9 and 3.

Friday, July 16 (Moon in Virgo) Career duties and responsibilities cannot be shortchanged under the prevailing aspects, as you may have to pinch-hit for an executive. Decisions are made for you that you wish were not. To hesitate too much or too long would be a mistake. Your lucky number is 2.

Saturday, July 17 (Moon in Virgo) For racing luck, try these selections at all tracks. Post position special: number 4 p.p. in the fourth race. Pick six: 7, 2, 5, 4, 6, 1. Be alert to the letters H, Q, and Z in the names of potential winning jockeys and horses. Hot daily doubles: 1 and 3, 2 and 2, 4 and 4. The give and take between a Capricorn companion and a Cancer can make your day. Dress casually; avoid binding garments. Lucky lottery: 4, 13, 22, 31, 40, 49.

Sunday, July 18 (Moon in Virgo to Libra 12:19 a.m.) This is a memorable day for friendships, group activities, long-range financial decisions, and charitable contributions. Libra will help you balance the rights and wrongs in your life. Your lucky number is 6.

Monday, July 19 (Moon in Libra) It's an excellent day for spending time outdoors with easygoing friends. A picnic and cookout will add to the pleasure of this cycle. There are also fine trends for church and club committee work and for pinch-hitting for a VIP member who is away on vacation. Lime and other pale greens are your colors; your lucky number is 1.

Tuesday, July 20 (Moon in Libra to Scorpio 10:30 a.m.)   A friend will help you close out some pesky work project, and you can count on Libra and Gemini to present new viewpoints and conclusions that you may have overlooked. Some good ideas will occur to you just before sleep, which can be connected with important decisions. Your number is 3.

Wednesday, July 21 (Moon in Scorpio)   Scorpio will make an ideal beach and water companion. You would love a brief respite from career concerns, and the children will love the idea of swimming and boating. The fresher air at the edge of your world amazes you. Today is fine for making social arrangements. Lucky lottery: 5, 14, 23, 32, 41, 50.

Thursday, July 22 (Moon in Scorpio to Sagittarius 10:48 p.m.)   It's a fine day for completing odd chores, tasks that don't interest you, and work that you really dislike. The Saturn keynote suggests excellent health maintenance and stability in matters associated with weight and exercise, yet efforts to get away on any lengthy vacation are still being blocked. Your lucky number is 7.

Friday, July 23 (Moon in Sagittarius)   Now in your lunar-cycle high, you can exceed production statistics, take on new responsibilities, and make good impressions on others. By showing self-confidence and self-reliance, you can move into the winner's circle and put yourself in line for a promotion. Salmon pink is your color; your lucky number is 9.

Saturday, July 24 (Moon in Sagittarius)   Another Sagittarius and an Aries have key roles, as you hold the initiative and soar ahead of the competition. Overtime effort won't be wasted under those intensely positive trends. Take advantage of your education, academic prowess, travel experiences, and career luck to get ahead. Lucky lottery: 2, 11, 20, 29, 38, 47.

Sunday, July 25 (Moon in Sagittarius to Capricorn 11:08 a.m.)   Immerse yourself in projects where you can distinguish yourself. Submit avocational and creative work to contests and evaluation by authorities. Push your chances of success with career and related interests. Cardinal is your color; your lucky number is 4.

Monday, July 26 (Moon in Capricorn)   Capricorn has good financial advice for you. You might stumble on an opportunity to earn extra income, or learn that some of your possessions are increasing in value. Over the rest of the month, your wealth production and the quality of your work will be higher. Your lucky number is 8.

Tuesday, July 27 (Moon in Capricorn to Aquarius 9:54 p.m.)   For racing luck, these selections at all tracks. Post position special: number 1 p.p. in the first race. Pick six: 1, 8, 4, 1, 6, 1. Stay alert to the letters H, Q, and Z in the names of jockeys and horses. Hot daily doubles: 1 and 1, 1 and 9, 2 and 8. Self-confidence and tapping your intuitive processes will work wonders. Your color is melon.

Wednesday, July 28 (Moon in Aquarius)   The lunar eclipse in your third house can pressure communications and short-distance travel, and cause you to be misquoted by a young troublemaker. Be ultra-cautious in parking lots and where children carelessly play. Ivory and pink are your colors. Lucky lottery: 3, 12, 21, 30, 39, 48.

Thursday, July 29 (Moon in Aquarius)   Freakish accidents can occur in the wake of yesterday's eclipse, so be cautious when climbing and descending and avoid heavily polluted areas. Encourage children to wash their hands more often, particularly before eating, and make sure that store clerks handling food are wearing gloves. Your lucky number is 5.

Friday, July 30 (Moon in Aquarius to Pisces 5:27 a.m.) The Venus keynote in your horoscope makes your job and assignments a big bore. You tire easily on the job and want to get away for an adventurous weekend, but your family may be less enthusiastic about your plans for them. A little more sleep than usual will help. Hot combination numbers: 7 and 3.

Saturday, July 31 (Moon in Pisces) Your family will probably get their way and force you to change your plans. Do so cheerfully to encourage their cooperation and approval later on. A boat trip or a drive to the beach can prove enjoyable. The day becomes more to your liking. Lucky lottery: 9, 18, 27, 36, 45, 6.

AUGUST 1999

Sunday, August 1 (Moon in Pisces to Aries 12:47 p.m.) As the month begins, Uranus, Neptune, Venus, and Mercury are all erratic, slowing down your work on and off the job, as well as technological changes. It's as though fate and destiny are taking a holiday. Your family can be out-of-sorts. Maroon is your color; your number is 8.

Monday, August 2 (Moon in Aries) Because your love life is stimulated by the moon today, emotions are strongly sensitized. Awareness of your beloved's needs is in focus as romance permeates the atmosphere. It's a fine cycle for making love, giving a party, and surrounding yourself with people you like. Your number is 3.

Tuesday, August 3 (Moon in Aries to Taurus 5:09 p.m.) Aries and Leo have dual roles in the day's scenario. For racing luck, try these selections at all tracks.

Post position special: number 5 p.p. in the fifth race. Remain alert to the letters I and R in the names of jockeys and horses. Pick six: 6, 4, 1, 5, 5, 3. An aggressive young jockey attracts major attention. Gold is your color. Hot daily doubles: 2 and 3, 1 and 4, 5 and 5.

Wednesday, August 4 (Moon in Taurus) Guard against summer complaints—sunburn, fatigue, and nausea. Encourage people handling takeout food to wear gloves. You could hear about some ignorance of sanitation and hygiene today. Work hasn't much appeal for you but you admire those who literally possess and control their work. Lucky lottery: 7, 16, 25, 34, 43, 3.

Thursday, August 5 (Moon in Taurus to Gemini 7:57 p.m.) What didn't get done yesterday can be mastered more easily now. Stay abreast of any changes in the well-being of an older loved one. Children tend to play too hard over the heat of the afternoon. More duties can be handled effectively when you organize your time. Hot combination numbers: 9 and 3.

Friday, August 6 (Moon in Gemini) The Mercury keynote in your horoscope speeds up financial payoffs. With the cosmic messenger now moving forward in your eighth house, security interests can be handled quickly. Taurus and Virgo figure prominently. Your winning color is champagne; your lucky number is 2.

Saturday, August 7 (Moon in Gemini to Cancer 9:53 p.m.) Work closely with your mate to complete household tasks. Brain-to-brain discussions are required where your children's attitudes are at stake. Joint investments of time, energy, and money will produce the desired results. Lucky lottery: 4, 13, 22, 31, 40, 49.

Sunday, August 8 (Moon in Cancer) Read the financial pages of your newspaper carefully to learn where the economy is headed. Good trends exist for you and your loved ones for working on a budget that includes cost of social affairs and some travel. It's a good dollar-stretching day. Your lucky number is 6.

Monday, August 9 (Moon in Cancer to Leo 11:56 p.m.) Pisces and Cancer are in the picture. Look for sales and unusual bargains; work on a menu for the rest of the month that will include fruits and vegetables. Buying curbside and in special greengrocer outlets will prove helpful. Your color is brown; your lucky number is 1.

Tuesday, August 10 (Moon in Leo) The Mercury keynote in your horoscope reactivates your yen to travel this month. You want to stay in touch with kin at a distance, and you can bond with them more closely when you write rather than phone. Your lucky colors are tawny brown and foxy brown. Hot combination numbers: 3 and 9.

Wednesday, August 11 (Moon in Leo) The solar eclipse increases the accident-producing potential of this cycle, so be cautious while driving in heavy traffic and in parking lots. Don't take chances and run lights when they are changing. Drive defensively and especially be careful climbing and descending. Lucky lottery: 5, 14, 23, 32, 41, 50.

Thursday, August 12 (Moon in Leo to Virgo 3:22 a.m.) For racing luck, try these selections at all tracks. Post position special: number 7 p.p. in the first race. Pick six: 7, 5, 1, 1, 3, 7. Watch for the letters I and R in the names of jockeys and horses. Hot daily doubles: 2 and 5, 1 and 6, 3 and 4. Invite an Aries and a Libra to accompany you.

Friday, August 13 (Moon in Virgo) The Saturn keynote in your chart indicates stability in health and work until around the 30th, when this orb of patience goes erratic. Virgo plumps for practicality rather than superstition. Your winning colors are primrose and amber; your lucky number is 9.

Saturday, August 14 (Moon in Virgo to Libra 9:24 a.m.)
Don't turn a minor household chore into a federal project because nobody seems eager to assist you. It's not a day to have fellow employees hanging around your home, distracting you from duties. There are some career uncertainties. Lucky lottery: 2, 11, 20, 29, 38, 47.

Sunday, August 15 (Moon in Libra)　　You relax well and choose your friends wisely today. There are fine trends for meeting a friend downtown for an unusual trek around a mall and into a restaurant with a good reputation. Sitting in a park or other shaded area can make your appreciation of this day all the more memorable. Your lucky number is 4.

Monday, August 16 (Moon in Libra to Scorpio 6:40 p.m.)　　The Venus keynote in your horoscope indicates a resurgence of the travel bug. Over the rest of the month, you gather travel information joyfully and scan brochures and magazines. Even so, this is a good day to recycle last year's travel joys in conversation with a kindred spirit. Your lucky number is 8.

Tuesday, August 17 (Moon in Scorpio)　　For racing luck, try these selections at all tracks. Post position special: number 1 p.p. in the first race. Pick six: 1, 7, 4, 1, 1, 3. Hot daily doubles: 1 and 7, 1 and 4, 1 and 1. Look for the letters I and R in the names of jockeys and horses. This can be an especially memorable day for you.

Wednesday, August 18 (Moon in Scorpio)　　Today is fine for using what you learned from past experiences to make this a day of achievement. It's fine also for completing projects, evaluating recent no-win involvements, and using your intuitive processes when making future plans. Your winning colors are yellow and red. Lucky lottery: 3, 12, 21, 30, 39, 48.

Thursday, August 19 (Moon in Scorpio to Sagittarius 6:32 a.m.)　　You are now in your lunar high cycle, when all things become possible. Push your personality assets—your strong confidence, self-reliance, intelligence, and helpful connections—for all they are worth. Hold the initiative and set the pace for those who follow. Blue is your color; your lucky number is 5.

Friday, August 20 (Moon in Sagittarius) Repeat yesterday's pattern as you go for the gold. Have faith in yourself and in the way you play teacher. You can win others over to your point of view. Air your ambitions cheerfully. Be proud but not condescending. Your winning color is cinnamon; your lucky number is 7.

Saturday, August 21 (Moon in Sagittarius to Capricorn 6:59 p.m.) By keeping on the go and searching, you can turn this into a good money day. It's not just what you earn, but what you set aside, and the goodwill you are building up for future earning power, that makes this such an unusual day. Capricorn and Aquarius are a wonderful team Lucky lottery: 9, 18, 27, 36, 45, 3.

Sunday, August 22 (Moon in Capricorn) Find bargains in your newspaper and in conversation with Virgo and Taurus. Good trends exist for ordering items by mail and phone. All of a sudden, you could hear some beneficial financial news and put it to use early tomorrow. Try to increase your earning power and you will succeed. Your color is pea green; your lucky number is 2.

Monday, August 23 (Moon in Capricorn) For racing luck, try these selections at all tracks. Post position special: number 6 p.p. in the fourth race. Pick six: 1, 6, 3, 6, 2, 8. Hot daily doubles: 1 and 5, 2 and 4, 3 and 3. Stay alert for the letters I and R in the names of jockeys and horses. Aries jockeys have that extra bit of courage and aggression.

Tuesday, August 24 (Moon in Capricorn to Aquarius 5:49 a.m.) Your career potential is picking up steam and the sun moves into your tenth house. You localize and concentrate well on what is at hand, and everyday routines get a big boost. You handle studies, communications, and local travel well. It's a fine day for feeling free and busy. Your lucky number is 8.

Wednesday, August 25 (Moon in Aquarius) Extra care must be taken in health maintenance and preventive-medicine routines, as mighty Jupiter, your planetary ruler, goes erratic in your sixth house. Be alert to the viruses making the rounds and to handwashing and kitchen hygiene. Lucky lottery: 1, 10, 19, 28, 37, 46.

Thursday, August 26 (Moon in Aquarius to Pisces 1:50 p.m.) The full moon in your fourth house illuminates all family and home matters. You can make good decisions now about real estate and other property and ownership interests. For racing luck, try these selections at all tracks. Post position special: number 3 p.p. in the ninth race. Pick six: 1, 3, 3, 12, 6, 9. Look for the letters I and R in the names of jockeys and horses. Hot daily doubles: 3 and 6, 3 and 9, 3 and 3.

Friday, August 27 (Moon in Pisces) Family values and devotion top your agenda. Discussions with your mate and children are a must under these favorable aspects. These are quality hours for better understanding your loved ones. Pisces and Scorpio will impact your thinking. Hot combination numbers: 5 and 2.

Saturday, August 28 (Moon in Pisces to Aries 7:09 p.m.) Beach, water, and boating activities fit in with the trends of this Piscean day. Quality time with your children should include an outdoor picnic lunch. Expect some nostalgia as children realize how soon their school break will end. Be generous. Lucky lottery: 7, 16, 25, 34, 43, 3.

Sunday, August 29 (Moon in Aries) Aries will match your passion, your desire, and your capacity for ecstasy. This is a romantic day, with favorable aspects for partying and entertaining. Your children may feel that they aren't given enough allowance and personal freedom. Turquoise is your color; your lucky number is 9.

Monday, August 30 (Moon in Aries to Taurus 10:41 p.m.) It may be difficult to get down to work after so pleasant a weekend. You could have the feeling that there is an increase of nagging at your job. This could be based on envy and jealousy, for some are going up and others are standing still. Your lucky number is 4.

Tuesday, August 31 (Moon in Taurus) You value your good health and abide strongly by preventive-medicine routines and schedules. The Saturn keynote in your horoscope indicates another slowing down of work. Is this due to a lack of cooperation among coworkers, or some hesitation and uncertainty in the front office? Chestnut is your color. Hot combination numbers: 6 and 1.

SEPTEMBER 1999

Wednesday, September 1 (Moon in Taurus) Today is fine for resolving to take care of your body, stabilizing your weight, watching your diet, and honoring your nutritional convictions. This is also a good day for exercising, walking, and jogging. It's an earthy day, with Taurus and Virgo in the picture. Autumnal beauty excites you. Lucky lottery: 5, 14, 23, 32, 41, 50.

Thursday, September 2 (Moon in Taurus to Gemini 1:25 a.m.) Pay attention to the needs of your mate. Business partners also could use a bit of well-articulated approval and appreciation. You derive more from sharing and cooperating than from trying to go it alone. New contracts and agreements can be signed. Gemini may seem somewhat critical. Your lucky number is 7.

197

Friday, September 3 (Moon in Gemini) The heart has its reasons, and on a day such as this hard, cold facts are not going to achieve what a bit of empathy and sympathy can. Brain crashes against brain, but hearts will beat joyfully in unison. Do what you can to improve the in-law situation. Mocha is your color. Hot combination numbers: 9 and 3.

Saturday, September 4 (Moon in Gemini to Cancer 4:10 a.m.) The Mars keynote in your horoscope gives you a burst of energy and the desire to solve personal problems. Capricorn and Cancer figure prominently in this busy day, when you are strongly bent on putting everything right around your home. Brown is your color. Lucky lottery: 2, 11, 20, 29, 38, 47.

Sunday, September 5 (Moon in Cancer) It's an excellent day for reviewing business and advertising mail. Keep abreast of stock market predictions and discuss the local economy with your neighbors and friends. Review advertisements pertaining to insurance and investment matters. Gold is your color; your lucky number is 4.

Monday, September 6 (Moon in Cancer to Leo 7:29 a.m.) Leo enters the picture with long-range views. Good trends exist for planning autumnal holidays, contacting friends who have been away the past month, and picking up the threads of local and charitable interests that were dropped over the summer. Orange is your color; your lucky number is 8.

Tuesday, September 7 (Moon in Leo) For racing luck, try these selections at all tracks. Post position special: number 1 p.p. in the first race. Pick six: 1, 3, 1, 5, 7, 1. Look for the letters A, S, and J in the names of jockeys and horses. This can be a memorable, as well as an adventurous day. Leo, Scorpio, and Aquarius want to be with you. Your color is emerald.

Wednesday, September 8 (Moon in Leo to Virgo 11:57 a.m.) There can be a minor conflict between what you want to do and career demands. Children are full of extensive plans this school year, and you may have to lay down some laws about study hours each evening. A friend has much to tell you about recent experiences. Lucky lottery: 3, 12, 21, 30, 39, 48.

Thursday, September 9 (Moon in Virgo)   The new moon in your tenth house illuminates career, professional, and authority matters. It's a day when a discussion with a top supervisor will clear up some nagging questions for you. There's nothing wrong in asking questions. Blue-green is your color; your lucky number is 5.

Friday, September 10 (Moon in Virgo to Libra 6:16 p.m.)   It's imperative that you give assignments your best shot, for your work is being evaluated under the prevailing aspects. It's no longer possible to depend on past high performance ratings. The old order is changing more than anybody expected. Hot combination numbers: 7 and 3.

Saturday, September 11 (Moon in Libra)   The Venus keynote in your horoscope alerts you to the possibility of desirable travel this month. In evaluating a change of hairstyle, don't be swayed too much by a current fad that won't last very long; choose the style that is really you. Primrose is your color. Lucky lottery: 9, 18, 27, 36, 45, 6.

Sunday, September 12 (Moon in Libra)   Persuade a kindred spirit to share your breakfast or brunch. It's an excellent day for discussing committee plans for the rest of the year. Church and social club membership and participation require renewal and review. Libra and Gemini are helpful. Tan is your color; your lucky number is 2.

Monday, September 13 (Moon in Libra to Scorpio, 3:08 a.m.)   It's an excellent day for completions, submitting finished work for approval, and depending on your intuitive processes to figure out what is happening behind the scenes. Scorpio and Cancer have key roles. Your winning colors are mauve and coppery gold; your lucky number is 6.

Tuesday, September 14 (Moon in Scorpio)   Extract the answers from past experiences. The spiritual side of your nature is strongly activated as the moon transits your twelfth house. It isn't too early to prepare for an upsurge of good luck on the 16th and 17th. The information you require is there in your own head. Your lucky number is 8.

Wednesday, September 15 (Moon in Scorpio to Sagittarius 2:35 p.m.)   Gather the information and tools you will need for a big push toward your goals. Know when to shift your attention from the past to the present and be willing to defend yourself. Your winning colors are magenta and khaki. Lucky lottery: 1, 10, 19, 28, 37, 46.

Thursday, September 16 (Moon in Sagittarius)   For racing luck, try these selections at all tracks. Post position special: number 3 p.p. in the third race. Pick six: 2, 4, 3, 3, 6, 1. Note the letters A, S, and J in the names of the jockeys and horses. Hot daily doubles: 1 and 2, 1 and 6, 1 and 9. Why shouldn't you be lucky today when you are in your lunar-cycle high?

Friday, September 17 (Moon in Sagittarius to Capricorn 3:14 a.m.)   Hold the initiative and act self-confident for best results under prevailing aspects. Air your ambitions and let the world see you at your best: intelligent, sophisticated, cosmopolitan. You can break into the realm of impossible dreams. Hot combination numbers: 5 and 2.

Saturday, September 18 (Moon in Capricorn)   It's a fine money day, with the moon stimulating your second house of earning power and income. Self-discipline and a strong sense of obligation will pay handsome dividends. You accept responsibilities that others have passed to you. Your winning color is ruby. Lucky lottery: 7, 16, 25, 34, 43, 3.

Sunday, September 19 (Moon in Capricorn)   Seek bargains in unusual places, and stick to your budget, despite the efforts of a loved one to seduce you into a major purchase. Older relatives may want to see you more often. Your presence means security in the minds of many associates. Earth is your color; your lucky number is 9.

Monday, September 20 (Moon in Capricorn to Aquarius 2:38 p.m.)   The more you concentrate on your work today, the more you will earn in the long run. Set the pattern for impressing top executives by your work and your suggestions related to quality control and increased production. You give more to the day than others. Your lucky number is 4.

Tuesday, September 21 (Moon in Aquarius)   Aquarius and Leo figure prominently. Studies, communications, transportation, and catering to the whims of siblings are all part of this picture. You don't stay in one place too long under the prevailing aspects. You supply the answers that others need. Hot combination numbers: 6 and 1.

Wednesday, September 22 (Moon in Aquarius to Pisces 10:51 p.m.)   Take care of everyday matters, the mundane, and all the little details. What you do today can save you from mistakes later in the month. Be sure your youngsters are not only able to read well but are withdrawing books from the library. Your winning colors are tawny and rust. Lucky lottery: 8, 17, 26, 35, 44, 2.

Thursday, September 23 (Moon in Pisces)   It's the first day of autumn, when family matters top your agenda. Pay attention to your property and to items you hope to acquire. You are conscious of your possessions and their worth. For racing luck, try these selections at all tracks. Post position special: number 1 p.p. in the first race. Pick six: 1, 1, 7, 4, 1, 6. Hot daily doubles; 1 and 1, 1 and 4, 1 and 7.

Friday, September 24 (Moon in Pisces)   Listen to your children's complaints about their school and teachers. If problems are posed, you can consider the alternative of home schooling. It's a day to clear away mental debris and make hard decisions. Cerulean blue is your color; your lucky number is 3.

Saturday, September 25 (Moon in Pisces to Aries 3:34 a.m.)   The full moon is in your fifth house of love, illuminating your social and parenting aspects. Good trends exist for entertaining in your own home and for expanding your social horizons. What you do with other people today can be translated into networking in the interest of your kids. Lucky lottery: 5, 14, 23, 32, 41, 50.

Sunday, September 26 (Moon in Aries)   Make love, enjoying the romance and sense of adventure of this Indian summer. An Aries and another Sagittarius have key roles. You are fascinated by the passionate outbursts of others and appreciate a show of moral and physical courage by your lover. Your lucky number is 7.

Monday, September 27 (Moon in Aries to Taurus 5:51 a.m.)   As the month wanes, consider a daily dose of herbal medicine. For every ailment, there is an herb at your health store. Your body is the type that will respond to the natural. Listen to the health complaints of older and younger loved ones. Your lucky number is 2.

Tuesday, September 28 (Moon in Taurus)   You can get a lot of work done if you ward off pleasant distractions. It's a work-all-day cycle, so let love come later. What you are doing this afternoon will attract the favorable attention of those in charge. Taurus and Capricorn are on deck. Melon is your color. Hot combination numbers: 4 and 7.

Wednesday, September 29 (Moon in Taurus to Gemini 7:21 a.m.)   For racing luck, try these selections at all tracks. Post position special: number 6 p.p. in the sixth race. Pick six: 1, 3, 5, 6, 8, 6. Hot daily doubles: 1 and 5, 1 and 1, 1 and 4. Note the letters A, S and J in the names of jockeys and horses. Gemini will bring in the long shots.

Thursday, September 30 (Moon in Gemini)   Share, cooperate, and be sure to listen to your partner's point of view. It's a fine day to bond more closely with your spouse and business partner. Joint efforts and investments turn out well. Walk at least a mile after the evening meal. Hot combination numbers: 8 and 3.

OCTOBER 1999

Friday, October 1 (Moon in Gemini to Cancer 9:31 a.m.)   Face the month ahead with your spouse, discussing joint investments of time, energy, and money. Also, discuss problem solving in the interest of your children and find ways to encourage them to study and set goals. Gemini and Libra are in the picture. Your colors are pinecone and flame; your lucky number is 8.

Saturday, October 2 (Moon in Cancer)   It's an excellent time to review the physical plan of your home and look for points of deterioration. Check locks on windows and doors. The day favors improvements all along the line of endeavor, so correct what could prove worrisome. Sapphire and navy are your colors. Lucky lottery: 1, 10, 19, 28, 37, 46.

Sunday, October 3 (Moon in Cancer to Leo 1:13 p.m.)   It's a good day for clearing away the debris of summer and early fall, and fine too for helping a neighbor or coworker with an onerous task. A strong sense of generosity permeates your mind and body and you reach out to give more than to take. Maroon is your color; your lucky number is 3.

Monday, October 4 (Moon in Leo)   It's a beautiful time of the year and, with the moon transiting your ninth house of travel, take time out to appreciate the gorgeous colors of nature. A walk in a park or the woods will demonstrate the advance of autumn. Gather some brilliantly colored leaves. Your lucky number is 7.

Tuesday, October 5 (Moon in Leo to Virgo 6:40 p.m.)   The Mercury keynote in your horoscope indicates a speeding up of the intangibles and an unveiling of what has been going on behind the scenes. This is a good day to complete outstanding chores, to pay bills, and to handle long-range matters. Leo wins out. Hot combination numbers: 9 and 3.

Wednesday, October 6 (Moon in Virgo)   Career demands can top your agenda as you find that some recent work isn't approved by supervision. You would rather be miles away from boring duties, responsibilities, and obligations on a fall day like this. Indigo and off-white are your colors. Lucky lottery: 2, 11, 20, 29, 38, 47.

Thursday, October 7 (Moon in Virgo)   It's a good career day, full of the aspects that make for wise use of authority. The more professional you are in your relations with bosses and coworkers, the more successful you will be. As the work advances, you feel good about the help you receive. Snow and ebony go well together. Hot combination numbers: 4 and 2.

Friday, October 8 (Moon in Virgo to Libra 1:52 a.m.)   The Venus keynote in your chart indicates a warming up to the work you have been assigned. A positive and friendly attitude to those who welcome you is called for, but don't overdo it. You could be tested by an executive. The end of the work week is to your liking. Ultramarine is your color; your lucky number is 6.

Saturday, October 9 (Moon in Libra)   The new moon in Libra illuminates your friendships and group activities. It's time to settle down and remember that the committee exists for getting input from all. Make sure that no one member is trying to dominate and make the decisions. Chestnut is your color. Lucky lottery: 8, 17, 26, 35, 44, 2.

Sunday, October 10 (Moon in Libra to Scorpio 10:01 a.m.)   Phone and write, inviting relatives and others to a nice at-home visit. The weather can put you in a fine autumnal frame of mind. You are strongly aware of this season, which puts you in your own element and recalls youthful fun. Scarlet and brown are your colors; your lucky number is 1.

Monday, October 11 (Moon in Scorpio)   Tackle jobs that can be finished today. For racing luck, try these selections at all tracks. Post position special: number 5 p.p. in the fifth race. Pick six: 1, 5, 7, 4, 5, 5. Watch for the letters B, K, and T in the names of jockeys and horses. Hot daily doubles: 1 and 4, 2 and 3, 5 and 5.

Tuesday, October 12 (Moon in Scorpio to Sagittarius 10:18 p.m.)   The answers you need are rooted in your past problem solving. You are strongly aware that intangibles and invisibles are very much in this day's scenario. You put your intuitive processes to good use. Your winning colors are pinecone and rust. Hot combination numbers: 7 and 3.

Wednesday, October 13 (Moon in Sagittarius) You are in your powerful lunar high cycle, when you can put your life on the right track. You have unbeatable courage now for seizing opportunities and remaining aware of your personal advantages. You can break through the red tape and do yourself a lot of good. Lucky lottery: 9, 18, 27, 36, 45, 3.

Thursday, October 14 (Moon in Sagittarius) Keep plugging away at the job that will rate you full attention from the front office. Hold the initiative and set the pace. If you're naturally self-confident, with your amazing Jupiter-ruled good luck, the day will belong to you. Wear gold and white. Hot combination numbers: 2 and 6.

Friday, October 15 (Moon in Sagittarius to Capricorn 10:04 a.m.) Keep your eye out for money that is headed your way. Fine trends exist for finding a new source of pin money. It's an excellent time to share your good luck with others. Capricorn and Virgo admire your methods. Silver and pink are your lucky colors. Hot combination numbers: 4 and 3.

Saturday, October 16 (Moon in Capricorn) Go for the gold on a day pattern made for your earning power and income. You can save money by shopping for bargains in the right places. Listen to any and all talk about the economy and the best ways of dealing with its surprising ups and downs. Old rose is your color. Lucky lottery: 6, 15, 24, 33, 42, 50.

Sunday, October 17 (Moon in Capricorn to Aquarius 11:17 p.m.) Discuss financial arrangements and concerns with Capricorn. Read the financial pages of your newspaper and consider changing some of your investments—after a good brain-to-brain talk with your broker. Plan your work week so that there is time to reorganize your money. Your lucky number is 8.

Monday, October 18 (Moon in Aquarius) Aquarius and Gemini are represented in the day's program. Narrow your sights today, concentrating on what can be done. Don't get into anything that seems impossible at this time. Communications, transportation matters, and studies will do well. Your lucky number is 3.

Tuesday, October 19 (Moon in Aquarius)   For racing luck, try these selections at all tracks. Post position special: number 5 p.p. in the third race. Pick six: 1, 3, 5, 8, 5, 2. Watch for the letters B, K, and T in the names of the jockeys and horses. Hot daily doubles: 2 and 3, 2 and 5, 3 and 5. A Capricorn companion will bring a notebook. Your color is magenta.

Wednesday, October 20 (Moon in Aquarius to Pisces 8:33 a.m.)   The Mars keynote in your horoscope pushes you in the direction of more money and a better job. Everyday routines and schedules are right for you. Pay strict attention to the little details and minuscule matters that others will overlook. Little moments add up to a winning hour and day. Lucky lottery: 7, 16, 25, 34, 43, 3.

Thursday, October 21 (Moon in Pisces)   Your family and their welfare dominate your agenda. It's a good cycle for bonding more closely with your growing youngsters and discussing them with your mate when they aren't present. It's time to look your home over for possible deterioration. Your number is 9.

Friday, October 22 (Moon in Pisces to Aries 1:42 p.m.)   Pisces and Cancer figure prominently. Your special consideration of loved ones makes this a wonderful day, as you reach out to the misunderstood and the unhappy, including neighbors. Real estate sales are favored. Your lucky number is 2.

Saturday, October 23 (Moon in Aries)   A magnificent cycle of good luck in your love and social department begins, as your ruling planet enters Aries. You can come to a better understanding of your children under the prevailing aspects. What your beloved expects from you is being illuminated by the moon. Lucky lottery: 4, 13, 22, 31, 40, 49.

Sunday, October 24 (Moon in Aries to Taurus 3:25 p.m.) The full moon illuminates your overall physical well-being and the work you should do. The Uranus keynote in your horoscope indicates that changes which have been threatening in neighborhood matters and everyday routines, can now go forward. You become aware of the passing of this year, as the sun enters your twelfth house. Your lucky number is 6.

Monday, October 25 (Moon in Taurus) Health and preventive-medicine routines are strongly emphasized. Keep tabs on the health of senior citizens in your clan. Good health should be treated as your most valuable possession under these Taurus and lunar aspects. Pumpkin is your color; your lucky number is 1.

Tuesday, October 26 (Moon in Taurus to Gemini 3:33 p.m.) For racing luck, try these selections at all tracks. Post position special: number 3 p.p. in the third race. Pick six: 1, 2, 3, 5, 3, 3. Hot daily doubles: 1 and 2, 3 and 3, 9 and 3. The letters B, K, and T are significant in the names of jockeys and horses. Getting away from the grind becomes therapeutic.

Wednesday, October 27 (Moon in Gemini) Gemini enters with advice for all. You may feel that the zodiacal scales are being balanced between the fire-sign Sagittarius and air-sign Gemini. Listen but remain your own person. Your intellectual processes are being stirred. Lucky lottery: 5, 14, 23, 32, 41, 50.

Thursday, October 28 (Moon in Gemini to Cancer 4:09 p.m.) You become aware of the many skills you possess, but have used infrequently. You may be conscious of some wrong turn you took in life. Why not work one of those skills into a day such as this and see what develops? It's a good day to turn over a new leaf. Gold is your color; your lucky number is 7.

Friday, October 29 (Moon in Cancer) It's an excellent day to check on the security of your windows, doors, and vehicles. Thievery in our present culture has become a leading profession. Today is fine for making improvements, corrections, and positive changes. You could feel that a business associate is at the edge. Hot combination numbers: 9 and 6.

Saturday, October 30 (Moon in Cancer to Leo 6:47 p.m.) Evaluate and keep on investigating the economy of your area and decide whether you are making wise investments of time, money, and energy. Changes are taking place that may be difficult to understand. Technology is speeding. Lucky lottery: 2, 11, 20, 29, 38, 47.

Sunday, October 31—Daylight Saving Time Ends (Moon in Leo) The Mercury keynote in your chart indicates a speeding up of your highly personalized interests. You could feel that things are about to go your way. Fine trends exist for sprucing up your personal appearance and acquiring a new fall wardrobe on sale. Lucky lottery: 4, 13, 22, 31, 40, 49.

NOVEMBER 1999

Monday, November 1 (Moon in Leo to Virgo 11:07 p.m.) You are apt to include today in a longer weekend and stay away from your job. Travel, visiting a former supervisor at a distance, and taking care of some long-range business can be in the picture. You are unsettled and restless, and you feel in need of a change of scene. Auburn is your color; your number is 5.

Tuesday, November 2 (Moon in Virgo) The Jupiter keynote in your horoscope warns against overspending socially. The Saturn keynote implies a need for taking the complaints of senior citizens more seriously. The work you do today can measure up to the best you have done this year and impresses supervisors. Hot combination numbers: 7 and 3.

Wednesday, November 3 (Moon in Virgo)   Virgo and Capricorn will listen to what you have to say about work. You feel duties, responsibilities, and obligations as though they are heavy burdens. A talk with your employer or supervisor can clear the atmosphere of this uncertainty. Lucky lottery: 9, 18, 27, 36, 45, 6.

Thursday, November 4 (Moon in Virgo to Libra 6;57 a.m.)   All work and no play isn't the answer or the key to your happiness. See a kindred spirit for lunch and know that with this person you can be yourself completely. The Saturn keynote makes for sluggishness at your work scene. Ruby and russet at your colors; your lucky number is 2.

Friday, November 5 (Moon in Libra)   The mercury keynote in your horoscope slows down your work effort. For racing luck, try these selections at all tracks. Post position special: number 4 p.p. in the fourth race. Be alert to the letters C, L, and U in the names of the jockeys and horses. Pick six: 1, 3, 4, 4, 7, 3. Hot daily doubles: 1 and 3, 2 and 2, 3 and 7. Your lucky color is alabaster.

Saturday, November 6 (Moon in Libra to Scorpio 4:46 p.m.)   It's an excellent day to appreciate the season, so take a walk under the trees with a loved one and note the colors of falling leaves. For Sagittarius, autumn is the most beautiful time, but also one that is filled with hard-to-identify sadness. All around you, nature is disrobing. Lucky lottery: 6, 15, 24, 33, 42, 50.

Sunday, November 7 (Moon in Scorpio)   You are sensitive to the completions of cycles as you glance about. There is a strong trend of spirituality represented. Love, trust, loyalty, and devotion permeate your thinking. Today is fine for church and club membership and participation. Scorpio supervises. Azure is your color; your lucky number is 8.

Monday, November 8 (Moon in Scorpio)   The new moon in the twelfth house of your chart illuminates past experiences and events. Good trends exist for completions and for presenting work for approval and evaluation. Your mind is strongly investigative and curious as you search for vital answers. Your lucky number is 3.

Tuesday, November 9 (Moon in Scorpio to Sagittarius 4:15 a.m.)   The Venus keynote in your horoscope indicates that you are warming up to friends and others who share your interests. You want to be more social, to be included more in celebrations, parties, and entertainment. It's time to expand your wardrobe and spruce up your appearance. Hot combination numbers: 5 and 2.

Wednesday, November 10 (Moon in Sagittarius)   There are conflicts between doing what you want to do and the limitations of your work. You are in your lunar-cycle high, when achievement is within your grasp, but Mercury, now leaving your sign and retrograding into your twelfth house, means that some work may have to be done over. Lucky lottery: 7, 16, 25, 34, 43, 3.

Thursday, November 11 (Moon in Sagittarius to Capricorn 5:00 p.m.)   It's full speed ahead and the devil take the hindmost. Throw caution to the winds and take the lead, setting the pace for others. The achievement that means so much to you can be chalked up as your self-confidence makes you the winner. Cherry and cardinal are your colors; your lucky number is 9.

Friday, November 12 (Moon in Capricorn)   Excellent money trends exist touching your earning power and income. Capricorn is all business but extremely helpful. You can make up for lost time and put all your figures in the black column. Pay bills and collect what is due you. Your winning color is taupe. Hot combination numbers: 2 and 6.

Saturday, November 13 (Moon in Capricorn)
Budgeting, bargain hunting, and anything else that saves cash will succeed once you put your mind to it. Scan the advertisements to see which store offers the lowest price. This holds true in foods, cleaning materials, wardrobe accessories, and cosmetics. Maroon and ivory are your colors. Lucky lottery: 4, 13, 22, 31, 40, 49.

Sunday, November 14 (Moon in Capricorn to Aquarius 5:46 a.m.)   Pause, then decide on your best agenda for today. Aquarius and Gemini add an airy, light, and intellectual touch, and these companions could be your best bet for a pleasant and worthy day. Siblings and neighbors also appreciate your company. What you want is nearby. Your lucky number is 6.

Monday, November 15 (Moon in Aquarius)   You communicate effectively, so keep on talking. Getting your ideas across to assistants will make this a valuable day. Your trusty vehicle may require attention from your favorite mechanic. Encourage youngsters not to give up on their studies, even when facing failure. Crimson is your color; your lucky number is 1.

Tuesday, November 16 (Moon in Aquarius to Pisces 4:21 p.m.)   For racing luck, try these selections at all tracks. Post position special: number 3 p.p. in the sixth race. Pick six: 1, 8, 3, 7, 2, 3. Note the letters C, L, and U in the names of jockeys and horses. Hot daily doubles: 1 and 2, 3 and 3, 3 and 6. Balance another Sagittarius companion with an intuitive Gemini. Wear plaids.

Wednesday, November 17 (Moon in Pisces)   Family values dominate the conversation, as those around you become more conservative. You don't want to sound too academic, but you can hardly help it when the conversation becomes heated. Loved ones may be expecting more from you than you can deliver. Lucky lottery: 5, 14, 23, 32, 41, 50.

Thursday, November 18 (Moon in Pisces to Aries 10:57 p.m.)   Your home requires a pre-winter inspection—the attic and basement especially. There is gossip about real estate values in your community sinking, but, as you know, talk is cheap. Everybody has an opinion on one of those mysteries that will never be solved. Hot combination numbers: 7 and 3.

Friday, November 19 (Moon in Aries)   Today and tomorrow are good love and social days, and it's up to you to make the most of them. Your beloved expects you to make the first move this time. Parties and entertainment will be more enjoyable than you realized. Children are doing better. Your color is turquoise; your lucky number is 9.

Saturday, November 20 (Moon in Aries to Taurus 1:26 a.m.)   The Saturn keynote in your chart indicates that lovemaking is therapeutic. Aries takes over and you like it this way. Passion and the potential for ecstasy permeate the early morning and late evening. It's one of those days when you admire much about your own home. Lucky lottery: 2, 11, 20, 29, 38, 47.

Sunday, November 21 (Moon in Taurus)   Preserve some of your abundant energies in the interest of preventive-medicine routines. Get rest and relaxation through doing some of those quiet, intellectual things that appeal so strongly to you—a good travel book, a television documentary, or a quiet walk in your own neighborhood. Your lucky number is 4.

Monday, November 22 (Moon in Taurus)   Taurus and Virgo have front seats. Pace yourself in your work so that you don't get fatigued early. Be on guard against viral infections, and watch children who are apt to keep their aches and pains to themselves rather than be housebound. Your lucky number is 8.

Tuesday, November 23 (Moon in Taurus to Gemini 1:14 a.m.)   The full moon illuminates marriage, other partnerships, and the teamwork others expect from you. For racing luck, try these selections at all tracks. Post position special: number 1 p.p. in the first race. Pick six: 1, 2, 1, 5, 7, 1. Hot daily doubles: 1 and 2, 1 and 10, 1 and 9. Gemini makes a good companion at the track, for your thinking patterns complement each other.

Wednesday, November 24 (Moon in Gemini)   With the sun in your sign, you are in your own element and take each day from now on to your heart. You excel when making difficult decisions and teaching, explaining, and advising. You won't be thrown by any event or news, taking it all in stride. Lucky lottery: 3, 12, 21, 30, 39, 48.

Thursday, November 25 (Moon in Gemini to Cancer 12:29 a.m.)   The Mercury keynote indicates stepped-up completions and a meeting of all deadlines in your work. It's an excellent day for improvements, corrections, and changes that meet the demands of technology advances. Savings, investments, and security matters are well aspected. Cerulean is your color; your lucky number is 5.

Friday, November 26 (Moon in Cancer)   Scorpio and Cancer make good companions, for they are interested in what you are doing. The prevailing aspects imply that you are thinking along saving, protecting, and defensive lines. Nobody is more aware of the need for caution than you. Your lucky number is 7.

Saturday, November 27 (Moon in Cancer to Leo 1:19 a.m.)   The Mars keynote in your horoscope indicates more aggressive actions locally. You speak up in your own behalf and also for the underdog. Your love of freedom and liberation is evident in what you say and do. Your winning color is pumpkin. Lucky lottery: 9, 18, 27, 36, 45, 6.

Sunday, November 28 (Moon in Leo) Your mind can wander, and it might be a good idea if you visited a kindred spirit at a distance from your home. You do well moving about by yourself, with your own secret thoughts and aspirations. You are thinking high, lofty, dignified thoughts that can only be shared with someone who understands the whole you. Orange and flame are your colors; your lucky number is 2.

Monday, November 29 (Moon in Leo to Virgo 5;11 a.m.) Your career and professional life demand the best from you, so try to arrive at work before the others and settle in before the distractions arrive. If they see how intent you are, they may leave you alone, and you can meet a monthly deadline to everybody's pleasure. Your lucky number is 6.

Tuesday, November 30 (Moon in Virgo) Duties, responsibilities, and obligations crowd in on you. If you have questions, go to the top for answers. Too much is lost or changed when it comes down too many channels. You can cash in yon your well-earned reputation for keeping things moving in the right direction. Auburn and amber are your colors; your lucky number is 8.

DECEMBER 1999

Wednesday, December 1 (Moon in Virgo to Libra 12:29 p.m.) While the moon is stimulating your career ambitions, a Saturn keynote indicates that overdoing physically must be avoided. Local interests are demanding some of your energy also, so stay in your own element with an Aries and Leo. Saffron is your color. Lucky lottery: 8, 17, 26, 35, 44, 2.

Thursday, December 2 (Moon in Libra)   Social requirements are emphasized. You're strongly aware that this is going to be a busy month. Start your list making, including those things you won't have time to do. Cherry and brown are your colors. Hot combination numbers: 1 and 7.

Friday, December 3 (Moon in Libra to Scorpio 10:35 p.m.)   Friendships, committee work, and group activities will get in the way of your household and family chores. Encourage your teenagers to put up the holiday decorations. Also, they can address some of your holiday greeting cards. Many phone calls come your way—some asking for financial help. Your lucky number is 3.

Saturday, December 4 (Moon in Scorpio)   It's a day for completions, such as holiday decorating of your home and grounds and mailing cards. Remember those wonderful people who lived next door to you way back when? Scorpio wants to be helpful. Lucky lottery: 5, 14, 23, 32, 41, 50.

Sunday, December 5 (Moon in Scorpio)   Try to finish some of the myriad household tasks that belong to this special month. When it comes to volunteering, give older loved ones first refusal. Keep a weather eye on your budget when it comes to gift buying. Plan some shopping at a distance, where prices will be lower. Your lucky number is 7.

Monday, December 6 (Moon in Scorpio to Sagittarius 12:27 p.m.)   The Venus keynote in your horoscope indicates intense passion and sexual fantasies, and this trend will be with you during most of this month. Venus-in-Scorpio, your twelfth house, used to be called, "the hushed-up aspect." In your case, secretiveness touches your lovemaking. Amber is your color; your lucky number is 2.

Tuesday, December 7 (Moon in Sagittarius) The new moon joins the sun in Sagittarius and the day becomes yours to take apart and put to your own personal use. For racing luck, try these selections at all race tracks. Post position special: number 4 p.p. in the fourth race. Pick six: 9, 2, 3, 4, 1, 4. Stay alert to the letters D, M, and V in the names of jockeys and horses. Self-confidence is your strongest weapon.

Wednesday, December 8 (Moon in Sagittarius to Capricorn 11:14 p.m.) Still in your lunar-cycle high, you must set the pace and pattern of this lucky day. Push your Sagittarius personality and character assets—your quick-witted mind, your ability to rationalize tings in a believable way, your winning learning processes, and your good luck. Lucky lottery: 6, 15, 24, 33, 42, 51.

Thursday, December 9 (Moon in Capricorn) It's a big money day, with the lunar accent on earning power, income, a special bonus, an annual stipend, or a financial gift. Capricorn and Virgo want you to be more practical in your gift giving and spending now. If you shop, take time to figure out what you shouldn't buy. Your lucky number is 8.

Friday, December 10 (Moon in Capricorn) Are there holiday services you might undertake in order to get more cash on hand? This is a good day for answering this question and making the phone call. Shop for housebound seniors; give a few hours each weekend to a travel bureau or other business. Encourage your children to immerse themselves in household chores. Hot combination numbers: 1 and 4.

Saturday, December 11 (Moon in Capricorn to Aquarius 11:59 a.m.) For racing luck, try these selections at all tracks. Post position special: number 3 p.p. in the third race. Pick six: 4, 2, 3, 5, 1, 3. Hot daily doubles: 1 and 2, 3 and 6, 3 and 9. Note the letters D, M, and V in the names of jockeys and horses. Your Jupiter-ruled good fortune is speeded up by Mercury's entry into your sign. Lucky lottery: 3, 12, 21, 30, 39, 48.

Sunday, December 12 (Moon in Aquarius)   Today is favorable for local, communications, movement around your favorite mall, and running into friends while shopping or arranging to meet them for brunch. Relatives and neighbors are in this picture. You have no difficulty finding the items you need. Your lucky number is 5.

Monday, December 13 (Moon in Aquarius to Pisces 11:18 p.m.)   Order items you need by phone. Gifts for service people (paper boy or girl, domestics, handyman; hardware store fixit, and so on) should top your agenda. You may write small checks for each, but present the money early enough so that they can include it in their holiday budget. Your lucky number is 9.

Tuesday, December 14 (Moon in Pisces)   It's a major day for buying family gifts, including the special one for your beloved. Don't ignore the items your children have been harping on for ages. Pisces makes a good consultant on a day like this, when your family and the love you have for them is dominant. Your color is blue. Hot combination numbers: 2 and 6.

Wednesday, December 15 (Moon in Pisces)   It's time to add some finishing touches to the decorations in your home and grounds. Catering to the special needs of the handicapped, giving extra ounces of sympathy to older loved ones, and going that extra mile for friends will make this a memorable day. Lucky lottery: 4, 13, 22, 31, 40, 49.

Thursday, December 16 (Moon in Pisces to Aries 7:30 a.m.)   Family values and love top the cosmic agenda. As the day advances, passion struggles to the top and lovemaking can take on an extra dimension. Perhaps it is because your children remind you of how fruitful your grand passion has been. Your lucky number is 6.

Friday, December 17 (Moon in Aries)   Bond more closely with your beloved as the moon in your fifth house moves toward a dynamic trine to the sun in your sign. It's one of those days when everybody is going to think either silently or remark aloud that you are a wonderful person. It's your loving nature that makes you so. Hot combination numbers: 8 and 2.

Saturday, December 18 (Moon in Aries to Taurus 11:45 a.m.)   For racing luck, try these selections at all tracks. Post position special: number 1 p.p. in the first race. Pick six: 1, 3, 1, 1, 7, 4. Note the telltale letters D, M, and V in the names of the jockeys and horses. Daily doubles: 1 and 1, 1 and 10, 1 and 4. Scorpio recommends his or her own betting system; yours is better.

Sunday, December 19 (Moon in Taurus)   You can get a lot of work done that is associated with the upcoming holidays, the social side of your job, and church and club participation matters. You may tire easily as evening arrives, and there is a warning against working and playing too hard. Your lucky number is 3.

Monday, December 20 (Moon in Taurus to Gemini 12:39 p.m.)   The Jupiter keynote in your horoscope assures you that good luck will be working in your love life and your socializing, and in the way children give great credit to you and your spouse. This is a fast-paced day, so you'll be ultra-tired by nightfall. Retire early. Your lucky number is 7.

Tuesday, December 21 (Moon in Gemini)   Gemini has a lot to say about what you aren't doing. Don't rise to the criticism or it will tire you, but Gemini never tires. Even so, this can be a good money day, when information that arrives in the mail can cheer you up. Nobody understands the good in you more than your beloved. Coppery gold is your color. Hot combination numbers: 9 and 3.

Wednesday, December 22 (Moon in Gemini to Cancer 11:52 a.m.)   The full moon in your eighth house illuminates all security matters, including savings, budgeting, investments, insurance, and tax shelters. It's a good day for improvements and definite changes. Certainly, you will adjust better to Uranus-sponsored changes imposed on you by the times. Reds and greens are in. Lucky lottery: 2, 11, 20, 29, 38, 47.

Thursday, December 23 (Moon in Cancer)   Neptune activated changes may be more elusive than those engineered by Uranus. They tend to impact your home, family, real estate, community, and ownership matters more. Some relatives may announce plans that baffle you. There can be erroneous gossip about property values. Your lucky number is 4.

Friday, December 24 (Moon in Cancer to Leo 11:32 a.m.)   You may cancel a short-distance trip in order to visit a senior citizen. The day moves quickly, with many odd and unexpected tasks confronting you. You are wondering how you can crowd that postponed trip into tomorrow's busy schedule. Hot combination numbers: 6 and 1.

Saturday, December 25 (Moon in Leo)   With the moon transiting your ninth house of travel, you can work that little trip into your late-afternoon schedule, and you will be happy you made this sacrifice. You and your beloved can trust an older child or a dear friend to pinch-hit for you in home celebrations. Choose Libra or Aquarius. Lucky lottery: 8, 17, 26, 35, 44, 2.

Sunday, December 26 (Moon in Leo to Virgo 1:34 p.m.)   Review your long-range plans as the year winds down. You keep on the move, although the day brings marvelous aspects for taking it easy. A Leo and another Sagittarius are front and center. This evening brings concentration on your job and what the week ahead may require. Scarlet and white are your colors; your lucky number is 1.

Monday, December 27 (Moon in Virgo)   There's a lot of work, some of which was shortchanged during the approach of the holidays. You could find a supervisor somewhat demanding now, but avoid disagreements—the less you say the more this supervisor will realize that he or she is wrong. Your number is 5.

Tuesday, December 28 (Moon in Virgo to Libra 7:14 p.m.)   Duties, responsibilities, and obligations connected with your professional life are strongly emphasized. Virgo and Capricorn figure prominently. End-of-year reports must be tackled, and other chores that you have been overlooking lately are begging your attention. Russet is your color. Hot combination numbers: 7 and 3.

Wednesday, December 29 (Moon in Libra)   Libra comes to your assistance and you cheerfully make room for pleasure, socializing in an otherwise busy day. Group activities and the social side of your job and career are spotlighted. Plan your New Year's Eve celebrations with a Scorpio. Lucky lottery: 9, 18, 27, 36, 45, 6.

Thursday, December 30 (Moon in Libra)   Today is fine for entertaining a few friends in your home. It's payback time, when you owe dinner to a couple who have treated you royally. You could hear some favorable news about a refund, rebate, or special stipend. Your lucky colors are gold and black. Hot combination numbers: 2 and 4.

Friday, December 31 (Moon in Libra to Scorpio 4:36 a.m.)   The Venus keynote in your horoscope indicates potential for changing your image or revamping your appearance. The Mercury accent suggests that you may be ignoring money earmarked for you. There are a lot of old traditions honored this evening, as the moon transits your twelfth house of past experiences. Chestnut is your color; your lucky number is 4.

Happy New Year!

JANUARY 2000

Saturday, January 1 (Moon in Scorpio) Much that is essential might be blocked from view. Proofread, work your way through a possible maze of confusion. Taurus, Leo, and Scorpio play significant roles, and will have these letters or initials in their names—D, M, V. Lucky lottery: 4, 40, 6, 20, 1, 18.

Sunday, January 2 (Moon in Scorpio to Sagittarius 4:33 p.m.) Today you will be told, "There is something sensual about you and, to tell the truth, at times I can hardly keep my hands off you!" A Scorpio "sweet whispers" you. There is a motive, but not necessarily an ulterior one. Have luck with number 5.

Monday, January 3 (Moon in Sagittarius) Attention revolves around personality, artistic tastes, the ability to beautify your surroundings. Finish what you start. Do not attempt to please everyone. Be up-to-date concerning fashion and international news. Taurus, Libra, and Scorpio are in the picture, and have these letters or initials in their names—F, O, X.

Tuesday, January 4 (Moon in Sagittarius) There are numerous contradictions—during the late afternoon you'll be told one thing and, around early evening, you'll be instructed to do something contrary to your original orders. Being forewarned is being forearmed. Much that happens is shrouded in mystery. If you expect everything to be crystal clear, you will be disappointed.

Wednesday, January 5 (Moon in Sagittarius to Capricorn 5:24 a.m.) The moon is entering that part of your horoscope associated with income, the ability to locate lost articles, a chance to pounce on legitimate financial counsel. The spotlight is on taking responsibility. You now have a chance to earn serious money. Lucky lottery: 20, 7, 18, 19, 2, 4.

Thursday, January 6 (Moon in Capricorn)   The new moon in Capricorn means that you gain privileged information, which ultimately will benefit clients and loved ones. A chance exists to start over. The new moon washes away business errors and misstatements. Aries and Libra play meaningful roles, and will have these initials in their names—I and R.

Friday, January 7 (Moon in Capricorn to Aquarius 5:53 p.m.)   You could experience a religious revelation. The sun keynote blends with your Jupiter ruler, so suddenly you'll see the future clearly. Follow your hunches. A dream or intuitive flash could contain important information. Leo and Aquarius plays exciting roles, with these letters or initials in a name—A, S, J.

Saturday, January 8 (Moon in Aquarius)   On this Saturday, attention revolves around these questions: where am I going, why am I here, what is next for me? The focus will be on whether you want to trod the road of life alone or to find somebody to go to the movies with! Have luck with number 2.

Sunday, January 9 (Moon in Aquarius)   Dispersal of funds relates to your association with people you trusted in the past and would like to trust in the future. Be receptive without being gullible. There is good news from another country, possibly associated with a display of your product or talent. Another Sagittarian is involved.

Monday, January 10 (Moon in Aquarius to Pisces 4:59 a.m.)   Today's Pisces moon relates to property values. Check for plumbing problems. Have confidence in yourself. Follow through on your inner feelings. Rewriting may be necessary, along with proofreading. Taurus, Leo, and Scorpio play fascinating roles, and will have these letters or initials in their names—D, M, V.

Tuesday, January 11 (Moon in Pisces)   Lucky numbers: 11, 2, 20. Focus on freedom, change, variety, a flirtation that could lead to something serious. Develop your skills as a writer. You'll be asked pertinent questions about marriage. A decision along those lines looms large. Gemini and Virgo play dominant roles.

Wednesday, January 12 (Moon in Pisces to Aries 1:48 p.m.)   Lucky lottery: 11, 12, 10, 4, 14, 22. The spotlight is on flowers, music, a reconciliation with someone who means much to you. Taurus, Libra, and Scorpio play meaningful roles, and will have these letters or initials in their names—F, O, X.

Thursday, January 13 (Moon in Aries)   What begins as a joke will become more serious as the day progresses. This includes a love relationship involving Aries who plays cards hot and heavy. Do not start something you cannot finish. A flirtation is no longer mild, and could eventually break the budget.

Friday, January 14 (Moon in Aries to Taurus 7:38 p.m.)   On this Friday, you'll be dealing with areas of children, challenge, a change of venue, and sexual attraction. Attention revolves around the pressure of responsibility, deadlines, a relationship that could get too hot not to cool down. Capricorn figures prominently.

Saturday, January 15 (Moon in Taurus)   What appeared to be long ago and far away could now be practically at your doorstep. The emphasis is on universal appeal, language and cultures, the personal habits of people in countries in which you might eventually be doing business. Libra is involved. Your lucky number is 9.

Sunday, January 16 (Moon in Taurus to Gemini 10:25 p.m.) A bright light shines. You have reason to be optimistic on this Sunday. What previously held you back will no longer exist. Be aware of it, and highlight independence and originality. Holding hands with a hot-blooded Leo could lead to something you did not originally anticipate.

Monday, January 17 (Moon in Gemini) Today's cycle highlights cooperative efforts, being able to fit in with people active in extraordinary causes. This cooperation leads to close association that eventually (if single) could lead to marriage. Be aware of the existence of an important legal document!

Tuesday, January 18 (Moon in Gemini to Cancer 11:01 p.m.) Don't take yourself too seriously! At the same time, trust your own opinions, follow through on projects related to resorts, cruises, and entertainment. Gemini and another Sagittarian play important roles, and will have these letters or initials in their names—C, L, U. Your lucky number is 3.

Wednesday, January 19 (Moon in Cancer) Stick to your original plan regarding durable goods, the value of property. Deal gingerly with a Cancer who once helped you learn the business. There are temperamental people around you tonight. Be kind, without being obsequious. Taurus, Leo, and Scorpio play outstanding roles.

Thursday, January 20 (Moon in Cancer to Leo 10:59 p.m.) The Mercury keynote relates to communications, a wry kind of humor, a blend of laughter with wisdom. Special: take care in traffic—some people, inadvertently, appear to aim their vehicles at you! Gemini, Virgo, and another Sagittarian play major roles and have these initials in their names—E, N, W.

Friday, January 21 (Moon in Leo) Plenty of romance! The full moon, lunar eclipse is in Leo, your ninth house. Translated, there is idealism in romance, sentiment, poetic ways of expressing your desires. An invitation to travel is high on your agenda. Pay special attention to the language and cultures of people in other lands.

Saturday, January 22 (Moon in Leo) You'll be regarding this as your lucky day. What begins as an adversity will boomerang in your favor. An element of deception is present, so be alert, and see people, places, and relationships in realistic light. Pisces and Virgo take center stage, and will have these letters in their names—G, P, Y.

Sunday, January 23 (Moon in Leo to Virgo 12:08 a.m.) Someone who pulled the wool over your eyes will confide, confess, and seek forgiveness. Don't be too hard a taskmaster; instead, declare, "All right this time, but do not let it happen again!" Capricorn and Cancer figure in this scenario, and could have these initials in their names—H, Q, Z.

Monday, January 24 (Moon in Virgo) Lucky numbers: 3, 2, 4. Focus on criticism, self-improvement, keeping resolutions concerning health. The spotlight is also on your career, promotion, standing in the community, conferring with bigwigs. A long-distance communication verifies your opinions about shipments, distribution, and advertising.

Tuesday, January 25 (Moon in Virgo to Libra 4:10 a.m.) The moon position coincides with your ability to win in matters of speculation. Focus on luck, and the ability to gain the confidence of people in high positions. Music, entertainment, and romance will play important roles. A Leo is in the spotlight and will work in your behalf.

Wednesday, January 26 (Moon in Libra) For racing luck, try these selections at all tracks. Post position special—number 6 p.p. in the fifth race. Pick six: 1, 5, 4, 2, 6, 7. Look for these letters or initials in the names of potential winning horses or jockeys: B, K, T. Hot daily doubles: 1 and 5, 2 and 4, 3 and 3. Hometown favorites ride into the winner's circle. Cancer jockeys excel.

Thursday, January 27 (Moon in Libra to Scorpio 12:02 p.m.) Within 24 hours, you learn a secret. Keep plans flexible. Let others know you intend to stay and to do things your way. On a personal level, a delightful time will be had tonight. You'll receive a unique honor for past contributions to charitable–political activities.

Friday, January 28 (Moon in Scorpio) Tonight, you'll be dealing with Leo and Scorpio who confide, confess, and seek your guidance. Check the reliability of source material. Proofread, rewrite, and revise, if necessary. At first, you react like a wounded bird. Later, your spirits revive; you'll once again be on top of the game.

Saturday, January 29 (Moon in Scorpio to Sagittarius 11:18 p.m.) Work your way through a maze. You have something important to say and people will listen, albeit reluctantly. You've been undergoing a test period. You are coming through like a champion. You'll win admirers and people who genuinely love you. Your lucky number is 5.

Sunday, January 30 (Moon in Sagittarius) The moon in your sign represents your high cycle. Your judgment and intuition are on target. You are capable of designating where the action will be—do so! The spotlight is on your home environment, marital status, ways of increasing your income. Wear shades of pink and purple. A gift represents a token of love; you receive it tonight.

Monday, January 31 (Moon in Sagittarius) On this last day of the first month of the year, you'll be surprised and amazed by people who appeared to be indifferent, but who now are showering you with affection. Define terms and pay attention to information relating to real estate. Pisces plays a definite role!

FEBRUARY 2000

Tuesday, February 1 (Moon in Sagittarius to Capricorn 12:10 p.m.)   There is much news about a family member on the move. The lunation for February highlights trips, ideas, and amusing situations. Taurus, Leo, and Scorpio today will play paramount roles, and have these letters or initials in their names—F, O, X. By shopping around, you obtain needed material for remodeling—at bargain prices.

Wednesday, February 2 (Moon in Capricorn)   Excitement prevails in connection with mystery, intrigue, the possibility of a romantic triangle. It will become obvious that, indeed, discretion is the better part of valor. Pisces and Virgo figure in this dramatic scenario, and have these letters or initials in their names—G, P, Y.

Thursday, February 3 (Moon in Capricorn)   Someone who tries to deceive will be caught red-handed. Focus on responsibility, the pressure of a deadline, a relationship that requires scrutiny. Be sure you are not taken for a ride in other than an automobile. Capricorn and Cancer figure in this complex scenario.

Friday, February 4 (Moon in Capricorn to Aquarius 12:31 a.m.)   The lunar position symbolizes reinforcement of your beliefs and principles. You'll successfully meet a challenge, and you could also win a contest. You'll be rid of an unnecessary burden. Get ready for a fresh start and possibly a new love. Aries and Libra play roles.

Saturday, February 5 (Moon in Aquarius)   The new moon, solar eclipse falls in that section of your horoscope associated with ideas that are vital, but require time to become viable and ultimately valuable. The answer to your question: Yes, let go of obligations that wear you down and are not constructive. Your lucky number is 1.

Sunday, February 6 (Moon in Aquarius to Pisces 11:02 a.m.) Much domestic scolding is involved. Don't make a federal case of minor imperfections. Instead, make intelligent concessions, and realize that relatives today tend to be ultrasensitive. Capricorn and Cancer declare in unison, "We are going to win despite the odds!"

Monday, February 7 (Moon in Pisces) Diversify without scattering your forces. Keep resolutions concerning exercise, diet, and nutrition. Focus on the value of your property, a plumbing situation. You'll be presented with a gift representing a geographical location written about by the poet Robinson Jeffers. Your lucky number is 3.

Tuesday, February 8 (Moon in Pisces to Aries 7:18 p.m.) On this Tuesday, it will be necessary to check prescriptions, to be sure of facts and figures. Taurus, Leo, and Scorpio will play amazing roles, and have these letters or initials in their names—D, M, V. Number 4 crops up in many areas.

Wednesday, February 9 (Moon in Aries) The Aries moon relates to that part of your horoscope associated with physical attraction, creativity, style, variety, and sex appeal. Keep your plans flexible. What might begin as dull routine will be transformed into an exciting venture. A flirtation lends spice, but keep it under control. Know when to say, "Enough is enough!"

Thursday, February 10 (Moon in Aries) Attention revolves around where you live, your children, the challenge of a different enterprise. The spotlight also falls on luxury, art objects, an invitation to visit a museum. Taurus, Libra, and Scorpio assert their views in a dramatic way, and actually have your best interests at heart.

Friday, February 11 (Moon in Aries to Taurus 1:21 a.m.) Your intuitive intellect is honed to razor sharpness. People comment on your natural talent as a teacher and psychologist. Interest in the New Age arts and sciences increases, including astrology. Project an air of mystery; let people play a guessing game. Remain confident that you are doing the right thing.

Saturday, February 12 (Moon in Taurus) For racing luck, try these selections at all tracks. Post position special—number 8 p.p. in the eighth race. Pick six: 4, 8, 1, 6, 5, 3. Look for these letters or initials in the names of potential winning horses or jockeys: H, Q, Z. Hot daily doubles: 4 and 8, 6 and 6, 1 and 7. Veteran jockeys ride favorites. Capricorn risks injury.

Sunday, February 13 (Moon in Taurus to Gemini 5:23 a.m.) On this Sunday, expand your interest in spiritual matters. Look beyond the immediate. Prepare for a possible journey. As metaphysical values surface, you'll learn once again that what goes around comes around. Aries and Libra are in the picture.

Monday, February 14 (Moon in Gemini) Romance! Why not? It is St. Valentine's Day. You receive more attention than usual, and you might find yourself inextricably involved. It's very exciting, but don't give away the farm for some sweet whispered nothings. Leo and Aquarius grab the spotlight, provide entertainment and information.

Tuesday, February 15 (Moon in Gemini to Cancer 7:46 a.m.) Within 24 hours a financial dilemma relating to your mate or partner will be solved. In the meantime, make no accusations; be willing to wait, observe, and listen. The spotlight is on direction, motivation, building material, your marital status. A Cancer plays a top role.

Wednesday, February 16 (Moon in Cancer) The moon in Cancer relates to additional information about computers, accounting procedures, being more accurate about debits and credits. It's an excellent evening for dining out. Social activities accelerate. You'll be called upon to be the umpire in a love triangle. Your lucky number is 3.

Thursday, February 17 (Moon in Cancer to Leo 9:12 a.m.) A Cancer helps educate you in connection with earnings, investments, gains, and losses. Proofreading is necessary; also be sure to read between the lines. Someone is trying to tell you something in a discreet way. Taurus, Leo, and Scorpio are represented, with these letters in their names—D, M, V.

Friday, February 18 (Moon in Leo) The moon in Leo enables you to elaborate on teaching methods or plans involving travel, which others consider grandiose. Don't stop now! You do have something of value going for you despite the objections by those who know the price of everything, the value of nothing.

Saturday, February 19 (Moon in Leo to Virgo 10:54 a.m.) The lunar position (full moon) highlights romance, extreme emotions, the need to maintain your equilibrium. Questions about partnership and marriage continue to loom large. Envious people can do evil things. Know it, and protect yourself at close quarters.

Sunday, February 20 (Moon in Virgo) Be ultracritical if necessary in order to get at the truth. A professional superior is on your side and this is true, even if not obvious. Line up your facts, figures, and priorities. Pisces and Virgo will be playing dynamic roles, and could have these initials in their names—G, P, Y.

Monday, February 21 (Moon in Virgo to Libra 2:21 p.m.)   Efforts made 36 hours ago will bear fruit. A Virgo plays an instrumental role, provides encouragement, and opens doors previously shut tight. Property is evaluated; it turns out that you might possess the key to riches! A deadline exists, so get going. Keep a steady pace.

Tuesday, February 22 (Moon in Libra)   See that you finish what you started—a project involved faraway places. Romance figures prominently. Travel is involved. You will see beyond the immediate. Some persons state, "You have an unfair advantage; you have talent!" Aries plays a top role.

Wednesday, February 23 (Moon in Libra to Scorpio 8:58 p.m.)   This is what you've been waiting for—a personal appearance by a loved one who recently declared, "I will never see you again!" Don't be arrogant. Instead, express appreciation: "I admire the fact that you tossed aside false pride, if you hadn't come or called I would have!"

Thursday, February 24 (Moon in Scorpio)   The lunar position highlights a clandestine operation, a secret meeting, activities that possibly "flirt with the law." Protect your assets, and protect yourself in clinches. Some appear determined to get something for nothing, and you could be the prime target. Capricorn plays a role.

Friday, February 25 (Moon in Scorpio)   On this Friday, get a second emotional wind. Survey the current situation and your life. A philosophical attitude is necessary. Give full play to your intellectual curiosity about the religions of the world. Gemini and another Sagittarian play dynamic roles, and have these letters or initials in their names—C, L, U.

Saturday, February 26 (Moon in Scorpio to Sagittarius 7:10 a.m.)   For racing luck, try these selections at all tracks. Post position special—number 4 p.p. in the fourth race. Pick six: 2, 2, 1, 4, 3, 8. Watch for these letters or initials in the names of potential winning horses or jockeys: D, M, V. Hot daily doubles: 2 and 2, 4 and 6, 4 and 4. Taurus and Scorpio jockeys ride long shots into the winner's circle.

Sunday, February 27 (Moon in Sagittarius) Your cycle is high. You'll breathe a sigh of relief and declare, "I am going to enjoy this Sunday, I am lucky, and I am going to appreciate that fact!" The spotlight is on reading and writing, dealing gingerly with Gemini and Virgo. Have luck with number 5.

Monday, February 28 (Moon in Sagittarius to Capricorn 7:45 p.m.) A blend of aspects highlights your personal environment, romance, desires, beauty, flowers, and music. This will be one Monday on which you state, "Do not stop the world—I'm not ready to get off!" A neighbor or relative introduces you to fascinating literature that concerns the lives of famous composers.

Tuesday, February 29 (Moon in Capricorn) On this last day of the month (leap year), you discover ways of increasing your income. Many people, only half-joking, claim you have the Midas touch. Your knowledge of basic values surfaces; your interest in places and people in foreign lands will be much in evidence.

MARCH 2000

Wednesday, March 1 (Moon in Capricorn) For racing luck, try these selections at all tracks. Post position special—number 2 p.p. in the fourth race. Pick six: 2, 4, 1, 2, 6, 7. Look for these letters or initials in the names of potential winning horses or jockeys: F, O, X. Hot daily doubles: 2 and 4, 6 and 6, 5 and 8. Taurus jockeys shine, and win with long shots.

Thursday, March 2 (Moon in Capricorn to Aquarius 8:14 a.m.)   Lucky numbers: 3, 7, 8. The lunar position relates to winning and losing. A loss will be followed by the start of a winning streak. This adds up to the message: "Keep the faith!" A relative returns from a trip with good news. Keep your aura of mystery—don't tell all!

Friday, March 3 (Moon in Aquarius)   On this Friday, you learn that unorthodox procedures will be necessary, if your goal is to be achieved. An Aquarian will play a major role, does have your best interests at heart, and will prove it. An overtime assignment is featured, which ultimately will give you the chance to prove your worth.

Saturday, March 4 (Moon in Aquarius to Pisces 6:31 p.m.)   On this Saturday, you'll meet visitors from foreign lands. Focus on social habits, language, idealized illusions about romance. A long-range project gets underway. Faith in yourself is restored, so get going without waiting for others. Your lucky number is 9.

Sunday, March 5 (Moon in Pisces)   Spirituality! Those close to you share in a serious discussion about life here and in the hereafter. The leadership role is yours; don't reject it! Stand tall for your beliefs. Be generous and open-minded, without being naive. Leo plays a dramatic role.

Monday, March 6 (Moon in Pisces)   The new moon in Pisces relates to a different view of your property, or home. You will be sensitive to the degree of being psychic. Discussions also revolve around the fact that both Babe Ruth and Ronald Reagan were born on February 6th. Cancer and Capricorn express intense interest in your views.

Tuesday, March 7 (Moon in Pisces to Aries 1:55 a.m.)   The key is diversification. You discover a package containing photographs; give full play to your curiosity. Ask questions, and share fascinating information.

234

Your interest in history is spurred. You'll be drawn particularly to events revolving around the Civil War.

Wednesday, March 8 (Moon in Aries) A minor miscalculation could throw your program off. Take time to make corrections. What escaped 48 hours ago will be recaptured—also to your benefit. Taurus, Leo, and Scorpio figure in this exciting scenario, and will have these letters or initials in their names—D, M, V.

Thursday, March 9 (Moon in Aries to Taurus 7:02 a.m.) Forces that had been scattered will be back in place. An Aries helps you remove a threat, and stands by during a crisis. There's joyous news later about an essay or contest. Gemini, Virgo, and another Sagittarian play significant roles, and could have these initials in their names—E, N, W.

Friday, March 10 (Moon in Taurus) A family member recovers from an illness, gives you credit for loyalty or aid. Special: take care of yourself; this applies especially to your voice and throat. Attention revolves around domestic activities that include where you live, and your marital status. Libra is involved.

Saturday, March 11 (Moon in Taurus to Gemini 10:46 a.m.) Your intuitive intellect is honed to razor sharpness. Show off your skill as a psychologist and astrologer. Family members may pull you in different directions, but maintain your emotional equilibrium. A coworker makes an unofficial call, seeks information generally prohibited. Clearance is required!

Sunday, March 12 (Moon in Gemini) On this Sunday, you are on more solid ground. People who sought proof will receive it, thanks to you. Money, payments, and collections are involved. A Capricorn remembers a past favor, declares, "You are a good person and I will never forget it!"

Monday, March 13 (Moon in Gemini to Cancer 1:52 p.m.)   Mission completed! The Mars keynote blends with your Jupiter, therefore the action gets started! Focus on universality, overcome distance and language obstacles. A reunion with a loved one follows a journey. Aries and Libra will play their cards close to the chest.

Tuesday, March 14 (Moon in Cancer)   On this Tuesday, with the sun keynote and moon in its own sign, you could find yourself "entangled" with people whose loyalties do not coincide with your own. Protect yourself! Do not even give the appearance of considering a double cross. A Leo says, "Please trust me!"

Wednesday, March 15 (Moon in Cancer to Leo 4:44 p.m.)   Lucky lottery: 2, 12, 22, 51, 48, 7. This could be your lucky Wednesday. The spotlight is on your family, home, and security. Keep valuables under lock and key. Someone close to you, recently divorced, needs encouragement. Capricorn is involved.

Thursday, March 16 (Moon in Leo)   Don't twist the tail of the lion! Cooperate with Leo. The moon is in that sign which represents philosophy, publishing, the ability to get your message across. A relationship that sizzled and then fizzled will once again sizzle tonight. Gemini is represented.

Friday, March 17 (Moon in Leo to Virgo 7:49 p.m.)   It's St. Patrick's Day, so have fun, join in the celebration, but go easy on adult beverages. Learn more about the holiday and St. Patrick. Taurus, Leo, and Scorpio present friendly challenges. Respond in a like manner. Have luck with number 4.

Saturday, March 18 (Moon in Virgo)   Make concessions, but do not abandon your principles. A Virgo who holds a responsible position, seeks to cooperate, and wants very much for you to succeed. Gemini and another Sagittarius also play important roles, and have these let-

236

ters or initials in their names—E, N, W. Your lucky number is 5.

Sunday, March 19 (Moon in Virgo to Libra 10:57 p.m.)   On this Sunday, fulfill a promise to a Taurus. . This involves study, recreation, or a stage play. Before the day is finished, let others know once and for all that when you make a promise, you keep it. Taurus will be the first in line to back you up.

Monday, March 20 (Moon in Libra)   Within 24 hours, many of your desires will be fulfilled. Seek perfection without being overly critical of your own efforts. Like ships that pass in the night, those who were close to you will come and go. Maintain a philosophical attitude. Pisces plays a top role.

Tuesday, March 21 (Moon in Libra)   Everything you waited for, but were afraid to ask for! The Saturn keynote and moon in your eleventh house means you should be realistic about what you need, what you are tempted to do. This scenario includes good fortune in finance and romance. A Cancer is involved.

Wednesday, March 22 (Moon in Libra to Scorpio 6:17 a.m.)   Lucky lottery: 9, 19, 14, 22, 18, 6. Reach beyond the immediate. You could grab the brass ring representing fame and fortune. You'll exude personal magnetism, an aura of sensuality and sex appeal. Wear shades of red. Pay attention to an opportunity relating to overseas travel.

Thursday, March 23 (Moon in Scorpio)   Don't brood about past mistakes! The slate could be wiped clean today. Do your own thing; do not follow others. Special: don't lift heavy objects! A recent back problem will return if you are not careful. Leo and Aquarius figure in this stunning scenario, and have these letters or initials in their names—A, S, J.

Friday, March 24 (Moon in Scorpio to Sagittarius 3:43 p.m.)   For racing luck, try these selections at all tracks. Post position special—number 2 p.p. in the second race. Pick six: 2, 2, 4, 8, 5, 3. Look for these letters or initials in the names of potential winning horses or jockeys: B, K, T. Hot daily doubles: 2 and 2, 6 and 6, 3 and 8. A popular Cancer-born jockey predicts he will win, and he does!

Saturday, March 25 (Moon in Sagittarius)   On this Saturday, the moon is in your sign, your first house. This coincides with the initiative. Elements of timing and luck are with you. This could be the start of a winning streak. Focus on social activities, writing, advertising, publishing, putting your message across effectively.

Sunday, March 26 (Moon in Sagittarius)   On this Sunday, you will be grateful that good fortune has smiled, although early today, you feared for the worst. Taurus, Leo, and Scorpio figure in this dynamic scenario, and will have these letters or initials in their names—D, M, V.

Monday, March 27 (Moon in Sagittarius to Capricorn 3:52 a.m.)   A debt will be paid, and a friendship will be restored. Your judgment and intuition are on target. Needed material can be acquired at favorable rates. It is Monday, but there is plenty of action, and many people who usually are retiring in nature will be aggressive. Virgo is involved.

Tuesday, March 28 (Moon in Capricorn)   You might be musing, "Is this déjà vu?" Today's scenario features familiar places and faces. A family member who once declared, "I am going out of your life," will return, albeit with a hangdog look. Be kind, diplomatic, show that you are big enough to forgive, and by doing so, perhaps love can be rekindled.

Wednesday, March 29 (Moon in Capricorn to Aquarius 4:35 p.m.)   Within 24 hours, excellent news is received concerning an investment, romance, the ability to be at the right place at a special moment. Your reputation as a square shooter stands you in good stead. Tell your story with confidence, you'll be believed! Pisces is involved.

Thursday, March 30 (Moon in Aquarius)   Attention revolves around responsibility, deadline pressure and investments, the need to locate a lost article. The odds are you will succeed. Pay little or no attention to naysayers who lack inspiration or talent. Organize your priorities. Be in rhythm with events that add up to a passing parade.

Friday, March 31 (Moon in Aquarius)   Round out a project. Stand tall for your principles; you are going places and in the direction you wish to go. An Aries you helped in the recent past will return the favor, big time! Finish what you start; open lines of communication with someone in a foreign land who seeks to be your representative.

APRIL 2000

Saturday, April 1 (Moon in Aquarius to Pisces 3:13 a.m.)   More than in past years, you will be intrigued by April Fools' Day. The Neptune keynote blends with your Jupiter. The Pisces moon adds another dimension that includes housing, property, dealings with an older person. The answer to your question: go slow. A deal might not be consummated until three days hence.

Sunday, April 2—Daylight Saving Time Begins (Moon in Pisces)   On this second day of April, a family member complains, "It seems my life goes up and down and I am never aware which way it will go." The key is to listen, offer tea and sympathy, but do not get inextricably involved. Capricorn and Cancer figure in this scenario and have these letters or initials in their names—H, Q, Z.

Monday, April 3 (Moon in Pisces to Aries 11:33 a.m.) The moon gets ready to enter Aries, which means that within 24 hours, you will be more sexually attractive. Look forward to an immediate, dynamic, fascinating future. Long-range prospects come into focus; the ultimate destination could be a foreign land. Aries plays a role.

Tuesday, April 4 (Moon in Aries) The new moon in Aries relates to a physical attraction, creativity, style, dealings with children. A different kind of love is featured; you might be musing, "Why did it take me so long to wake up?" Leo and Aquarius figure in this dynamic scenario. Your lucky number is 1.

Wednesday, April 5 (Moon in Aries to Taurus 3:30 p.m.) Lucky numbers: 3, 1, 0. Focus on improving your lifestyle, adding furniture to your home, relating to a Cancer-born person who cooks up a storm. A recent injury to your left eye should not be ignored. A family member pulls you in one direction, while a friend or lover says, "Instead, come with me and live!"

Thursday, April 6 (Moon in Taurus) For racing luck, try these selections at all tracks. Post position special—number 7 p.p. in the third race. Pick six: 1, 2, 7, 4, 5, 8. Be alert for these letters or initials in the names of potential winning horses or jockeys: C, L, U. Hot daily doubles: 1 and 2, 4 and 7, 3 and 5. Long shots are featured. A Sagittarian jockey burns up the track.

Friday, April 7 (Moon in Taurus to Gemini 3:59 p.m.) During this Friday, previous complications will dissolve. Imprint your style, determine to have a creative, enjoyable weekend. Taurus, Leo, and Scorpio will play a memorable role, and have these letters or initials in their names: D, M, V. Have luck with number 4.

Saturday, April 8 (Moon in Gemini)   The Gemini moon relates to public affairs, legal agreements, and marriage. Show off your writing skills. Realize your own power. Don't bow to anyone. Stand tall, express and stick to your principles. A flirtation is exciting, but lacks solidity. Lucky lottery: 50, 1, 5, 15, 22, 18.

Sunday, April 9 (Moon in Gemini to Cancer 8:16 p.m.)   Peace, calm, what a change of pace! Everything seems in order. There is quiet after the storm, in this case an emotional storm. Focus on decorating, remodeling, learning more about plant life, restoring domestic harmony. Taurus, Leo, and Scorpio are in this picture, and could have these initials in their names—F, O, X.

Monday, April 10 (Moon in Cancer)   People owe you plenty, including money. Terms have yet to be clearly defined. The moon in the eighth house relates to the assets of other people. You might be surprised to learn how much of value is involved. Don't point an accusing finger—if anyone is to blame, it is you for not remaining alert.

Tuesday, April 11 (Moon in Cancer to Leo 9:16 p.m.)   Follow a hunch; your intuitive intellect is honed to razor sharpness. On this Tuesday people take you seriously. This is positive. Your cycle is such that you put across points in a dramatic, profitable way. Capricorn and Cancer figure in this sensational scenario.

Wednesday, April 12 (Moon in Leo)   Lucky lottery: 12, 5, 50, 1, 15, 18. The Leo moon lends spice and drama. Foreign affairs are involved, especially foreign exchange rates. Open lines of communication. Contact a representative who can develop markets for your product or talent. Aries plays a top role.

Thursday, April 13 (Moon in Leo) The ninth house emphasis highlights publishing, travel, a renewed interest in religions of the world. Look beyond the immediate; study various possibilities within the mantic arts and sciences. In matters of speculation, stick with number 1. Consult a Leo concerning the possibility of upset winners.

Friday, April 14 (Moon in Leo to Virgo 3:19 a.m.) The dust settles. People line up for their beliefs. You'll be called upon by your family to be an umpire. The wise course is to have none of it. If you get involved, you'll be blamed, for better or for worse. Cancer and Capricorn play dominant roles, and have these letters or initials in their names—B, K, T.

Saturday, April 15 (Moon in Virgo) For racing luck, try these selections at all tracks. Post position special— number 3 p.p. in the third race. Pick six: 1, 7, 3, 5, 8, 2. Be alert for these letters or initials in the names of potential winning horses or jockeys: C, L, U. Hot daily doubles: 1 and 7, 3 and 3, 4 and 5. Long shots have a field day. Gemini and Sagittarian jockeys ride the winners.

Sunday, April 16 (Moon in Virgo to Libra 8:36 a.m.) Within 24 hours, sudden changes take place. Luck will not be a stranger. The moon is moving into the eleventh sector of your horoscope. Tomorrow, you'll win friends and influence people. You'll be accepted among the high and mighty. Taurus, Leo, and Scorpio figure in this dramatic scenario, and have these letters in their names—D, M, V.

Monday, April 17 (Moon in Libra) Get ready for change, travel, and variety. The Libra moon relates to fun, games, speculation, music, dancing, and increased romantic activity. Listen, Sagittarius: "Can you handle it, are you ready for all this?" Gemini and Virgo will be leading the way.

Tuesday, April 18 (Moon in Libra to Scorpio 3:36 p.m.) The full moon position in Libra accentuates the positive, eliminates the negative. Don't have anything to do with "Mister In-Between!" Today's cycle highlights romance, creativity, style, proposals that include business, career, and marriage. A domestic adjustment relates to the possibility of a new residence.

Wednesday, April 19 (Moon in Scorpio)   Lucky lottery: 7, 17, 22, 33, 5, 10. Don't look back. Something could be gaining on you! Please go forward. Realize you cannot unscramble an egg. Predict your own future. Puzzle pieces fall into place, so act in a positive, confident way. Pisces is involved.

Thursday, April 20 (Moon in Scorpio)   Power play! A lost love returns in an unexpected, inexplicable way. The passing parade, time marches on. As the author Thomas Wolfe said, "You can't go home again!" A delicate situation prevails. Personal survival is the order of the day. Capricorn plays a role.

Friday, April 21 (Moon in Scorpio to Sagittarius 12:59 a.m.)   Your cycle moves up. What evaded you previously is now available. You need only to pick-and-choose. One phase of life is over; another is just beginning. Enthusiasm replaces gloom. You will be counseling others on how to live and profit. Your lucky number is 9.

Saturday, April 22 (Moon in Sagittarius)   Everything points to a new start in a different direction. You'll exude personal magnetism, an aura of confidence. You also have an abundance of sex appeal. Your vitality has made a dramatic comeback. Some people claim you have partaken of a magic potion. Your answer: "That is for me to know and for you to find out!"

Sunday, April 23 (Moon in Sagittarius to Capricorn 12:48 p.m.)   Put together the pieces of a financial transaction. An investment in the arts, including motion pictures, would prove profitable. Don't do this behind the back of your partner or mate. Be up-front, and you cannot go wrong. Others may lack your perception, so take the time to explain and instruct.

Monday, April 24 (Moon in Capricorn)   A change of pace from serious to lighthearted. An entertaining event intrigues. You could be a part of it, financially, creatively, or both. Friends and family are skeptical. "When did you think you became a producer?" they ask in a sarcastic way. Another Sagittarian is involved.

Tuesday, April 25 (Moon in Capricorn)   You are on more solid ground. Agreements are no longer merely verbal. A Scorpio has been your secret ally, working in your behalf. Knowing this boosts your morale. You are going places and today you are sure of it. Taurus plays a role.

Wednesday, April 26 (Moon in Capricorn to Aquarius 1:43 a.m.)   Today's Mercury keynote relates to communication via words, verbal and written. A mathematical equation is solved—whether for entertainment or other purposes. Eccentric actions on the part of a relative command attention. Remember: "It is fun to be fooled, not fun to be deceived."

Thursday, April 27 (Moon in Aquarius)   Attention revolves around where you live, decorating and remodeling, arranging an entertainment program for the purpose of charitable–political activity. The Venus keynote emphasizes beauty-flowers, delight to the taste buds. Taurus and Libra play featured roles.

Friday, April 28 (Moon in Aquarius to Pisces 1:06 p.m.)   Get your second wind! By tomorrow, the moon will be in Pisces, your fourth house; translated, the spotlight is on your parents, property, negotiations, the settlement of family differences. Pisces and Virgo play "secret" roles. Have luck with number 7.

Saturday, April 29 (Moon in Pisces)   Discussions revolve around the various enterprises in which names were changed. The question arises, "Should I change my name?" The accurate answer is that your name must be compared with your birth number. You can change your name, but you cannot change your birth date. Have luck with number 8.

Sunday, April 30 (Moon in Pisces to Aries 8:55 p.m.)   Finally you are relieved of a burden which had amounted to a losing proposition. Coincidentally, a love relationship flourishes. You're on the precipice of beginning a new life. You'll be musing, "For the life of me, I don't know why I waited so long!" Aries is involved.

MAY 2000

Monday, May 1 (Moon in Aries)   On this Monday, the first day of May, the moon in Aries reflects physical attraction, creativity, the need for a change of routine, the need for the fresh air of companionship with dynamic, ambitious people. Capricorn and Cancer will play outstanding roles and have these letters or initials in their names—H, Q, Z.

Tuesday, May 2 (Moon in Aries)   For racing luck, try these selections at all tracks. Post position special—number 8 p.p. in the first race. Pick six: 8, 1, 2, 4, 6, 7. Look for these letters or initials in the names of potential winning horses or jockeys: I and R. Hot daily doubles: 8 and 1, 3 and 6, 4 and 8. Track records are broken. Aries jockeys display exceptional skills. Favorites run out of the money.

Wednesday, May 3 (Moon in Aries to Taurus 12:54 a.m.)   The answer to your question: affirmative; make a fresh start, show your originality. Have the courage of your convictions. Further answer: new love is on the horizon—your instincts are correct. Reassurance is required, if a relationship is to continue. Leo will play a colorful role. Your lucky number is 1.

Thursday, May 4 (Moon in Taurus)   The new moon in Taurus relates to your work methods, taking a fitness test and emerging with flying colors. Focus on where you are going and why—what to do about it when your goal is achieved. Capricorn and Cancer will play fascinating roles, and have these letters in their names—B, K, T.

Friday, May 5 (Moon in Taurus to Gemini 2:24 a.m.)   This could be the precursor to a lively, dynamic weekend. The Jupiter keynote, together with your natal Jupiter significator, adds up to too much of a good thing! This is your lucky day, and it could be the start of a winning streak. Another Sagittarian is involved.

Saturday, May 6 (Moon in Gemini)   On this Saturday, there will be obstacles, social and otherwise. The Gemini moon relates to how the world looks to you and how you appear to the world. The seventh house influence is associated with public relations, partnership, cooperative efforts, and marriage. Have luck with number 4.

Sunday, May 7 (Moon in Gemini to Cancer 3:14 a.m.) Words mean a lot. In Biblical discussions, you will remind people that first came the word and what followed was the remainder of God's creation. Lively debates and discussions are featured. Make it crystal clear that no hurt feelings will result in changed opinions.

Monday, May 8 (Moon in Cancer)   Focus on mystery, intrigue, fantastic tales of the occult. The moon in its own sign relates the ways and means of fulfilling your dreams. Learn more about accounting procedures and how to handle the money of others entrusted to you. A Libra figures prominently.

Tuesday, May 9 (Moon in Cancer to Leo 5:02 a.m.) The moon moves into Leo, which represents education, travel, publishing, getting your spiritual message across. In matters of speculation, stick with these numbers—1, 1, 5. Following a meditation, you will wake up with the answers to perplexing questions. Pisces is involved.

Wednesday, May 10 (Moon in Leo) The emphasis is on production, promotion, serious consideration of a relationship that might have gone too far and too fast. An older person advises, "Go with the tide, let what will happen take its course." The Leo moon tells of luck in connection with travel, discovery, writing.

Thursday, May 11 (Moon in Leo to Virgo 8:42 a.m.) Long-term negotiations are finished. You'll be happy, free, and, as result of what you did during tough times, you win recognition and possibly fame and fortune. You will encounter an Aries who is bilingual, and who takes more than a mild liking to you. This person could propose a journey or at the very least, a business relationship.

Friday, May 12 (Moon in Virgo) Make room for yourself at the top! Avoid heavy lifting; speak out from the heart. Imprint your style; accept a leadership role. You'll be asked to oversee a project requiring strength blended with diplomacy. A love relationship could be on the rebound; it was of-track and now is back on.

Saturday, May 13 (Moon in Virgo to Libra 2:28 p.m.) On this Saturday, you will be with companions who are knowledgeable about sports. Be comfortable, enjoy repartee that includes a wide variety of subjects within the realm of sports. Remind others that this is the birthday of Joe Louis. And a good time was had by all!

Sunday, May 14 (Moon in Libra) The Libra moon relates to your eleventh house, that section of your horoscope associated with good fortune in finances and romance. You'll have special luck with the number 3. Gemini plays the role of devil's advocate. Keep your emotional equilibrium. Show that you can take criticism as well as give it.

Monday, May 15 (Moon in Libra to Scorpio 10:18 p.m.) Your winning streak continues. The Libra moon means music, style, and romance. The Pluto key-note represents an upsetting sound—someone who loses control makes a threat. Stand stall, without being pugnacious. Taurus, Leo, and Scorpio figure in this scenario, and could have these initials in their names—D, M. V.

Tuesday, May 16 (Moon in Scorpio) The spotlight is on intellectual curiosity, questions about life and death and celebrities. A challenge arises, "Was Joe Louis really buried at Arlington Cemetery?" Your correct answer: "Burial at Arlington National Cemetery, by presidential waiver. It was the thirty-ninth exception to the eligibility rules for burial in Arlington Cemetery."

Wednesday, May 17 (Moon in Scorpio) Lucky lottery: 17, 20, 8, 33, 1, 10. A financial deal is on the horizon, and will elevate your prestige as well as your bank account. A domestic adjustment is featured. Your friends and family figure prominently. Music plays a role. A Libra helps entertain and inform.

Thursday, May 18 (Moon in Scorpio to Sagittarius 8:10 a.m.) The full moon highlights romance, creativity, and denotes an upswing in your cycle. You will not be rebuffed romantically or career-wise. You might be humming, "Everything is going my way!" Avoid seeing people and places merely as you wish they could be. Be realistic, and avoid self-deception.

Friday, May 19 (Moon in Sagittarius) On this Friday, you come to the conclusion, "I ain't such a bad person after all!" That's putting it lightly. You deserve many pats on the back. The moon in your sign means that your judgment and intuition will be on target. Capricorn plays a top role.

Saturday, May 20 (Moon in Sagittarius to Capricorn 8:02 p.m.)   What goes around, comes around. Tonight, you subscribe to that theory wholeheartedly. Someone who played a major role in your life and then unexpectedly left returns with hat in hand. A project started three years ago can be completed. You'll get deserved credit along with a financial reward.

Sunday, May 21 (Moon in Capricorn)   Your spiritual values unlock. This means discussions flow freely. A young person is duly impressed, elevates your morale by declaring, "I don't think I would know anything at all if I didn't know you!" Leo and Aquarius will play intriguing roles, and will have these letters in their names—A, S, J.

Monday, May 22 (Moon in Capricorn)   People comment, "It takes a strong character to handle these crises that seem to follow one after another!" Reference is being made to financial fluctuations associated with inflation followed by depression. Place your valuables under lock and key. Events will transpire, enabling you to improve your income potential.

Tuesday, May 23 (Moon in Capricorn to Aquarius 9:01 a.m.)   For racing luck, try these selections at all tracks. Post position special—number 5 p.p. in the seventh race. Pick six: 5, 5, 7, 1, 2, 2. Look for these letters or initials in the names of potential winning horses or jockeys: C, L, U. Hot daily doubles: 5 and 5, 6 and 2, 4 and 3. Speed horses win. Gemini and Sagittarius jockeys ride long shots.

Wednesday, May 24 (Moon in Aquarius)   Lucky lottery: 4, 2, 12, 11, 22, 9. The Aquarian moon relates to family members on the go. Trips and visits are featured. You'll receive a gift that finally will end up in the closet. (But don't tell anyone!) Taurus, Leo, and Scorpio figure in this unusual scenario.

Thursday, May 25 (Moon in Aquarius to Pisces 9:08 p.m.) Get ready for a change of scene—and plans. Stress versatility and intellectual curiosity, read and write, and disseminate information. A Virgo beseeches, "Could you help me get rid of my writing dry spell?" Be cooperative, but let it be known that you do not have all the answers.

Friday, May 26 (Moon in Pisces) Attention revolves around home repairs, plant life, beautifying your surroundings. Special: tend to a plumbing problem pronto! The Pisces moon relates to property value and negotiations. Attend a meeting relating to your community. Taurus, Libra, and Scorpio play outstanding roles.

Saturday, May 27 (Moon in Pisces) Lucky lottery: 7, 12, 11, 22, 6, 3. Permit logic to share equal time with emotions. The temptation is to allow emotions to run away with clear thinking. The key is to remember, "Tomorrow is another day and I must face myself!" Pisces and Virgo will play dynamic roles.

Sunday, May 28 (Moon in Pisces to Aries 6:08 a.m.) As a dinner guest of a Capricorn chef, it will be up to you to pretend food is palatable. In reality, it is not. Promise yourself to refuse an invitation from Capricorns who have had no experience in the art of cooking and food preparation. A Cancer is also in the picture.

Monday, May 29 (Moon in Aries) The finish line! The Aries moon relates to creativity, style, challenge, children, variety, and sensuality. It is getting toward the end of the month. You are saying, "Almost the finish line!" You will be fascinated by the creative arts. You could try your hand at painting.

Tuesday, May 30 (Moon in Aries to Taurus 11:03 a.m.) Within 24 hours, there's a new outlook. This involves repairs, remodeling, getting things done without making a federal case of it. Stress independence and originality.

Do not back away from controversy. People fight for your right to self-expression. A Leo figures prominently.

Wednesday, May 31 (Moon in Taurus)   Lucky lottery: 31, 41, 8, 10, 12, 1. Attention revolves around income, personal possessions, decorating, remodeling, and making living quarters a pleasant, happy place. The focus is also on cooperative efforts, proposals that include partnership or marriage.

JUNE 2000

Thursday, June 1 (Moon in Taurus to Gemini 12:35 p.m.)   Focus on communication, the ability to finish what you start. A very unusual relationship could dominate. You are in a quandary, not knowing whether you want to remain or to leave. Aries and Libra play dominant roles, and could have these letters or initials in their names—I and R.

Friday, June 2 (Moon in Gemini)   On this Friday, with the new moon in that part of your horoscope associated with cooperative efforts, public relations, legal affairs, and marriage, you'll have a point of view previously obscured. The spark that brought you together with a special person reignites. Does love conquer all?

Saturday, June 3 (Moon in Gemini to Cancer 12:31 p.m.)   You are called back from your mission. This means don't wander too far from home ground. Your cycle is such that you are asked to repeat steps. Review material, and rehearse out loud if necessary. Cancer and Capricorn play top roles, and have these initials in their names—B, K, T.

Sunday, June 4 (Moon in Cancer)   On this Sunday you'll feel, "My life has been worth living!" Delve into mysteries, explore the lives of Sir Oliver Lodge and Sir Arthur Conan Doyle. Knowing more about karma and

251

Gina Cerminara (*Many Mansions*) would not hurt, either. Gemini encourages study.

Monday, June 5 (Moon in Cancer to Leo 12:47 p.m.) This Monday gets off to a slow start, but then picks up steam. Taurus, Leo, and Scorpio will play dramatic roles, and could have these letters or initials in their names—D, M, V. Someone you regarded as an opponent will turn out to be an ally who up to this time has kept views quiet.

Tuesday, June 6 (Moon in Leo) Get ready for a change of scene. A family member announces: "I need more love and I'm not getting it here!" Stay calm; keep your emotional equilibrium. An important domestic adjustment is taking place which will work to your advantage, as well as that family member who appears starved for love.

Wednesday, June 7 (Moon in Leo to Virgo 2:58 p.m.) Some lessons are repeating to such an extent that you ask, "Is this déjà vu?" Today's scenario features dramatic, bold uses of color. Some people proclaim, "Your color selections are too bold!" Don't let it bother you. People who so state are themselves lacking in color. Have luck with number 6.

Thursday, June 8 (Moon in Virgo) Today's scenario features a blend of skepticism with fantasy. A taste of both! Focus on your interest in real estate, motion pictures, storytelling. The Virgo moon relates to distance, language, and prophesy. Pisces and Virgo will play outstanding roles, and have these letters or initials in their names—G, P, Y.

Friday, June 9 (Moon in Virgo to Libra 8:00 p.m.) The emphasis is on what is real, including deadlines, promotion, production, and budget. A relationship is intense, but not without controversy. It could get too hot not to cool down. Your money position is

252

much better than you originally anticipated. It turns out that your choice of stocks was excellent.

Saturday, June 10 (Moon in Libra)   On this Saturday, you will rule the roost. The Mars keynote, with your Jupiter, tells of a run of good luck. People gather around you, "Say," they ask, "what is going on here, where do you get all that luck?" Response: "I am always lucky on Saturday nights!"

Sunday, June 11 (Moon in Libra)   Let go of the past. Stop hitting yourself with sledgehammer words. Today, make this resolution: "I am independent and free and intend to live my life in the future!" Accent showmanship and drama. Express feelings of love. Leo will play a dramatic role.

Monday, June 12 (Moon in Libra to Scorpio 3:56 a.m.)   The Scorpio moon tells of secret meetings, clandestine arrangements, a relationship that is exciting but could border on the illicit. A family member seems to want to take you aside and say, "Please be careful, there is such a thing as too much, too soon!" Capricorn is in the picture.

Tuesday, June 13 (Moon in Scorpio)   You're likely to dub this a "confusing Tuesday." So many things happen at a rapid pace. Another Sagittarian is involved, along with an ambitious Gemini. In matters of speculation, both agree, stick with number 3. A close relative returns from a trip with vital information.

Wednesday, June 14 (Moon in Scorpio to Sagittarius 2:19 p.m.)   Lucky lottery: 8, 40, 3, 10, 12, 18. Within 24 hours, your cycle moves up. You will be where the action is; you will be in charge of direction, motivation, and deadline. A legal tangle gets straightened out. The sword of Damocles is removed as a result. Scorpio is involved.

Thursday, June 15 (Moon in Sagittarius)   For racing luck, try these selections at all tracks. Post position special—number 5 p.p. in the fifth race. Pick six: 1, 2, 3, 8, 5, 1. Look for these letters or initials in the names of potential winning horses or jockeys: E, N, W. Hot daily doubles: 1 and 2, 5 and 5, 6 and 7. Speed horses win, and pay big prices. Gemini and Virgo jockeys in outstanding rides.

Friday, June 16 (Moon in Sagittarius) Winning numbers: 3, 1, 0. The full moon in your sign emphasizes romance, creativity, style, the ability to overcome obstacles and to prove that indeed love conquers all. As one outstanding physician put it, "Save full moon nights for romance, not surgery." Libra plays a role.

Saturday, June 17 (Moon in Sagittarius to Capricorn 2:27 a.m.) On this day, the lesson driven home is that there is a difference between obsequious-type friendship and the real thing. Some people can talk but cannot do the walk. See people, places, and relationships as they are, not merely as you wish they might be. Pisces is involved.

Sunday, June 18 (Moon in Capricorn) Power play! Express your desires, along with the possible solution to a dilemma. Use the elements of timing and surprise. Focus on durable goods and steel products. Capricorn and Cancer figure in this dynamic scenario, and could have these letters or initials in their names—H, Q, Z.

Monday, June 19 (Moon in Capricorn to Aquarius 3:26 p.m.) A relationship is on the precipice. It will either once again get going, or will be finished. The choice is your own. Money is involved. Future prospects require clarification. The emphasis is on distance, language, travel, a reunion that will be warm, warmer, hot. Aries is represented.

Tuesday, June 20 (Moon in Aquarius) A decision is reached. Follow through. Make a fresh start in a new direction without looking back and suffering pangs of conscience. What passed for romance became more and more a matter of carrying someone else's loads and debts. Leo plays a dramatic role.

Wednesday, June 21 (Moon in Aquarius)   Lucky lottery: 2, 11, 22, 18, 4, 40. Focus on where you stand in a current relationship; this could involve business, career, or romance. A special investment advisory deserves scrutiny. A Cancer is involved, and is willing to lend the benefit of his or her experience.

Thursday, June 22 (Moon in Aquarius to Pisces 3:52 a.m.)   Winning numbers: 3, 3, 8. The Pisces moon relates to property value, decisions about your home, security, family, and marriage. A psychic adviser should not be taken too seriously! Gemini and another Sagittarius play fascinating roles, and have these letters or initials in their names—C, L, U.

Friday, June 23 (Moon in Pisces)   For racing luck, try these selections at all tracks. Post position special—number 4 p.p. in the fourth race. Pick six: 1, 4, 3, 4, 2, 2. Be alert for these letters or initials in the names of potential winning horses or jockeys: D, M, V. Hot daily doubles: 1 and 4, 2 and 2, 1 and 8. Favorites will be in the money. Scorpio jockeys ride record breakers.

Saturday, June 24 (Moon in Pisces to Aries 1:56 p.m.)   Within 24 hours, a love relationship heats up. You'll find a constructive outlet for your creative capabilities. Currently a relationship helps build your morale; it will improve, getting better until tomorrow it becomes red hot. Lucky lottery: 5, 50, 1, 8, 22, 51.

Sunday, June 25 (Moon in Aries)   On this Sunday, a family reunion would be a perfect setting. The emphasis is on voice, sounds, a theatrical performance. The spotlight falls on domestic adjustment where you live, your ultimate financial goal, and marital status. Taurus, Libra, and Scorpio are in this picture.

Monday, June 26 (Moon in Aries to Taurus 8:20 p.m.)   See through someone who knows the price of everything, the value of nothing. It is fun to be fooled, but not to be deceived. The Aries moon relates to your children, sensuality, a variety of experiences. Pisces and Virgo play outstanding roles, and have these letters or initials in their names—G, P, Y.

Tuesday, June 27 (Moon in Taurus)   There's much discussion today about a change of names. Talk revolves around numbers, numerology, movie stars and their names and, finally, if your name is right for you, your career or business. Capricorn and Cancer have strong opinions. Look for these letters in their names—H, Q, Z.

Wednesday, June 28 (Moon in Taurus to Gemini 11:01 p.m.)   For racing luck, try these selections at all tracks. Post position special—number 8 p.p. in the ninth race. Pick six: 1, 2, 7, 3, 8, 8. Be alert for these letters or initials in the names of potential winning horses or jockeys: I and R. Hot daily doubles: 1 and 2, 6 and 8, 4 and 4. Foreign horses and jockeys will be in the money.

Thursday, June 29 (Moon in Gemini)   Make a fresh start; let go of past errors, and sledgehammer words. Imprint your style; highlight drama, showmanship, and color coordination. You'll be told, "You are so vibrant that you exude sex appeal!" Leo and Aquarius play dramatic roles. Your lucky number is 1.

Friday, June 30 (Moon in Gemini to Cancer 11:11 p.m.)   The emphasis is on a relationship that is serious enough to result in marriage. If married, there's a renewed resolution to be together no matter what the emotional weather. The focus is also on payments, collections, improving your financial status. A Cancer is involved.

JULY 2000

Saturday, July 1 (Moon in Cancer)   The new moon, solar eclipse in Cancer relates to exciting, secret plans that could involve the Fourth of July. Tonight, romance is highlighted. You'll feel renewed, stylish, and sexy. Wear bright colors, and let the world know, "Here I am!" Your lucky number is 1.

Sunday, July 2 (Moon in Cancer to Leo 10:39 p.m.)   During the entire month of July there will be an aura of mystery in connection with a relationship, finance, career, the possibility of hidden wealth. On this Sunday, a Cancer prepares dinner, a blend of wholesomeness and the exotic. Tonight, you are one lucky Sagittarian!

Monday, July 3 (Moon in Leo)   Focus on experimentation, exploration, travel, photography, and publishing. You will have visions that will be transformed into realities. Some will claim you are psychic. Don't attempt to explain otherwise; let people believe what they want. Gemini is represented.

Tuesday, July 4 (Moon in Leo to Virgo 11:20 p.m.)   Take special care near explosives. This is not to put a damper on holiday activities, but it is to warn that you might be susceptible to injuries or burns. Taurus, Leo, and Scorpio help you celebrate. You will learn more about subtle innuendos relating to American history.

Wednesday, July 5 (Moon in Virgo)   Get ready for a cycle relating to a change of plans, variety of sensations, a flirtation that becomes more serious than you originally anticipated. There's gain via words, both verbal and written. You'll meet a lively member of the opposite sex who revels in a clash of ideas. Your lucky number is 5.

Thursday, July 6 (Moon in Virgo)   Attention revolves around the need to move furniture. Today's scenario features beautifying your surroundings, flowers, music, and gifts. Someone who shares your love of art objects and luxury items will play a major role. Taurus, Libra, and Scorpio are involved.

Friday, July 7 (Moon in Virgo to Libra 2:48 a.m.) Lie low, play the waiting game. Overcome a tendency to see people and relationships as you wish they might be, instead of the way they actually are. You get your wish! The Libra moon is in your eleventh house, which equates to good fortune in finance and romance.

Saturday, July 8 (Moon in Libra) Lucky lottery: 8, 16, 24, 6, 12, 9. Focus on the pressure of responsibility, an intense relationship. Frustration results from attempting to be in two places at once; it cannot be done! Capricorn and Cancer play outstanding roles, and have these initials in their names—H, Q, Z.

Sunday, July 9 (Moon in Libra to Scorpio 9:45 a.m.) The solution to a mystery is practically at hand. You are on the precipice of added recognition, perhaps fame and fortune! What previously appeared impossible is now within the realm of reality. Your marital status figures prominently, and could involve Aries and Libra.

Monday, July 10 (Moon in Scorpio) You have been through an emotional wringer. Now it's a new day! You will wake refreshed, musing, "I would not want to go through what I went through again, but I would not miss it for the world!" Leo and Aquarius are in the picture, and could have these initials in their names—A, S, J.

Tuesday, July 11 (Moon in Scorpio to Sagittarius 8:06 p.m.) The Scorpio moon relates to a secret mission. You are dispatched to help solve a marital problem experienced by a Gemini relative. Be subtle; don't be frightened of what you hear. Put your common sense above all else. And don't forget to laugh at your own foibles!

Wednesday, July 12 (Moon in Sagittarius)   For racing luck, try these selections at all tracks. Post position special—number 3 p.p. in the third race. Pick six: 1, 4, 3, 6, 4, 1. Watch for these letters or initials in the names of potential winning horses or jockeys: C, L, U. Hot daily doubles: 1 and 4, 6 and 6, 3 and 3. Long shots will be in the money; Gemini and Sagittarius jockeys win.

Thursday, July 13 (Moon in Sagittarius)   Patience is a virtue which enables you to emerge victorious. Be aware of mechanical defects at home and in your automobile. If you're wise, you'll stick close to familiar ground. Going too far, too soon would be a grievous error. Taurus and Scorpio play roles.

Friday, July 14 (Moon in Sagittarius to Capricorn 8:28 a.m.)   You'll be fascinated by additional information concerning French history. You'll learn more about Nostradamus, his predictions and his life. Different aspects of the French Revolution will also come to light. Read, write, teach, and disseminate information. Your lucky number is 5.

Saturday, July 15 (Moon in Capricorn)   Attention revolves around where you live. A major decision affects your residence, lifestyle, marriage. If diplomatic, you win. Conversely, if you attempt to force issues, you will lose. Taurus, Libra, and Scorpio play important roles, and have these letters or initials in their names—F, O, X.

Sunday, July 16 (Moon in Capricorn to Aquarius 9:27 p.m.)   The full moon, lunar eclipse falls in Capricorn, that section of your horoscope associated with your earning potential. A shake-up is due; what blocked your cash flow will be removed. You win friends and allies effortlessly. People seem suddenly to become aware of your personality and talent.

Monday, July 17 (Moon in Aquarius)   The Aquarian moon symbolizes experimentation, exploration, pleasure resulting from a friendship or creative endeavor. An overtime assignment should be regarded as a healthy challenge, an opportunity to once again prove your worth. Capricorn could dominate this scenario.

Tuesday, July 18 (Moon in Aquarius)   What goes around comes around—this time to your advantage. An Aries says (and means it) "You are creative, sensual, sexy and, at times, I can hardly keep my hands off you!" These statements reflect the chemistry of two fire signs—you and Aries. Have luck with number 9.

Wednesday, July 19 (Moon in Aquarius to Pisces 9:45 a.m.)   Lucky lottery: 1, 12, 10, 19, 18, 11. The answer to your question: affirmative, make a fresh start, be open to the possibility of a new love. Within 24 hours, you will be on more solid ground, possibly buying or selling property. A Leo exhibits showmanship, which works to your advantage.

Thursday, July 20 (Moon in Pisces)   A decision revolves around direction, motivation, food, home, and security. A relative with a gourmet appetite also discloses a minor digestive problem. Relate this original aphorism: "It is fun to be a gourmet, not a gourmand!" Practical matters dominate.

Friday, July 21 (Moon in Pisces to Aries 8:10 p.m.)   Get your second emotional wind. Deal with those who have a sense of humor, are artistic, who have been around the world and know how to enjoy life. Gemini and another Sagittarius dominate, and could have these letters or initials in their names—C, L, U. Your lucky number is 3.

Saturday, July 22 (Moon in Aries)   For racing luck, try these selections at all tracks. Post position special—number 4 p.p. in the fourth race. Pick six: 8, 5, 1, 4, 3, 7. Watch for these letters or initials in the names of potential winning horses or jockeys: D, M, V. Hot daily doubles: 8 and 5, 4 and 4, 3 and 7. Scorpio jockeys ride favorites into the winner's circle.

Sunday, July 23 (Moon in Aries)   Focus on exploration, gaining knowledge combining the material and the spiritual. The Aries moon relates to your intellectual curiosity, stirring creative juices. The spotlight is on words, either verbal and written. Gemini and Virgo will make declarations of loyalty.

Monday, July 24 (Moon in Aries to Taurus 3:45 a.m.)   The lunar position emphasizes basic issues, durable goods, ideas that can be transformed into realities. You'll feel loved; you will also be inspired to help others understand the power of love. A Taurus says, "You inspire me to do the right thing and I appreciate it!"

Tuesday, July 25 (Moon in Taurus)   Take it easy, slow the pace, take stock of where you are going and what you intend to do about it. Focus on fitness and resolutions about health. A coworker declares, "Please set the pace; you are a role model!" Pisces and Virgo play exciting roles, and have these letters in their names—G, P, Y.

Wednesday, July 26 (Moon in Taurus to Gemini 8:03 a.m.)   Within 24 hours, questions relate to your partnership. Public relations and marriage issues will loom large. Serious talk revolves around responsibility, promotion, production, timing, a special and serious relationship. Be open to suggestions, but also put forth your own ideas and concepts.

Thursday, July 27 (Moon in Gemini)   What held you back will release its grip. Focus on your freedom to travel, to express feelings of love. You'll exude universal appeal. People want to be with you and to overcome distance and language barriers. Aries and Libra figure in this exciting scenario.

Friday, July 28 (Moon in Gemini to Cancer 9:31 a.m.) You'll sigh, "At last, there's an opportunity to do things my way, to express my style and feelings!" The Gemini moon continues to relate to credibility, reliability, legal rights, partnership, and marriage. Imprint your style, highlight showmanship, and use bright colors when wrapping gifts.

Saturday, July 29 (Moon in Cancer) Focus on secrets pertaining to the occult, to hidden wealth, to a yen for somebody who belongs to someone else. A liberal point of view is fine, but going too far means freedom with license, without responsibility. A Cancer is involved.

Sunday, July 30 (Moon in Cancer to Leo 9:24 a.m.) A Cancer of late has played a key role in your life. Focus on diversity, versatility, the appreciation of beauty, art, and food. Gemini and another Sagittarian will join this Cancer in playing instrumental roles in your future. Your lucky number is 3.

Monday, July 31 (Moon in Leo) A blue moon, solar eclipse falls in Leo, that part of your horoscope representing philosophical subjects, the higher mind, spirituality, the possibility of a journey overseas. Some people, places, and faces are familiar enough for you to muse, "Could this be déjà vu?" Scorpio plays a top role.

AUGUST 2000

Tuesday, August 1 (Moon in Leo to Virgo 9:28 a.m.) On this first day of August, the moon appropriately is in Leo, which means you have fire in your belly regarding travel, a special assignment associated with improving living conditions for people. Cancer and Capricorn play leading roles, and have these letters in their names—B, K, T.

Wednesday, August 2 (Moon in Virgo)   For racing luck, try these selections at all tracks. Post position special—number 7 p.p. in the first race. Pick six: 7, 3, 1, 4, 2, 8. Watch for these letters or initials in the names of potential winning horses or jockeys: C, L, U. Hot daily doubles: 7 and 3, 3 and 3, 1 and 8. Horses that get in front with a display of dazzling speed will win.

Thursday, August 3 (Moon in Virgo to Libra 11:32 a.m.)   A Virgo who proves to be a valuable ally is sincere and has resolved to make you a winner. You may learn later about an ulterior motive, but for now don't ask too many questions. Along with Virgo, it will be Taurus, Leo, and Scorpio who play important roles in your life today.

Friday, August 4 (Moon in Libra)   Puzzle pieces fall into place. Some things happen in an inexplicable manner. It sort of reminds you of Charles Fort, also of apports (objects appearing out of nowhere) which are common occurrences at some seances. Today represents a learning experience.

Saturday, August 5 (Moon in Libra to Scorpio 5:05 p.m.)   This Saturday night will not be one of blaring music or bold actions. It will highlight the subtle approach, expressions of love, family relationships, your marital status. You can pick and choose your companions and relationships. Your lucky number is 6.

Sunday, August 6 (Moon in Scorpio)   Some people will state, "You seem always to fit in with the rhythm of the day's events." That basically is true, and is especially applicable to this Sunday. What was lost will be recovered, possibly your driver's license or passport. Pisces plays a top role.

Monday, August 7 (Moon in Scorpio)   What a Monday! What you expected two days ago will practically materialize. Today's scenario is bathed in mystery, glamour, and intrigue. Out of a maze, you will appear holding the victory sign because you will win despite the odds. Capricorn and Cancer play dynamic roles.

Tuesday, August 8 (Moon in Scorpio to Sagittarius 2:31 a.m.) Claim to fame! Your views are verified, a project is near completion, you will get the credit deserved. On a personal level, there's a reunion with a loved one. You will know once and for all that you belong together, despite opposing concepts or politics. Aries figures prominently.

Wednesday, August 9 (Moon in Sagittarius) Finally, victory is official! Focus on independence, creativity, originality, the courage of your convictions. Wear blends of yellow and gold; make personal appearances and statements. Leo and Aquarius will play fascinating roles. Lucky lottery: 1, 12, 10, 28, 30, 7.

Thursday, August 10 (Moon in Sagittarius to Capricorn 2:45 p.m.) The moon in your sign highlights initiative, attractiveness, and sex appeal. A decision relates to marriage—you'll be pleased and rewarded. Your judgment and intuition are on target. Follow your instincts and your heart. Break free from foolish restrictions. Express yourself with candor; fate is in the making!

Friday, August 11 (Moon in Capricorn) Your intuitive intellect is honed to razor sharpness. Good fortune seems endless, so much so that some people will accuse you of having a money tree. Keep your emotional equilibrium and humor. Another Sagittarian fills in the blanks, helps to complete your story.

Saturday, August 12 (Moon in Capricorn) A challenging Saturday! A Capricorn shares the secrets of financial success. A lost article is returned. The spotlight is on embarrassment, pride, achievement, the ability to fight prejudice. A barrier that seems insurmountable will be surmounted—by you. Have luck with number 4.

Sunday, August 13 (Moon in Capricorn to Aquarius 3:44 a.m.) Family relationships are slightly strained. A Virgo says, "I would like to be on my own, to see what I could achieve without the aid or hindrance of family." Don't fight the obvious. Ride with tide, and give your blessings. Take notes and keep records.

Monday, August 14 (Moon in Aquarius) The Aquarian moon relates to relatives, trips and visits, bright ideas that require time to become viable. A domestic adjustment is featured. A gift received represents a token of love. Expect the unexpected, and you won't be surprised! Libra plays a role.

Tuesday, August 15 (Moon in Aquarius to Pisces 3:42 p.m.) There's romance under the full moon. A relative surprises you by introducing you to a fabulous person. Today might take on a fascinating hue. Pisces and Virgo play artful roles. Don't attempt to figure out everything at once! Play the waiting game; follow your hunch.

Wednesday, August 16 (Moon in Pisces) Lucky lottery: 8, 12, 7, 3, 30, 14. The value of your property is up for serious discussion, possibly sale. Learn more about accounting procedures; the difference between net and gross. You actually know more than most people give you credit for; tonight you'll prove it.

Thursday, August 17 (Moon in Pisces) An element of deception exists, deliberates or otherwise. Be aware, protect yourself in close quarters. Some juggling seems to relate to your Social Security number or bank account. Be on top of any major question or controversy. Aries and Libra play astounding roles.

Friday, August 18 (Moon in Pisces to Aries 1:45 a.m.) You get out of a tight spot. You prove your skill and worth. Others declare, "You are tops on our list!" Make a fresh start, retain creative control, and do not give up something of value for a mere whispered promise. Leo and Aquarius will play terrific roles.

Saturday, August 19 (Moon in Aquarius)   This is a Saturday you will not soon forget! The Aries moon in your fifth house relates to romance, the stirring of your creative juices, the ability to express yourself in a dramatic way. Some will approach you, asking, "Do you believe in love at first sight?" Capricorn is in the picture.

Sunday, August 20 (Moon in Aries to Taurus 9:32 a.m.) Highlight diversity, investigative reporting. Tonight there's fun and frolic. The scenario blends charm and humor with passion. Some people insist, "We do love you at first sight!" Gemini and another Sagittarius will play exemplary roles, and will have these initials in their names—C, L, U.

Monday, August 21 (Moon in Taurus)   Be willing to revise, rewrite, to proofread, to tear down for the purpose of rebuilding on a more solid base. The Taurus moon means you will get work done. Those who previously disappeared at crucial moments will be available and will help. Have luck with number 4.

Tuesday, August 22 (Moon in Taurus to Gemini 2:56 p.m.)   A Gemini insists on trying to guess your age. Maintain secrecy. How old you are is nobody's business but your own. Your ideas are youthful, creative, dynamic, and that is what counts. The written word contains power. Use words today to attain your goal.

Wednesday, August 23 (Moon in Gemini)   A Gemini who of late has been playing a major role in your life will explain. The story is confusing, but amusing. Smile awhile! Much of this tale relates to publicity, added recognition, the solution of a legal tangle, marriage. Focus on where you live, your lifestyle, the restoration of domestic harmony.

Thursday, August 24 (Moon in Gemini to Cancer 6:00 p.m.) Contact someone who helps tie up loose ends. Gemini makes a serious request—give it serious consideration. Much that happens relates to the outside world, changing your lifestyle, your marital status. Pisces and Virgo play creative roles, and could have these letters or initials in their names—G, P, Y.

Friday, August 25 (Moon in Cancer) As August nears its end, you will review results; you will be pleased, albeit grudgingly so. Tonight a relationship is controversial. A deadline must be met. This scenario highlights timing and surprise. Capricorn and Cancer will attempt to run the show. Your lucky number is 8.

Saturday, August 26 (Moon in Cancer to Leo 7:17 p.m.) Long-range negotiations are completed; turn on your charm. Show off your writing, publishing, and language skills. You'll hear these words, "I truly love you!" Aries and Libra play meaningful roles, and will have these letters in their names: I and R. Lucky lottery: 12, 18, 24, 6, 10, 7.

Sunday, August 27 (Moon in Leo) On this Sunday, suddenly the world seems bright—and, yes, you had plenty to do with it! A Leo sings your praises; you deserve it. Stick to your own style, stress independence, originality, the courage of your convictions. Your lucky number is 1.

Monday, August 28 (Moon in Leo to Virgo 7:56 p.m.) Crossroads! Choose a path that leads to home, family, property, and basic issues. Don't be tempted to go off the deep end. A Cancer invites you to dinner— waste no time accepting. Seafood is served, possibly broiled swordfish. I can detect the aroma!

Tuesday, August 29 (Moon in Virgo) The new moon in Virgo relates to your career or business. It's time for a fresh start, new personnel. Some people say you are too critical. What they might not know is that you are your own most severe critic. Let it be known you advocate fair play and that business is business. Another Sagittarian is involved.

Wednesday, August 30 (Moon in Virgo to Libra 9:34 p.m.)   You are proved correct—the original shipment was flawed. Now you will be dealing with quality goods. People learn that you really do mean business and that you expect the best and intend to get it. Taurus, Leo, and Scorpio figure in today's dynamic scenario, and have these letters in their names—D, M, V.

Thursday, August 31 (Moon in Libra)   On this last day of August, you'll be encouraged to write, to express your views, to criticize and to be criticized. A flirtation lends spice, so reveal your dreams and visions. Do not fear fantasy! Turn the pages of your life, and create your own future. A Virgo figures prominently.

SEPTEMBER 2000

Friday, September 1 (Moon in Libra)   What a Friday! The spotlight falls on the fulfillment of your hopes and desires. You will also be lucky in matters of speculation, especially with these three numbers: 2, 11, 5. A Libra previously regarded as a mild relationship will be your enthusiastic ally.

Saturday, September 2 (Moon in Libra to Scorpio 1:56 a.m.)   Much that happens will be of a clandestine nature. People might be demanding, "Open the books!" Be meticulous with regard to your accounting procedures. Focus on galleries, theaters, institutions, and hospitals. A Scorpio wants to do right by you, is sincerely seeking "how to do it."

Sunday, September 3 (Moon in Scorpio)   A lively Sunday! A clash of ideas is featured. Someone who lurked behind the scenes will emerge, expressing ideas that are controversial to say the least. Gemini, Virgo, and another Sagittarian play outstanding roles, and will have these letters or initials in their names—E, N, W.

Monday, September 4 (Moon in Scorpio to Sagittarius 10:10 a.m.)   Attention revolves around your family, home, security, debts which for a time are inexplicable. Tonight, the whole story emerges—keep your emotional equilibrium. Taurus, Leo, and Scorpio figure in this dynamic scenario, and have these letters or initials in their names—F, O, X.

Tuesday, September 5 (Moon in Sagittarius)   In your high cycle, you can afford to play the waiting game. Follow a hunch and your heart. Some persons will be annoyed, rightfully or wrongly. Pay heed only to your own feelings even if it appears on the surface to be selfish. Pisces and Virgo dominate today's scenario.

Wednesday, September 6 (Moon in Sagittarius to Capricorn 10:10 a.m.)   Lucky lottery: 8, 10, 12, 9, 3, 13. The spotlight is on responsibility, reward, a strong love relationship. An overtime assignment is featured, which could be a blessing in disguise. Capricorn and Cancer play major roles, and have these initials in their names— H, Q, Z.

Thursday, September 7 (Moon in Capricorn)   Mission completed! This is one Thursday you won't soon forget! Today's scenario features recognition, the possibility of a journey, participation in a humanitarian project. A love relationship gets hot and heavy! Aries will play an instrumental role.

Friday, September 8 (Moon in Capricorn)   Make a fresh start; stress originality; have the courage of your convictions. Special: don't lift heavy objects! A dynamic Leo comes into your life like a storm! The lunar position coincides with your ability to locate lost articles, to improve your income potential. Your lucky number is 1.

Saturday, September 9 (Moon in Capricorn to Aquarius 10:46 a.m.) This is an enjoyable Saturday—the financial pressure is relieved. A reunion with a sibling is highlighted. Emphasize versatility, diversity, a willingness to accompany a relative on a short trip. Legal papers are involved. Make it crystal clear that you do not intend to get caught up in a wild-goose chase.

Sunday, September 10 (Moon in Aquarius) Social activities accelerate; you are encouraged to pursue your hobby by an Aquarian knowledgeable in metaphysical subjects. A question continues to loom large concerning an association with someone who asks for more than you feel you are capable of delivering, at least at this time.

Monday, September 11 (Moon in Aquarius to Pisces 10:35 p.m.) In your high cycle, you will be at the right place at a special moment, almost effortlessly. Ideas are plentiful. Choose quality; avoid scattering your efforts. Take notes of dreams and predictions. Taurus, Leo, and Scorpio play astonishing roles.

Tuesday, September 12 (Moon in Pisces) You'll be encouraged to write, write, write! You will meet someone who thinks you are the cat's meow! Avoid being obsequious or overly modest. Carry yourself with pride; act as if you are well aware of your talents. Another Sagittarian is involved.

Wednesday, September 13 (Moon in Pisces) For racing luck, try these selections at all tracks. Post position special—number 2 p.p. in the fourth race. Pick six: 2, 5, 1, 2, 3, 6. Watch for these letters or initials in the names of potential winning horses or jockeys: F, O, X. Hot daily doubles: 2 and 5, 7 and 3, 1 and 1. Local favorites win. Taurus and Libra jockeys turn in exceptional performances.

Thursday, September 14 (Moon in Pisces to Aries 8:01 a.m.) Within 24 hours, excitement prevails. Someone of the opposite sex elevates your morale by confessing, "I have always had a thing for you!" Tonight you will participate in a mystery. Something is going on behind your back and you will solve it.

Friday, September 15 (Moon in Aries) What had been nebulous will be solid. You'll be dealing in durable goods. Your emotions run high, so allow a certain amount of excitement to color your decisions. However, know when to say, "Enough is enough!" Capricorn and Cancer will play top roles.

Saturday, September 16 (Moon in Aries to Taurus 3:06 p.m.) Highlight universal appeal, make contact with someone who is bilingual, has previously hinted, "I would like to represent you here and overseas." Above all, you might find yourself inextricably involved—seriously in love. Aries is in the picture.

Sunday, September 17 (Moon in Taurus) New work methods help you get organized. You'll now have more time for recreation. A Taurus is very much drawn to you and is not afraid to show it. Leo and Aquarius are also in the picture, and have these letters or initials in their names—A, S, J.

Monday, September 18 (Moon in Taurus to Gemini 8:23 p.m.) Focus on popularity, public relations, ways and means to earn more money. Your marital status figures prominently as it does almost daily these days! Change your routine: dine out, if practical. Capricorn and Cancer figure in this dynamic scenario, and have these initials in their names—B, K, T.

Tuesday, September 19 (Moon in Gemini) A written report on your personality and work will be featured. The moon position (Gemini) highlights the way you look to the world and how the world appears to you. Focus on legal affairs, a clash of ideas, and marital status. Gemini will play a fascinating role.

Wednesday, September 20 (Moon in Gemini to Cancer 12:16 p.m.)   Legal complications can be resolved if you're persistent. Go slow, be deliberate, let it be known, "I am not a quitter and I don't intend to quit now!" Taurus, Leo, and Scorpio edge their way into the scenario, and could have these letters in their names— D, M, V.

Thursday, September 21 (Moon in Cancer)   Favorable results are due to recent efforts, including improved writing skills. A flirtation is featured, and lends spice to your life. A rebellious Virgo suggests a shortcut, but wait before accepting, if you accept at all. A Gemini and another Sagittarian are in the picture. Look for these letters in their names—E, N, W.

Friday, September 22 (Moon in Cancer)   Stress harmony; toss aside false pride; let a relative know, "I always want to be with you on a warm, friendly basis." Attention revolves around your ability to beautify your surroundings, to decorate and remodel, to take charge of your own fate, to dance to your own tune.

Saturday, September 23 (Moon in Cancer to Leo 3:01 a.m.)   Meditation is featured. If you are quiet within, you'll wake up with answers. The Leo moon relates to philosophy, theology, your interest in the cultures of people in foreign lands. Plan a unique entertainment program. Invite those who have expressed interest in special studies or writings.

Sunday, September 24 (Moon in Leo)   The emphasis is on practicality, responsibility, a chance to hit the financial jackpot. Be sensitive to elements of timing and surprise. An older person says, "I am perfectly willing to share my experience with you!" Capricorn and Cancer play major roles. Your lucky number is 8.

Monday, September 25 (Moon in Leo to Virgo 5:03 a.m.)   By keeping resolutions about exercise, diet, and nutrition, you emerge with a clean bill of health. The moon position highlights prestige, pride, your standing in the community, conferring with people in positions of authority. Aries and Libra figure prominently, and have these initials in their names—I and R.

Tuesday, September 26 (Moon in Virgo)   Throw off shackles of depending on others. Lead the way; don't follow anyone; imprint your style; display inventiveness; have the courage of your convictions. Leo and Aquarius display sincere interest in your welfare. These letters or initials are likely to be involved—A, S, J.

Wednesday, September 27 (Moon in Virgo to Libra 7:23 a.m.)   The new moon in Libra relates to hopes, desires, and popularity, a chance to hit the financial jackpot. Music and entertainment are involved. In matters of speculation, stick with number 2. Strive to be first in line; promote new products; be ready for a different kind of love.

Thursday, September 28 (Moon in Libra)   A lively Thursday. Attend a social gathering during which you meet people who laugh easily and might make your life more pleasant. The moon position continues to encourage your ability to win friends and influence people and to exploit your popularity and talent.

Friday, September 29 (Moon in Libra to Scorpio 11:31 a.m.)   Down to Earth! Stress practicality, and discover ways to untie legal knots. People appreciate your basic theme and your honest approach. You no longer will feel alone in promoting integrity, reliability, and loyalty. Taurus, Leo, and Scorpio play dominant roles.

Saturday, September 30 (Moon in Scorpio)   On this Saturday, the last day of September, the thrill and excitement of secret meetings and clandestine arrangements

273

will be featured. Focus on disseminating information, and gain via words, verbal and written. A clash of ideas leads to a physical attraction and after that, who knows? Your lucky number is 5.

OCTOBER 2000

Sunday, October 1 (Moon in Scorpio to Sagittarius 6:51 p.m.) Within 24 hours, your potential will be fulfilled in an exciting way. Tonight, play your cards close to the chest. Someone who has no business asking personal questions will nevertheless ask. Circumstances are moving in your favor. Scorpio and Taurus will play outstanding roles.

Monday, October 2 (Moon in Sagittarius) The moon in your sign coincides with your high cycle. It's a time to take the initiative, to imprint your style, to refuse to follow others. Wear shades of pink and purple, if possible. Make personal appearances. Gemini, Virgo, and another Sagittarian figure in this scenario.

Tuesday, October 3 (Moon in Sagittarius) The spotlight revolves around a secret mission. Don't take it or yourself too seriously! Focus on domestic areas, decorating and remodeling, major questions about marriage. Taurus, Libra, and Scorpio play leading roles, and will have these letters or initials in their names—F, O, X.

Wednesday, October 4 (Moon in Sagittarius to Capricorn 5:44 a.m.) Lucky lottery: 4, 6, 46, 10, 12, 18. Go slow in connection with money, payments, and collections. Someone might have misappropriated funds. Unless you have definite proof, however, say nothing. Within a matter of hours, your money situation will be resolved.

Thursday, October 5 (Moon in Capricorn) What a relief! The solution is found to money and how it got

274

that way. A lost article is located; a writing dry spell will no longer exist. Get your thoughts on paper. Express your ideas in an entertaining and dramatic way. Capricorn and Cancer figure in this fascinating scenario.

Friday, October 6 (Moon in Capricorn to Aquarius 6:34 p.m.)   Focus on universal appeal, the ability to get the job done and to plan your future moves in a dynamic way. A relationship is tested; it will be the beginning or the ending, and you will know what to do about it. Aries will play what might be considered a sensational role.

Saturday, October 7 (Moon in Aquarius)   For racing luck, try these selections at all tracks. Post position special—number 7 p.p. in the third race. Pick six: 1, 7, 7, 3, 8, 2. Look for these letters or initials in the names of potential winning horses or jockeys: A, S, J. Hot daily doubles: 1 and 7, 2 and 2, 5 and 6. An apprentice jockey, possibly a Leo, sets a record, brings home long shots.

Sunday, October 8 (Moon in Aquarius)   The Aquarian moon relates to funding, earning power, locating lost articles, moving in a circle with those who understand the stock market and how it works. Attention revolves around your family, home, building material, investments that take courage and foresight.

Monday, October 9 (Moon in Aquarius to Pisces 6:37 a.m.)   You'll be saying, "No blue Monday for me!" Highlight diversity, versatility, exploration, a trip involving a relative who of late has been in hiding. You receive a gift that adds to your apparel, brings you up-to-date in connection with fashion. Your lucky number is 3.

Tuesday, October 10 (Moon in Pisces)   Be willing to revise, review, rewrite, and to rebuild on a more solid structure. The moon position highlights dealings with parents, negotiations concerning property, an important decision relating to your partnership or marriage. Taurus, Leo, and Scorpio will play memorable roles.

Wednesday, October 11 (Moon in Pisces to Aries 3:52 p.m.)   Lucky lottery: 4, 12, 7, 1, 8, 18. Within 24 hours, a dispute is settled. This concerns the removal of a fire hazard. Do what must be done. An Aries tries to take charge. Be lenient, but know when to say, "Enough is enough!" Gemini asserts, "I know what is best for you!"

Thursday, October 12 (Moon in Aries)   Be diplomatic when dealing with a fiery Aries. Otherwise, you will be asking for trouble; it will not be pleasant. Say to Aries, "You may very well know what is best, but I intend to live my own life!" Taurus, Libra, and Scorpio are also in the picture, with these letters or initials in their names—F, O, X.

Friday, October 13 (Moon in Aries to Taurus 10:06 p.m.)   The full moon is in your fifth house, and this is Friday the 13th. Maintain your emotional and intellectual equilibrium. The spotlight is on children, challenge, a variety of sensations. Your creative juices are activated; you'll feel alive, dynamic, vital, and sexy.

Saturday, October 14 (Moon in Taurus)   Lucky lottery: 14, 8, 26, 38, 50, 51. The emphasis is on overtime, the pressure of added responsibility. You win recognition by meeting and beating a deadline under budget. A relationship smolders, gets warm and then hot and could be too hot not to cool down. Capricorn is involved.

Sunday, October 15 (Moon in Taurus)   Look beyond the immediate; an opportunity beckons if only you will accept the invitation. A Taurus helps get the job done, and also provides enlightenment, enabling you to break free from a losing proposition. Aries and Libra also figure in this scenario. Your lucky number is 9.

Monday, October 16 (Moon in Taurus to Gemini 2:19 a.m.)   A bright Monday! The keynote is the sun that blends with your Jupiter. Elements of timing and romance ride with you. Imprint your style, and realize that you can do and perform the impossible! Leo and Aquarius will play fascinating, romantic roles. Have luck with number 1.

Tuesday, October 17 (Moon in Gemini)   Attention revolves around decisions associated with direction, motivation, the sale or purchase of property. Proposals are received relating to your career, business, and marriage. A Cancer extends a dinner invitation, and less than two hours later is forced to withdraw it due to unforeseen circumstances.

Wednesday, October 18 (Moon in Gemini to Cancer 5:38 a.m.)   The lunar position emphasizes your marital status. Confusion exists in connection with a journey or vacation. Toss aside your false pride; make inquiries and buy a gift relating to fashion. Keep your recent resolutions about diet, exercise, or nutrition. Your lucky number is 3.

Thursday, October 19 (Moon in Cancer)   The focus is on the need to revise, review, rewrite. By proofreading, you'll uncover a hidden clause. Had it not been discovered, it would have been costly and embarrassing. Taurus, Leo, and Scorpio play fascinating roles, and could have these letters in their names—D, M, V.

Friday, October 20 (Moon in Cancer to Leo 8:43 a.m.) Tonight could be the precursor to an exciting weekend. You'll be haunted by the question, "Am I in love or in lust?" Before this weekend is over, you will have added insight into where you are going, who you are, greater knowledge of your own life and why you are here. Virgo is represented.

Saturday, October 21 (Moon in Leo)   On this Saturday, music plays a major role. Someone from a foreign land talks and plays and turns on the charm in a fascinating way. Protect yourself in emotional clinches. Written material concerning your home beautiful will fascinate and inform.

Sunday, October 22 (Moon in Leo to Virgo 11:54 a.m.)   You are pulled in two directions. Someone who fooled you once is attempting to do it again—play the waiting game. Focus on meditation, direction, the ability to absorb information and to come up with the answers when needed. Pisces and Virgo play astounding roles. Have luck with number 7.

Monday, October 23 (Moon in Virgo)   A job that should have been done eight days ago remains untouched. The spotlight is on responsibility, a deadline, an upcoming meeting with the top employer. Put your house and priorities in order. Capricorn and Cancer will play bold roles, and could have these initials in their names—H, Q, Z.

Tuesday, October 24 (Moon in Virgo to Libra 3:31 p.m.)   On this Tuesday, you'll experience sensations associated with more freedom of thought and action. You become acquainted again with the power of words. Your libido is activated, and you might be musing, "I'm in the mood for love!" Aries and Libra will play fascinating roles.

Wednesday, October 25 (Moon in Libra)   Shake off your emotional lethargy. Get ready for a fresh start in a new direction. Avoid lifting heavy objects; imprint your style; let others know you are vital, dynamic, and ambitious. Leo and Aquarius step into the breach when most needed. Lucky lottery: 50, 1, 5, 7, 18, 13.

Thursday, October 26 (Moon in Libra to Scorpio 8:25 p.m.)   For racing luck, try these selections at all tracks. Post position special—number 6 p.p. in the fifth race. Pick six: 5, 6, 2, 1, 6, 3. Watch for these letters or initials in the names of potential winning horses or jockeys: B, K, T. Hot daily doubles: 5 and 6, 2 and 4, 1 and

278

7. Home-grown jockeys display growing mastery bringing in long shots.

Friday, October 27 (Moon in Scorpio)   The new moon in Scorpio relates to good fortune in matters of finance and romance. Your popularity soars. You win friends and influence people. In a way, you are Svengali; the world can be considered your Trilby. Gemini and another Sagittarian will play dramatic roles. Have luck with number 3.

Saturday, October 28 (Moon in Scorpio)   You'll be dealing with two Scorpios—more than almost anyone can handle! A clash of ideas and temperaments is featured. Much that occurs will be in secret, behind the scenes. You will have to take time to dredge up information. Taurus will also be in this picture, playing an investigative role.

Sunday, October 29—Eastern Standard Time (Moon in Scorpio to Sagittarius 2:42 a.m.)   The moon in your sign highlights direct action, the return of vitality, elements of timing and luck. Pay no attention to naysayers who know the price of everything and the value of nothing. Announce, "There are two ways to do things, the right way and my way!" Another Sagittarian is involved.

Monday, October 30 (Moon in Sagittarius)   Go slow, be diplomatic, and permit the music to play while you dance to your own tune. The focus is also on art, literature, and on your ability to take notes in a way that serves a grand purpose when necessary. Tonight get used to hearing, "Your voice is different!"

Tuesday, October 31 (Moon in Sagittarius to Capricorn 1:03 p.m.)   Magicians perform tricks, youngsters are in disguises; not only is it Halloween, but also National Magic Day in memory of Houdini. Keep your own aura of mystery; don't reveal how tricks are performed. Let others play guessing games. Psychic impressions will hit the mark.

NOVEMBER 2000

Wednesday, November 1 (Moon in Capricorn)   Write your way in and out of anything! Put forth your most adorable self. A mental survey of upcoming holidays helps promote a better sense of security. Continue to prepare your gift list. Gemini, Virgo, and another Sagittarian play outstanding roles, and have these initials in their names—E, N, W.

Thursday, November 2 (Moon in Capricorn)   Focus on your home, the necessity for handling a Capricorn with kid gloves. The Venus keynote blends with your Jupiter and a good time is had by all! A Libran who once was out of your life could return in a dramatic way. The spotlight is also on your earning capacity, a gift representing a token of love.

Friday, November 3 (Moon in Capricorn to Aquarius 1:41 a.m.)   Caution marks the spot! This could be the precursor to a weekend involving plumbing problems, flood damage, a disappointment in someone who makes promises and then breaks them. Some people assure, "What you are going through is good for you because you are paying off your karma."

Saturday, November 4 (Moon in Aquarius)   The emphasis is on power, authority, practical affairs, special recommendations, meeting people who have the wherewithal to fund projects. Some say, "You are like a bad penny, always popping up!" Smile while adding, "I am the best penny you'll ever have!" Your lucky number is 8.

Sunday, November 5 (Moon in Aquarius to Pisces 2:15 p.m.)   Focus on spirituality, the realization that once again you survived a crisis. Family members who at first were recalcitrant will be at your side, offering encouraging words. Aries and Libra take their places at the head of the line. Your lucky number is 9.

Monday, November 6 (Moon in Pisces)   Make a fresh start in a new direction. Keep resolutions about diet, exercise, and general health. You are unique, special, and talented, and all of us need you—and you owe us your best efforts! Leo and Aquarius will play exciting, dramatic roles.

Tuesday, November 7 (Moon in Pisces)   Overcome moods via meditation. You are on solid ground despite skepticism. The emphasis is on direction, motivation, a decision that looms large in connection with your marriage. Change your routine, dine out, and invite a Cancer to join you. Capricorn also plays an important role.

Wednesday, November 8 (Moon in Pisces to Aries 12:03 a.m.)   Lucky lottery: 12, 8, 1, 10, 9, 19. In your high cycle, you win a public opinion poll in connection with a controversial concept or action. Someone close to you says, "I bet you could run for president and win!" Gemini and another Sagittarian play manipulative roles.

Thursday, November 9 (Moon in Aries)   Initiate policies that coincide with your desires. Accept a leadership role, imprint your style, wear shades of red, and make personal appearances. A skirmish with Taurus and Scorpio will not amount to much, so respond accordingly. Read between the lines to discover the hidden clause.

Friday, November 10 (Moon in Aries to Taurus 6:13 a.m.)   It's a lively Friday! Someone who usually remains in the background will step forth and declare, "I have always wanted to talk to you, to present myself but I have been too shy until now!" Gemini, Virgo, and another Sagittarian play exciting roles, and could have these letters in their names—E, N, W.

Saturday, November 11 (Moon in Taurus)   The full moon relates to romance, style, creativity, and an aura of mysticism. A family member talks about the music of the spheres. Your voice sounds different. People comment, "There's something about you that is both fascinating and frightening." Your lucky number is 6.

Sunday, November 12 (Moon in Taurus to Gemini 9:29 a.m.)   Perfect your techniques, and streamline procedures. Within 24 hours, you might be sorry you pressed issues about which you know little or nothing. A passionate love relationship commands attention. Protect yourself in clinches. Know when to say, "Enough is enough!"

Monday, November 13 (Moon in Gemini)   Results! People implied you might be falling down on the job because of a lack of results. No more implications! By tonight, results will be obvious and you will be treated as some kind of hero. Capricorn and Cancer play stunning roles, and have these letters or initials in their names—H, Q, Z.

Tuesday, November 14 (Moon in Gemini to Cancer 11:22 a.m.)   What goes around, comes around. A love relationship at one time hot and then cool will once again be a part of your life. Focus on continuation, philosophy, and higher education. The feeling persists, "I am so close to my goal that I can almost touch it!" Aries plays a magnificent role.

Wednesday, November 15 (Moon in Cancer)   For racing luck, try these selections at all tracks. Post position special—number 7 p.p. in the third race. Pick six: 1, 2, 7, 4, 3, 1. Look for these letters or initials in the names of potential winning horses or jockeys: A, S, J. Hot daily doubles: 1 and 2, 3 and 7, 4 and 6. Horses that run well in mud will have an easy time. Leo jockeys ride winners paying long-shot prices.

Thursday, November 16 (Moon in Cancer to Leo 1:20 p.m.)   Puzzle pieces fall into place. A family member who has the money will finally agree to provide funding. Be kind, without being obsequious. Be grateful, but also maintain your own independent stance. If the truth be known, you are providing a favor for that family member.

Friday, November 17 (Moon in Leo)   Lucky numbers: 3, 17, 12. The lunar position emphasizes the financial status of someone who would like to be your partner or mate. Much that is visible is showing; the situation is colorful but lacks solidity. Dig deep for information. It is possible that you could locate a treasure map.

Saturday, November 18 (Moon in Leo to Virgo 4:17 p.m.)   On this Saturday, talk will concern long ago and far away. Open lines of communication. Consider the possibility of a representative overseas. Your product or talent deserves more distribution. Idealism in romance is fine, but don't give away the farm due to sweet, whispered promises.

Sunday, November 19 (Moon in Virgo)   On this Sunday, you'll be musing, "Once again I feel alive, vital, ambitious, and I know that life is worth living!" You'll be asked to attend an engagement party. Write original material; let people know once again that you are unusual, attractive, and sensual.

Monday, November 20 (Moon in Virgo to Libra 8:36 p.m.)   Lucky numbers 6, 5, 11. The Virgo moon relates to your career, pride, conferring with community leaders, and realizing you do belong among the high-and-mighty. People who criticize your criticism will come to realize you are your own most severe critic. Libra is involved.

Tuesday, November 21 (Moon in Libra)   Is this déjà vu? Suddenly, it seems there are familiar places and faces. You can deal with it and do so! Define terms, outline boundaries, protect yourself in emotional clinches. Pisces and Virgo play astounding roles, and have these initials in their names—G, P, Y.

Wednesday, November 22 (Moon in Libra)   For racing luck, try these selections at all tracks. Post position special—number 8 p.p. in the ninth race. Pick six: 2, 5, 7, 3, 7, 1. Watch for these letters or initials in the names of potential winning horses or jockeys: G, P, Y. Hot daily doubles: 2 and 5, 4 and 4, 7 and 2. Veteran jockeys win, and will ride favorites that pay fair prices.

Thursday, November 23 (Moon in Libra to Scorpio 2:34 a.m.)   Thanksgiving! What might appear to be clichés will be sincere, as many will express "thanksgiving." Someone from a foreign land talks about different customs, expresses gratitude for being in your company, and almost literally smacks lips while enjoying a traditional turkey dinner.

Friday, November 24 (Moon in Scorpio)   Make a fresh start; let it be known, "I intend to rule the roost— if I am cruel, it is because you made me so!" Have your say, hold no grudges, speak from your heart and you cannot go wrong. Leo and Aquarius will play leading roles, and have these initials in their names—A, S, J.

Saturday, November 25 (Moon in Scorpio to Sagittarius 10:34 a.m.)   The new moon in your sign coincides with creativity, sensitivity, emotional responses, and romance. Focus on personality, a willingness to take risks, the courage of your convictions. A different approach may be necessary to win your way with a Cancer person who admires you, but remains skeptical.

Sunday, November 26 (Moon in Sagittarius)   Put your point across in a charming, humorous way. People will term you delightful, fascinating, and spiritual. Refuse to economize on goodwill. Set an example for some people who are downright cheap. Gemini and another Sagittarian will play dynamic roles. Your lucky number is 3.

Monday, November 27 (Moon in Sagittarius to Capricorn 8:58 p.m.)   Within 24 hours, you will know that your recent efforts will pay dividends. The moon moves into your second house, relating to lost articles and income potential. The Pluto keynote means nothing remains the same. A lowbrow individual attempts to take over. Taurus plays a dominant role.

Tuesday, November 28 (Moon in Capricorn)   Expect more freedom of thought and action. A Capricorn returns an article that had been missing. Take notes, write down your dreams, get in the habit of writing something, no matter what, each and every day. Gemini, Virgo, and another Sagittarian will play exciting roles.

Wednesday, November 29 (Moon in Capricorn) The lunar position continues to coincide with your high cycle, especially where finances are concerned. Get more information from trade papers. You have winning ways, but could lack some technical data. Taurus, Libra, and Scorpio play music. Lucky lottery: 12, 6, 16, 2, 3, 5.

Thursday, November 30 (Moon in Capricorn to Aquarius 9:27 a.m.)   On this last day of November, the moon is leaving Capricorn. Within 24 hours, you receive some good news about a sibling. You'll be active, dynamic, creative, and some will say you are very sexy! Pisces and Virgo help you say goodbye to November!

DECEMBER 2000

Friday, December 1 (Moon in Aquarius)   The lunation falls into your first house. The Aquarian moon relates to trips and visits in connection with relatives who insist, "I cannot get along without you for another day!"

The holiday atmosphere prevails, so begin making plans for Christmas and New Year.

Saturday, December 2 (Moon in Aquarius to Pisces 10:24 p.m.)   Today, you will be bathed with an aura of mystery. People confer with you regarding psychic impressions. Your personality is dominant; you exude an aura of sensuality and sex appeal. No matter what your chronological age, married or single, people feel as if you are their mentor.

Sunday, December 3 (Moon in Pisces)   Get down to business! Focus on property value, leases, learning more about accounting procedures. Your potential is so great that people sense it and want to be near you. The key is for you, yourself, to have confidence, to know that your future will be bright.

Monday, December 4 (Moon in Pisces)   You might be getting ahead of yourself! Check your calendar for social and other dates or commitments. Be aware of your budget in connection with gift planning. Already, you are feeling the spirit of Christmas. Aries and Libra are playing dominant roles. Let go of a foolish obligation.

Tuesday, December 5 (Moon in Pisces to Aries 9:19 a.m.)   Clear away your emotional debris. Imprint your style, lead the way, do not follow others. Wear bright colors, make personal appearances and statements. Don't be shy when it comes to giving opinions, political and otherwise. A Leo figures prominently.

Wednesday, December 6 (Moon in Aries)   People question you, "What do you intend to do with your life and what about marriage?" Response: "Whatever I do, I intend to live my own life and as far as my marital relationship, that is strictly personal and my business!" Lucky lottery: 12, 18, 33, 22, 8, 5.

Thursday, December 7 (Moon in Aries to Taurus 4:28 p.m.) A very sensitive day in history! As you remember Pearl Harbor, express your gratitude that you remain free to develop your rare talents. Look behind the scenes for the answers; don't fall into the trap of giving away everything, just so you can hear sweet whispered words. This means above all else, avoid self-deception.

Friday, December 8 (Moon in Taurus) During a get-together with friends on this Friday, the atmosphere is close with intellectual curiosity. People let loose with knowledge concerning art, music, literature, and sports. Hold your fire, then let loose with the fact that today marks the birthday of Diego Rivera and James Thurber.

Saturday, December 9 (Moon in Taurus to Gemini 7:52 p.m.) On this Saturday, you will feel good. Your morale soars, a flirtation lends spice. Gemini, Virgo, and another Sagittarian figure prominently, and could have these letters or initials in their names—E, N, W. Efforts turn to writing; you do not fail to develop your talent along this line. Your lucky number is 5.

Sunday, December 10 (Moon in Gemini) Arguments among relatives will amount to a tempest in a teapot. This means that those who speak the loudest are merely letting off steam. Know it, and don't become involved in a debate over what can really never be settled. Taurus, Libra, and Scorpio are featured, with these letters or initials in their names—F, O, X.

Monday, December 11 (Moon in Gemini to Cancer 8:50 p.m.) The full moon relates to love, romance, partnership, and marriage. You might discover that double-dealing is involved in a legal agreement. Time is on your side, so play the waiting game. Don't equate delay with defeat. A Pisces individual becomes your ally when most needed and at the last possible moment.

Tuesday, December 12 (Moon in Cancer)   This is a power play day! The lunar position highlights the occult, the hidden, financial status of someone who knows the price of everything and the value of nothing. Refuse to be impressed by those who do the talking but cannot do the walk. A Cancer plays a major role.

Wednesday, December 13 (Moon in Cancer to Leo 9:10 p.m.)   You'll marvel at the long arm of coincidence. Remember: enough coincidences make a face. Reach beyond the immediate; you gain acceptance from bilingual people who welcome you into the intellectual circle. Lucky lottery: 36, 18, 9, 44, 51, 6.

Thursday, December 14 (Moon in Leo)   The answer to your question: Yes, do it up brown! This means apply principles of showmanship in making a fresh start in a new direction. A question about love: be ready, willing, and able. This applies, no matter what your chronological age. A Leo plays a dramatic role.

Friday, December 15 (Moon in Leo to Virgo 10:31 p.m.)   On this Friday, include a family member in a special entertainment or performance. A long-distance call is the precursor to a possible journey. Accent publishing, advertising, a unique promotion. Today's scenario highlights children, home, security, your marital status. A Cancer is involved.

Saturday, December 16 (Moon in Virgo)   For racing luck, try these selections at all tracks. Post position special—number 3 p.p. in the third race. Pick six: 7, 1, 3, 8, 2, 5. Watch for these letters or initials in the names of potential winning horses or jockeys: C, L, U. Hot daily doubles: 7 and 1, 3 and 3, 6 and 7. Speed horses win. Jockeys with racing luck include Gemini and Sagittarius.

Sunday, December 17 (Moon in Virgo)   Someone close to you seeks counsel, whether or not to change a name. Plenty of proofreading is necessary. A hidden clause is contained in a legal agreement. Be willing to tear down in order to rebuild, check the words and music. A Scorpio figures prominently.

Monday, December 18 (Moon in Virgo to Libra 2:02 a.m.)   Take special care with words, either verbal and written. The Libra moon relates to elements of luck, timing, and love. A spectacular run of right choices is featured. This is not only what could be something big but is something of value. Gemini and Virgo will play featured roles.

Tuesday, December 19 (Moon in Libra)   Attention revolves around home, your voice, the restoration of domestic harmony. Don't force issues. If you're patient and diplomatic, you gain a tremendous advantage. The moon position continues to emphasize success in dealings with people of means. Your lucky number is 6.

Wednesday, December 20 (Moon in Libra to Scorpio 8:13 a.m.)   Within 24 hours, a well-kept secret will be exposed. You'll be amazed, slightly concerned, but mostly pleased. Take time to define terms, outline boundaries, and to see people and places, as well as relationships, in a realistic way. A Pisces figures prominently.

Thursday, December 21 (Moon in Scorpio)   The emphasis is on the responsibility of meeting a deadline. A love relationship, no matter what your chronological age, can best be described as hectic. On this Thursday, nothing happens halfway for you—it is either hot or cold, not lukewarm. Capricorn is involved.

Friday, December 22 (Moon in Scorpio to Sagittarius 4:58 p.m.)   Your goal is in sight. Let go of the status quo, pronto. Highlight universal appeal; you need not remain in cramped quarters. An Aries talks freely: "I know that, without you I would be as if lost in a desert!"

express gratitude for the compliment, without being obsequious.

Saturday, December 23 (Moon in Sagittarius) This is one Saturday you won't soon forget! The sun keynote and moon in your sign indicates love in bloom! You'll have good fortune in matters of love, money, and health. A Leo will become much more, possibly a partner or mate. Lucky lottery: 10, 9, 12, 13, 18, 22.

Sunday, December 24 (Moon in Sagittarius) Your cycle continues high, so take the initiative, make personal appearances, imprint your style and above all, do not follow others! At a Christmas Eve family reunion, gifts received include large home appliances. Your marital status will figure prominently during this memorable holiday.

Monday, December 25 (Moon in Sagittarius to Capricorn 3:55 a.m.) On this Christmas Day, the new moon and solar eclipse are in Capricorn, along with the Jupiter keynote. This adds up to a major surprise in the area of finance. Yes, it is possible you could win a contest. The status quo gets a shake-up. You'll have more freedom of expression, more opportunity to win, and this could be the start of something big.

Tuesday, December 26 (Moon in Capricorn) A lost article is located, which relates to an engine or tools required for major repairs. You feel stronger and more vital. Get your emotional second wind as you prepare for a New Year's Eve celebration. Check the list of those you will be with and where the party is to take place.

Wednesday, December 27 (Moon in Capricorn to Aquarius 4:27 p.m.) On this Wednesday, you will know for sure that financial pressure is being relieved. Activity is indicated in connection with your siblings, trips and visits, ideas that eventually will prove profitable. Gemini, Virgo, and another Sagittarian are in the picture. Your lucky number is 5.

Thursday, December 28 (Moon in Aquarius)   The Aquarian moon relates to unusual news about your neighborhood, a relative who makes a surprise announcement. Attention revolves around your home, where you live, your income potential, and marital status. Taurus, Libra, and Scorpio boldly state they intend to play outstanding roles.

Friday, December 29 (Moon in Aquarius)   Slow the pace. Keep your resolutions about exercise, diet, and nutrition. Steer clear of adult beverages, at least for 24 hours. A glamorous Pisces will do a number on you. A Virgo puts forth details on how to get organized in connection with your product or talent.

Saturday, December 30 (Moon in Aquarius to Pisces 5:29 p.m.)   Lucky lottery: 8, 2, 12, 3, 7, 18. An older person, parent, or teacher, shares experience, and gives you an unqualified vote of confidence. Check further details in connection with a New Year's Eve celebration. Confidence is restored; your older person is likely to be a Capricorn or Cancer.

Sunday, December 31 (Moon in Pisces)   This Sunday, New Year's Eve, watch for false statements, canards. Some persons under the influence of adult beverages will say things they will be sorry for tomorrow. Be sure you are not one of those people! You will be told, "You are too good for this place and these people!" Take this with a proverbial grain of salt.

Happy New Year!

ABOUT THE AUTHOR

Born on August 5, 1926, in Philadelphia, Omarr was the only person ever given full-time duty in the U.S. Army as an astrologer. He also is regarded as the most erudite astrologer of our time and the best known, through his syndicated column (300 newspapers) and his radio and television programs (he is Merv Griffin's "resident astrologer"). Omarr has been called the most "knowledgeable astrologer since Evangeline Adams." His forecasts of Nixon's downfall, the end of World War II in mid-August of 1945, the assassination of John F. Kennedy, Roosevelt's election to the fourth term and his death in office . . . these and many others are on the record and quoted enough to be considered "legendary."

ABOUT THIS SERIES
This is one of a series of twelve
Day-to-Day Astrological Guides
For the signs of 2000
by Sydney Omarr

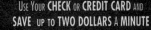

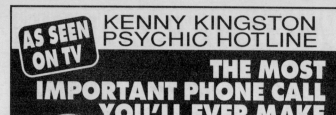